DATE DUE

MAY 1 5 1991		
OCT 1 9 1992		
NOV 0 9 1992		
NOV 30		
Dec. 21		
MAR 2 5 1995		
APR 1 2 1995		
MAY 2 6 2005		
JAN 0 3 2005		
NOV 2 1 2012		
GAYLORD		PRINTED IN U.S.A.

THE BOYS IN
THE BARRACKS

THE BOYS IN THE BARRACKS

Observations on American Military Life

LARRY H. INGRAHAM
Walter Reed Army Institute of Research

With Critical Commentary by
FREDERICK J. MANNING
Walter Reed Army Institute of Research

A Publication of the
Institute for the Study of Human Issues
Philadelphia

Manufactured in the United States of America

1 2 3 4 5 6 7 8   90 89 88 87 86 85 84

Library of Congress Cataloging in Publication Data

Ingraham, Larry H.
  The boys in the barracks.

  Bibliography: p.
  1. United States. Army—Military life.   2. Sociology,
Military—United States.   3. Soldiers—United States.
I. Manning, Frederick J.   II. Title.
U766.I73   1983   355.1'0973   83-250
ISBN 0-89727-048-7

For information, write:

Director of Publications
ISHI
3401 Science Center
Philadelphia, Pennsylvania 19104

*Chapter opening photos courtesy of the Defense Audio-
visual Agency and Larry H. Ingraham.*

*To Sergeant Wiley Fox
and the boys in the barracks
all over the world*

CONTENTS

PREFACE

This is a study of American soldiers in garrison. In other times and contexts the subjects of this book have been called "doughboys," "dogfaces," "grunts," "GIs" and heroes. They are the nameless sinews and muscles of the U.S. Army below the rank of sergeant. Most often they come to the attention of the general public only when they are killed—in combat or in training—or when they misbehave while drinking, rioting or using illegal drugs. Consequently, they have been often studied but seldom understood. This study of their everyday lives in garrison, particularly their leisure, nonduty activities, is therefore a somewhat unusual account of the American fighting man.

It seems a long time since the observations began in 1973. Both the Army and its "drug scene" have changed in the intervening years. Some of the drug and alcohol observations now seem quaint, almost archaic, as the argot has moved beyond "heads," "juicers" and "speed freaks." Conclusions like "drug use does not invariably result in unacceptable duty performance" were once viewed as radical but are now seen as merely common sense. The Army has also changed, especially since 1978, with policy initiatives designed to improve small unit cohesion, and command emphasis, at least in Europe, on getting leaders concerned and involved with after-duty barracks activities.

Despite these changes, "the boys in the barracks syndrome" has become a common topic of conversation in military circles. The underlying issue—how soldiers relate to one another—concerns not only military leaders, but all thoughtful citizens concerned about the future of American society.

In one sense, this book is addressed to soldiers and students of the contemporary American Army. It will prove useful in discussions of leadership and diverse policy issues ranging from barracks design to drug and alcohol abuse prevention. It should be useful to those chiefly concerned with problems of behavior in Army barracks: chaplains, mental health personnel, drug/alcohol counselors and company level leaders.

In a larger sense, this study will be of interest to behavioral scientists of all kinds. These include scholars of the contemporary military, as well as psychologists, sociologists, and anthropologists who are comfortable with qualitative data.

Reader response to earlier drafts of the book was conflicting. Some called for more documentation; others recommended a less formal treatment. The present work follows the latter, but mainly because time and events conspired to make it impossible to take up the former. As an aid to students and scholars alike, my colleague, Frederick Manning, agreed to provide a critical commentary which places the descriptions in theoretical perspective.

Judging from letters received from parents and other concerned citizens, the book should be of decided interest to the general reader. Even some Army recruiters have noted that while such candid reports make their work more difficult, it is better to take up the issues in straightforward dialogue than to ignore them or add another chorus to the disappointed recruit's marching song, "The Recruiter Didn't Tell Me. . . ."

A note seems necessary on the "colorful language" quoted in this study. Earlier drafts were criticized for the presence of "raw commentary demeaning of enlisted people." Some colleagues wryly observed that they had just come to terms with the "sociology of the absurd" when they encountered the "sociology of the obscene." The purpose of the descriptions included here is not to shock or titillate, but to give an accurate reflection of what was experienced during the study. Criticisms of the language some soldiers use and disgust at what some soldiers do reveals a moral righteousness that we can ill afford to entertain. The descriptions reveal enormous social distances across the ranks, sometimes to the point of disclosing three different armies: the army of the enlisted man, the army of the noncommissioned officer, and that of the commissioned officer. To bridge such chasms it is necessary to go beyond merely telling new lieutenants, "some of your troops will have values different from yours." It is necessary to reveal exactly what they do and what they say, if leaders are to respond in terms other than moral indignation and prejudicial notions of the way "those kinds of people" behave.

The publication of this book owes much to the thoughtful criticism and generous encouragement of friends and colleagues. It is my pleasure and duty to acknowledge a few of the many people who contributed to the completion of this project.

I owe a special debt to Harry C. Holloway, M.D., former Director of the Division of Neuropsychiatry, and to David H. Marlowe, Chief of the Department of Military Psychiatry at the Walter Reed Army Institute of Research. Both were constant in their encouragement, stimulation, and criticism from the time the project was initiated, through the data collection, to the drafting of the preliminary report. This book may not be all that they would hope, but it has been greatly improved by their commitment to excellence.

The work of the observers is evident throughout. Their notes were of such quality that I often felt more like a copy editor than an author. Robert W. Matthews and Stephen M. Way were the principal observers in the barracks. They were assisted by Specialist James M. Maedke, Sergeant First Class Charles I. Taylor and Lieutenant Colonel John H. Newby, Jr. To all of them go my deepest thanks for their sense of duty, loyalty and absolute honesty.

Six secretaries assisted in typing various drafts. I am grateful to Marsha Sotzky, Anne Rutuskas, Gale Skarupa, Eileen O'Brien, Wilhelmina Frederick, and Sherrilyn Lee for their patience and perseverance.

Because reader response to earlier drafts was often confusing and conflicting, I might well have laid the whole project aside, had it not been for William E. Datel, also of the Walter Reed Army Institute of Research. He insisted that I allow the publisher to specify the revisions that would be needed. As I stalled, hedged and dawdled, he patiently set about constructing a system of social supports that obligated me to push ahead despite my lack of resolve. I am especially indebted to Lieutenant General (ret.) Phillip B. Davidson, Jr., who offered both critical suggestions for improving the text and advice on navigating manuscript clearance through the Army bureaucracy. Without Bill Datel and General Davidson, this book would never have had a public reading.

I am also indebted to three directors of the Walter Reed Army Institute of Research and to a commanding general of the United States Army Medical Research and Development Command. To Colonel Edward L. Buescher, M.D., Colonel Robert J. T. Joy, M.D., Major General Garrison Rapmund, M.D., and Major General William S. Augerson, M.D., I owe a special debt. I refer not only to their criticism and encouragement, but to their vision of science in the military. All of them, as much by personal example as policy, maintained a spirit of free inquiry with the Army Medical Department. For them no question was closed to inquiry, first by scholarship and argument, then, if possible, by empirical means. My working instructions were always, "Tell the truth—no matter what." They then left me alone to pursue the truth as best I could discern it. The manuscript was therefore cleared for publication on the basis of scientific standards, and has not been modified in any way to conform to other standards.

Finally, I acknowledge my debt to many colleagues at the Walter Reed Army Institute of Research. Frank J. Sodetz, Frederick J. Manning, Robert J. Schneider and Joseph M. Rothberg provided a constant source of provocative criticism and unflagging encouragement. To all of them I extend my humble thanks. My claim to authorship in the face of the significant roles played by others is mitigated only by the knowledge that I alone bear the responsibility for errors of both omission and commission.

Larry H. Ingraham

INTRODUCTION

This book examines the daily lives of American enlisted men and considers the use of drugs and alcohol in barracks living. With the possible exception of college sophomores, no other category of Americans has been so thoroughly subjected to intelligence assessments, aptitude batteries and inventories of attitudes, beliefs, perceptions, feelings and values. Yet this enormous literature stands silent in response to simple questions about the lives of soldiers outside of combat settings.

What do soldiers actually do when they are not fighting a war? How do they structure their time? With whom do they associate and why? What is it like to live in an Army barracks? How much control does the Army really exert over their lives? These and similar questions are addressed in the chapters to follow.

The central theme is affiliation: how soldiers sort themselves into informal cliques after duty hours when the fact of military rank does not obtain. The central problems for barracks-dwelling soldiers include finding companions, establishing status and maintaining orderly interaction over time. Readers who experienced the U.S. Army of the 1940s, the 1950s, or even the 1960s may wonder how the question of affiliation came to be problematic; after all one was simply drafted into the Army and was told what to do, where to go, what to say, how to dress and what to eat. The problem for soldiers in those eras may well have been finding privacy and respite from enforced social interaction.

With respect to social structure the Army changed radically in the 1970s. The demography changed with the end of the draft, resulting in more married soldiers, even among the lower enlisted ranks, and fewer soldiers with post-high-school educational experience. The work week changed, too, with the abandonment of Saturday morning duties and inspections. The old pass policy, which permitted only a percentage of soldiers to be absent from the post, gave way to freedom for all soldiers to go and do as they pleased when not on duty. Open dormitories were replaced by smaller two- and three-person rooms, and the small unit dining halls were merged into consolidated facilities.

Most important of all, soldiers became relatively well paid. Many could afford automobiles, portable televisions, tape decks and attractive civilian clothing. Gone are the days of soldiers loitering in uniform outside the gates of the post, killing time until lights out. Now they can afford to eat away from Army dining halls, drink away from Army canteens, and entertain themselves without recourse to Army theaters or other facilities. Some even avoid the barracks entirely by renting apartments off post, without authorization or extra pay. As a measure of their wealth, it is interesting to note that not one high-stakes card or dice game was observed in 14 months of research, nor was a single loan shark identified.

The development of the multiphase study that gave rise to this book is the subject of the opening chapter. The aims, problems and insights of the project's formative years are discussed in detail, along with the makeup and responsibilities of the team of observers who carried out the fieldwork. Chapter 2 sketches the contemporary soldier's world, the structure of the duty day, and his evening and weekend activities. The discussion takes up the isolation of soldiers geographically, socially and psychologically. Appreciation of this isolation is essential in understanding how soldiers come to associate with each other and how they come to do what they do after duty hours. Such isolation also prevents certain phenomena from occurring. For example, it is very difficult for drug distribution rings to be organized by soldiers to push drugs onto other soldiers. Soldiers simply do not have enough contact with the civilian world outside, or even sufficient ties on post, for organized trafficking to occur.

Chapter 3 describes barracks living and takes up the affiliation theme more directly. Within their isolation, soldiers are restricted in the choice of companions by work group, rank, residence, race, and even by the physical layout of their barracks. The barracks of assignment exerts extraordinary influence on both choice of companions and choice of after-duty activities. This means that company leaders could, if they chose, exert enormous influence on what goes on in the barracks—including the use of drugs and alcohol. Soldiers in the barracks are neither "contaminated" nor "corrupted" by contacts in the civilian environs, nor for that matter by contacts in sister military units. They have scant commerce with either. Whatever they do and whatever antics they contrive are pretty much of their own making.

Chapter 3 also details the four major rules of barracks living: being a regular guy, damning the Army, refraining from squealing and confining theft to other barracks. These rules must be learned and followed if the soldier is to find respite from his ubiquitous isolation and if he is to have any hope of becoming incorporated into the social order of barracks living. These rules form the boundaries of the arena in which specific social behaviors (like using drugs and alcohol) are played out.

Chapters 4 and 5 describe drinking and drug use among soldiers. The study was initially conceived as an enquiry into drug and alcohol use, but it quickly became apparent that these behaviors were not deviant, but intimately entwined with the problems of affiliation and barracks living. The occupational role of soldier has a complex relation to drug and alcohol use. For many hard drinking is part and parcel of being a good fighter and warrior. Alcohol use is compatible with the soldier role, and leaders sometimes remark, "He drinks too much, but when the chips are down, there is none better." Leaders never say, "He does dope occasionally, but when the chips are down. . . ." For the leaders, and some privates with career aspirations, drug use is incompatible with soldiering, but few users subscribe to this belief.

The main connection between drug use and soldiering was the anti-Army norm of barracks living. Drug use was the governing metaphor to express private soldiers' anti-Army sentiments. It was the ultimate in "getting over on the system," a disapproved behavior which cannot be regarded as mutiny or refusal.

But there was more to the use of drugs and alcohol than simply baiting authority or being macho. The critical social problem for the boys was creating a sense of stability in their social relationships in circumstances in which they had little choice of companions, in which all relationships were confined to the immediate past or the here-and-now, and in which social activities permitted maximum participation with minimum requisite skill. Drinking bouts provided one effective mechanism for soldiers to build a distinctive history of group association that bound the members closer together. Drugs provided still another mechanism for group formation in that most barracks residents had enough experience with drugs to assure commonalities.

Chapter 6 examines the influence of Army leaders on behavior in the barracks and concludes that the influence is negligible. Typically, leaders chose not to get involved in barracks activities after normal duty hours; they tended to judge their people by duty performance which included the observance of traditional military courtesies and appearance standards. So long as the job was done, the leaders held, there was no cause to inquire into a soldier's private life. What information the leaders had about drug and alcohol use came largely from visible "problem soldiers" who were below standards in military appearance, deportment or job performance.

In exceptional cases, as with Sergeant Wiley Fox (a real soldier with a fictitious name), leaders could influence what went on in the barracks, but at great cost. The army of Beetle Bailey, with the platoon sergeant living in the barracks with his charges, is long gone. Most sergeants are now married; most live some distance from the post; few live in the barracks. Thus increasing misunderstanding and social distance are inevitable. It is one thing to order sergeants to visit the barracks after duty hours; it is quite another to find commonalities—things to talk about—once they are there.

As the observers' descriptions confirm throughout, soldiers spend much time in pointed, sometimes cruel, verbal banter and rough-housing. The primary result of these activities is status-ordering in the work group—defining who can tell whom what to do when, where and how. The notion that the Army runs exclusively on orders and formal symbols of rank is incomplete. In the typical workday, and in most other activities as well, those in formal authority have little to do with the actual, moment-to-moment execution of the assigned task. To divide the labor, coordinate activities and work efficiently as a team, a system of super- and subordination is necessary. Informal status-ordering—the verbal banter, the rough-housing, the talk about sexual escapades, the interpersonal bonding, the sharing of drugs and alcohol—achieves such a system. The status system reduces and absorbs interpersonal conflict among soldiers of equivalent formal rank and helps insure that assigned tasks are accomplished. The authority to give directions and to insist on correct procedures derives from the seemingly "meaningless and juvenile" interchanges that serve to put and keep everyone in place. Greasing battery terminals, checking motor seals, tightening lug nuts, and other such minor aspects of work may appear to be trivial and hardly worth the time devoted to put-downs and rough-housing, but it is precisely for want of such "horseshoe nails" that battles are lost.

The recreational activities in the peer group also have important status-sorting consequences. In the slack times of the duty day and in the barracks at night, the individuals come to know and define their own potential, and that of others. It is in gossiping, carousing, smoking and playing that consensus emerges as to who in the group can act and who can talk, who has sound judgment and who is a fool, who is reliable and who is untrustworthy, who gets into trouble and who stays out. Such social comparisons are critical for effectiveness in combat, for the ability to make accurate judgments has much to do with the appropriate deployment of unit resources. In the final analysis, it is the ability to make such determinations with confidence that distinguishes the "seasoned" military unit from the "green" one.

The ability to make accurate interpersonal assessments is also essential for any present or future sergeant, thus the barracks becomes the prep school. Army life at the level of the common soldier is a series of intensely personal, face-to-face encounters that often border on the violent and call for fine-tuned judgments. As a boy in the barracks, the future NCO learns when to fight and when to flee, when to bluff and when to be deadly serious, when to mobilize the group and when to handle it man-to-man, when to ridicule and when to reason, when to shout and when to whisper.

The informal interaction among common soldiers in the barracks provides the individual with a highly adaptive code of conduct. The soldier incorporated into the barracks can request another to cover for him during an unauthorized absence, to file a punishment document in such a way that it never appears on his record, to account for a field jacket or blanket he has lost, to lend him money or a car, and to tell him where to go and what to do when he is in trouble. When caught in a punishable indiscretion, the soldier incorporated into the social structure learns to tell "Top" [the First Sergeant] that he screwed up and that he's sorry, rather than using the tired lies, "My grandmother died" or "My car ran out of gas." He learns how to maintain his barracks area in conformity with local standards (the only ones that count), how to dress and conduct himself without incurring the wrath of the peer group, how to maintain his equipment, how to do his job, and how to save time and work. Information on how to behave also extends to nonduty times and includes how to conduct oneself with women ("nice girls," "whores" and "sweathogs"), where to go without increasing the risk of a fight, what to wear, and how to act in a "nice" restaurant.

The boys learn from each other both how to behave as soldiers and how to behave as men. In an informal but nonetheless influential apprenticeship, they learn to push the Army system to the limit to benefit themselves and their buddies. Later, if they have learned their lessons well, they push, pull, bend and twist the system for their subordinates as well.

There is a final, overriding reason for becoming incorporated into the social order of the barracks: the soldier's sanity and very life depend upon it. Impoverished and constrictive as it may seem, the social order of the barracks provides the individual with the only bonds of caring, respect, affection and affiliation that he has in the Army. These bonds, built up over countless jokes, put-downs, drinking bouts, joints and "sweathog" stories, are the ties that bind the men together to sustain themselves and perform as a team. Once these webs of interpersonal commonality and sentiment are rent asunder, the unit falls apart. It requires the loss of surprisingly few men for a unit to become combat-ineffective. The celebrated order, "Stand and fight to the last man," can be obeyed only in the most unusual circumstances.

Group structure is critical not only in sustaining unit performance, but also in sustaining individual performance. This fact, while not systematically researched until 1964 by Little, was discovered in World War I with cases of "shell shock" and rediscovered in World War II when the number of "combat exhaustion" evacuations from the North African theater exceeded the number of replacements. The importance of the group for sustaining the individual was persuasively argued by the Bartemeir study in 1946:

> It is a very obvious fact that the psychiatrically disabled soldier cannot function well in the close-knit combat unit, but this is not our point of emphasis. Here we mean to emphasize the fact that the organized pattern of the unit and its emotional bonds constitute the dominant constructive and integrative force for the individual soldier in his fighting function. This group life is his inner life. When an individual member of such a combat group has his emotional bonds of group integration seriously disrupted, then he, as a person, is thereby disorganized. The disruption of group unity is, in the main, a primary causal factor, not a secondary effect, of personality disorganization.

Ultimately, drugs and alcohol as used by the boys in the barracks contribute to the formation of these "emotional bonds of group integration." This is not to say that other social behaviors do not also serve this purpose. Nor is it to deny that there may also be negative consequences attached to the use of drugs and alcohol by barracks dwellers. It is simply to assert that the use of drugs and alcohol facilitates the bonding between isolated individuals who find themselves living together largely by chance rather than choice and who are held in place by a number of specific environmental structures, both physical and social.

Emphasizing the bonding effect of drugs and alcohol does not wash away the differences between smoking and drinking with regard to their legal status. Nor does it explain the psychological and physiological "high" that comes from a six-pack or a joint. The bonding yield referred to comes from the clustering of prior and present commonalities which soldiers can identify and construct while they are using; semidurable meanings and memories are ascribed to these commonalities and a semblance of social stability emerges from the mutual participation.

It may well be that drug use in an Army unit is positively correlated with unit cohesion and morale, rather than negatively correlated, as is generally supposed. The present data strongly suggest that the patterns of drug and alcohol use are largely determined by the patterns of social interaction in the barracks after duty hours which in turn are bounded by the patterns of interaction permitted within the formal structure during the duty day. The soldiers we studied tended to spend their leisure time with those they knew best, and those they knew best were usually those with whom they spent the most time during working hours. Therefore, insofar as the mission, structure and operations of a military unit encourage soldiers to know one another better, these factors also generate those conditions of interpersonal knowledge and trust that enable efficient drug distribution and discreet use. It should follow, all else being equal, that military units at highest risk for drug use are those that are most cohesive. However, those with the least cohesion will appear to be highest in drug use because they have insufficient group solidarity to prevent or mask public exposure of drug involvement.

For whatever reason and for whatever purpose, the fact is that drug use among common soldiers in the United States Army is now endemic, just as alcohol use has always been in the American military. It becomes essential to understand what is involved in this phenomenon. The findings and interpretations presented here demonstrate the need to understand the soldiers' lives in general before meaningful comment is possible on any single aspect of them, whether it be drug and alcohol use, venereal disease, absenteeism, performance effectiveness or whatever. There has been enough whispering and denial. It is time to define the nature of the existent social order so that the behaviors which occur within it will be predictable and manageable rather than unexpected and alarming.

As a rejoinder someone is certain to ask, but just who are these boys in the barracks? Whom do they represent? Dare we allow them to speak for the entire Army? Are they not merely a tiny minority of common soldiers—support troops at that—stationed at a "backwater" post with every reason to be dispirited and uninspired, and in constant search of manufacturing their own excitement? Had one of the elite combat units been the focus of observation, would the findings have been quite different?

The question of generalizability is a matter for future research. Unknown are the limits under which drug and alcohol use facilitates group bonding. Unknown, for example, are the consequences on group cohesiveness of drug use by soldiers deployed to a combat zone. Unknown as well is the extent to which gains in social solidarity are offset by immediate physiological costs. Mythology would have it that soldiers traditionally drink hard during pauses in battle, but we do not know in any kind of systematic fashion how such diversions affect group functioning or individual performance in the heat of the conflict.

However, to ask *who* our boys are is the wrong question when it comes to shedding light on the generalizability issue. The domain of generalization is defined by the barracks, not by the boys. Given common social structures, common behavioral patterns result. These patterns can take the form of horseplay, verbal banter, roughhousing, sex talk, whoring, smoking and drinking, clique formations and affiliations, among many others. The personalities and demographics of the individuals housed by the social structures are essentially irrelevant to the generalization question. Social structures determine the patterns of social behavior; individual differences determine who specifically fills what role (the script for which is already written), or who in particular is assigned which label (the content of which is already fixed). It matters little if the soldiers are black or white, rich or poor, tall or short, high school dropouts or college graduates, and, most probably, male or female. The important question is: How similar are the social structures?

Readers of drafts of this book have reacted with shock, dismay, and even disgust at some of the descriptions of barracks living. The tone of barracks life is often thought to be bleak and depressing, if not thoroughly repulsive and obscene. But it is well to remember that the boys in the barracks are not deviants or delinquents. They are American soldiers who do their jobs as they have been trained—and constrained—to do them. They are the next generation of Army sergeants. They will fight America's next war.

In the final analysis we are not talking about titillating tales and bawdy humor. We are concerned with the fate of our country, with the ability of our army to maintain itself on the field of battle. Obviously the picture that emerges here does not conform to the highest American middle-class values, aspirations and ideals regarding either the Army or American youth, but that is all beside the point. The lives of the soldiers in the barracks—bleak as these barracks may seem—depend on each other's, and ours on theirs.

STUDYING
THE BOYS

*DRUG USE
IN ARMY*

THE FORMATIVE YEARS

Today it is difficult to recapture the national mood toward drugs and the Army that prevailed as the seventies decade began. It was a time of deep discontent marked by war protests, Haight-Ashbury, hippies, yippies and social radicals of every kind. Through the medium of drugs the "flower children" envisioned peace and contentment as they sought freedom from an "establishment" that saw all drug users as lurid and depraved, conforming to the "junkie model" of Harry Anslinger.

Drug use in the Army at that time was privately acknowledged to exist at all levels of command, but was publicly denied. The most favored response to discovered use was legal prosecution and, if possible, discharge from service. That was a time when concerned sergeants adjusted duty assignments for those "on dope" without distinguishing between marijuana and barbiturates or heroin. That was a time when only the most daring garrison commanders permitted a simple survey of drug use out of fear that the results would reflect unfavorably upon their careers.

Circumspection about drug use in the Army ended abruptly in the summer of 1971 when two congressmen announced that up to 40 percent of the enlisted men serving in Vietnam were addicted to heroin. Drug abuse suddenly became a national concern. The President declared heroin use national enemy number one, and appointed a drug "czar" to plan and coordinate a federal response. In the Army urine screening procedures were developed and implemented for soldiers leaving Vietnam, and treatment programs were instituted to prevent the hoard of addicted veteran junkies from ravaging the countryside upon their return home. Almost overnight it became fashionable to speak of and propose research into "the drug abuse problem" in the Army.

The mounting national concern about drug abuse bordered on hysteria and contrasted starkly with the concerns of rank-and-file soldiers. Interview respondents imprisoned in stockades or referred to the mental hygiene service tended to fit the junkie characterization of drug use. These were regular users of heroin with extensive histories of drug use and ineffective military performance. Their concern was discharge from the Army, not addiction to drugs. A second group of soldiers also used drugs, but had not been "captured" or otherwise identified as users. Interviews with them became focused on positive benefits of drug use, the contrasting effects of different substances, how to roll a joint, where to buy, and how to improve enjoyment of drug-induced sensations. Their concern was to convert others to the delights of use while at the same time completing their Army tours with a minimum of hassle. The third group of soldiers did not use drugs, and were not particularly knowledgeable or concerned about those who did. Their objective was to complete their Army tours without hassles.

None of these groups viewed drug users as particularly dangerous, necessarily ineffective, or in need of rehabilitation. For the investigator imbued with the popular images of the dangers of drug use, the reports of the soldiers in the line were both dissonant and disconcerting. What was "the drug abuse problem" in the Army?

Interviews conducted in 1971 cast further doubt on common assumptions about drug use in the Army. Soldiers were interviewed who had been labeled "opiate-positive" as a result of the urine screen required upon leaving Vietnam. These data contradicted several popular assumptions about heroin use by American soldiers in Vietnam.

The respondents neither presented nor viewed themselves as street junkies. Quite the opposite, they despised the junkie and attendant stereotypes with as much fervor as did other Americans, and they saw themselves as good American soldiers who happened to get caught with heroin in their system when they left Vietnam. There was little evidence in the interviews that heroin necessarily resulted in reduced job proficiency. There was no evident association between heroin use and criminal behavior in the form of thefts or personal assaults. Heroin use in Vietnam was generally preceded by the use of other drug substances. Heroin use did not appear to result from mental illness or any other behavioral disorder that would distinguish the detected user from the undetected user or from the nonuser.

Heroin use did not result from combat stress. "Boredom" was not a satisfactory explanation of use. Heroin use in Vietnam was not embedded in an "anti-establishment, antimilitary countercultural" ideology.

Despite massive evidence of national and Army concern about the "drug abuse problem" in the form of detection strategies, educational materials, and treatment centers, and despite the ever-growing number of surveys reporting widespread use of various substances, the next logical research step was unclear. The admittedly limited data available indicated that the concerns of common soldiers were not those of policy planners, and that even in the extreme case of a heroin epidemic, popular assumptions of drug use were untenable. In such a context the research strategy was to go back to basics and inquire, "How many soldiers are using what kinds of drugs with what frequency and with what effect on individual and group behavior?"

A proposed research strategy, entitled "Drug Ecologies and the Military Community," was initiated under the direction of Dr. David H. Marlowe, a social anthropologist at the Walter Reed Institute of Research. The proposal explicitly recognized that a military community or Army post was not, in the main, a "total" institution, but rather a composite of radically different social structures that could be expected to exert varying influences on the behavior of its members. The proposal also recognized that a military community could not be studied in isolation, for there were numerous and complex links to the immediate civilian community. It followed, therefore, that drug use was to be viewed within the total milieu of the users, including hometowns, families, and friends. The military environment represented simply another segment, albeit an important one.

Given these assumptions a series of studies was planned to examine (1) the distribution of unauthorized drug use among low-ranking young soldiers; (2) the demographic, personal, social, organizational, and leadership variables which influenced the maintenance of such use; (3) the social networks that provided the occasion, the accompanying communication, the social reference points, and the physical supply in drug use; (4) factors which influenced individuals to present themselves voluntarily or involuntarily for treatment; and (5) the implications of the resultant epidemiologic picture for the design of prevention and treatment programs.

A medium-sized Army post in the eastern United States was selected as the study site and was dubbed "Fort S.L.A. Marshall" after the noted military historian. Whether Fort Marshall was representative or typical of Army posts in general is problematic. Army posts range in size from tiny Fort Hamilton in Brooklyn, New York, to the vastness of Fort Sill in Oklahoma and Fort Bliss in west Texas. They also vary in their principal functions from induction training centers like Fort Dix, New Jersey, and administrative centers like Fort Monroe, Virginia, to division garrison posts like Fort Riley, Kansas, Fort Hood, Texas, and Fort Polk, Louisiana. Determining what kind of post is typical of the "real Army" depends on one's vision of the Army. Fort Marshall was selected because of its proximity and because it contained a manageable number of garrisoned soldiers not in introductory training status. It was conceded at the outset that the generalizability of findings ultimately rests upon replications at other locations.

A multidisciplinary team carried out the studies. It consisted of anthropologists, sociologists, psychologists, psychiatrists, social workers, epidemiologists, a biomathematician, and secretarial personnel. The work proceeded in three phases.

Phase I: Initial Observations

Research began even before the research proposal was officially approved. Team members visited Fort Marshall to become familiar with its geography and to observe post activities in the evenings and on weekends. Some of these observations are worth recounting in detail as they provide a sense of the atmosphere in which the work began.

On the one hand some of the observations encouraged fantasies of mystery, intrigue, and danger at the prospect of penetrating the local "drug scene." One observer noted:

> 8:45 P.M.: Bowling alley. Twenty 20 out of 24 lanes in use constantly by possibly 80 to 100 people, mostly families and dependents. In both the male and female toilets are heavy steel boxes chained to the wall with a sign, "Drop your drugs here, no questions asked." People didn't seem to be hanging around; the principal activity was bowling, but a big sign above the door reading "No Loitering" suggests they may have had problems in the past.

Thus the bowling alley was noted as a possible "copping" area (it was still fashionable to use such terms as "copping" in the early seventies), although it was not possible to ask questions because of the observer's unofficial status on the post. Another rumored place to buy and sell drugs was a nearby fastfood outlet, and casual observation fed suspicion. The observer noted:

9:30 P.M.: McDonald's. At least 30 cars in the lot. Mostly long hairs, 15 to 16 years old. Two civilian deputy sheriffs are politely discouraging loitering. Some long hairs moved on quickly, some responded grudgingly, and others bought food and went to the patio area. The young teens leave a car, get into someone else's car, drive off, and return a short time later. Two enlisted men (judging from their short hair), parked in the back of the lot, met another group, and then came back to their car. They seemed to be just hanging; the deputy approached and asked them to move on.

During this time many on the research staff were skeptical about the possibility of ever really penetrating the "drug scene," believing that no user would really tell the truth, let alone permit observation of illegal activities. Drug drop boxes at the bowling alley and deputy sheriffs at McDonald's made for interesting speculations during staff meetings but were little more than curiosities.

On one of these initial "birdwatching" trips, the author chanced to meet Willie and Joe, two previously known Vietnam veterans. They both were using drugs regularly, including heroin, and although they were still in the Army, their hair was far beyond regulation length, they wore cut-offs and T-shirts, and their apperance was dirty and disheveled. Their company first sergeant had informed them that they were such a disgrace to the Army that he did not want to see them in the company area until the day of their discharge. Since that time they had lived off post in a rundown trailer situated in the middle of an automobile junkyard. There they maintained a drug store and shooting gallery for their friends and associates on post. They invited the author to their trailer where he observed marijuana smoking, needle use, and heroin sales. Now the activities at the fast-food places assumed a different character:

Stan and his family drove into Gino's. His car was immediately recognized by Willie, and both of them waved. Stan ordered at the counter, came over to our table, spoke cordially to them, and nodded to me in recognition of our meeting at the trailer. Joe asked how business was going. Stan said he only had three ounces left, and Joe said, "What a pity." I assumed that meant there was no chance for Stan to front them for the evening. Joe asked when the next shipment would be available. Stan said it would not be in before Friday, but that he would be really hustling until then to get orders lined up for pay day.

Having demonstrated that direct observation of drug use and sales were possible among soldiers, the research staff became concerned about how to react in the event of a drug bust. Lists were made of the various law enforcement agencies and jurisdictions in the vicinity of the post with an eye to informing them of the research interests and activities.

While the drug-related observations whetted appetites for the research effort, the initial reconnaissance forays were, by and large, a collossal bore. Nothing much seemed to be happening on the post after duty hours. On the weekends it was possible to drive around the post without seeing more than a dozen people, not counting the family quarters or shopping areas. The barracks areas seemed deserted. Weekday evenings were scarcely more active with the exception of intramural athletic events and social activities that gave the post the ambience of a small town or a suburban development. Activities in the barracks areas were more evident during the work week, but certainly were not dramatic:

> All tennis courts were in use at the corner of X and Y streets. Several men were standing in the street in the 800 area and a party of six was grilling food at a picnic table set up between the barracks. In the MP area six men were involved in washing and polishing cars. [At] the Service Club . . . there was no sign of activity. In the medical battalion six enlisted men were tossing a football in a rather desultory fashion. Two men were watching the whole scene from the steps of a nearby barracks, and three men watched from the fire balcony on the second floor. One man sat on a garbage can listening to a transistor radio.

And so the observations continued, both on post and in the immediate environs, revealing very pedestrian activities in small, informal groups that seldom exceeded half a dozen members.

In the fall of 1972 the research plan received final approval, and the research staff began interviewing sergeants and company grade officers to inform them of the effort, enlist their support, and get an initial sense of their perceptions of drug use on the post. Those interviewed were supportive of the work and willing to cooperate, but they did not view drug use as a particular problem in their units. Perceived drug use seemed to vary considerably among companies, and the informants attributed these differences to the number of short-term Vietnam returnees assigned, the amount of mission-relevant work given the unit, and the quality of leadership and morale. With the exception of a shooting in a company with reputedly heavy drug use, the principal problems reported by the leaders were barracks thefts, pay disputes, absences without leave, excessive drinking, and maintaining discipline in the permissive climate of the new Volunteer Army.

The next objective in the initial research phase was to acquire a sense of the history of Fort Marshall and to define its relationship wtih the adjacent civilian communities. Visits to the post museum and an interview with the post archivist revealed that Fort Marshall had been built during World War I as an embarkation point, training center, and remount station, and had been declared a permanent Army facility following World War II. Surveys of local newspaper files indicated a predominance of murder, assault, and drunk-driving stories involving soldiers assigned to the post, but little in the way of antipathy toward the post itself. The initial interviews with the company grade sergeants and officers indicated that most soldiers left the post on weekends; a long-time community resident indicated that this had always been the pattern as he recalled World War I soldiers literally "hanging off the train" on their way to the cities on pass.

Another project in the initial phase of research was to examine the post's record sources. Of principal interest were the personnel records, which provided data on the demographic composition of the post. The records of the provost marshal's office, the hospital, and the pharmacy were also examined for possible usefulness in characterizing on-post drug use. Two results of these efforts are especially noteworthy. First, the demographic composition of the post in terms of the distribution of rank, education, race, and marital status remained virtually unchanged throughout the two-year course of the study. Second, the demographic character remained unchanged despite massive personnel turnovers that in some units represented in- and out-migrations of 300 percent per annum.*

The final project in the initial research phase was a sociometric questionnaire mailed to every enlisted person assigned to the post. The questionnaire asked the respondent to name two individuals whom he regularly chose as associates during duty hours and three individuals with whom he spent time after duty hours. Thirty percent of the population returned usable questionaires. The responses were then checked against the master personnel roster, and the unit of assignment was noted. On the during-duty-hours question, 85 percent of the named associates were assigned to the same unit as the respondent; the percentage during nonduty hours was only slightly lower at 79 percent. Obviously unit of assignment exerted powerful effects on the choice of associates. Fully as interesting as the quantitative counts, however, were the numerous volunteered comments

---

*I am indebted to my colleague, Dr. Joseph M. Rothberg, for providing extensive analysis of the personnel records and demographic data.

written by soldiers who did not live in the barracks: "I don't hang around with Army people after duty"; "I spend my nonduty time with my family"; and "When off work I get as far away from the fucking Army as possible."

At the conclusion of the initial phase, the feasibility of observing drug consumption and sales firsthand had been established. It was evident that there was little activity on post after duty hours with the exception of family-oriented athletic programs, movies, and attendance at the NCO and officers' clubs. Facilities designed for use by the enlisted people were largely deserted. Interviews with company grade officers and sergeants indicated that units varied widely in drug use, that soldiers spent little time around the units when off duty, and that drugs did not present a particularly troublesome problem to the leaders. Inquiries indicated a long history of amicable military/civilian relations. Inspection of the post records showed considerable personnel instability in some units, and those with the greatest turnover rates and the largest number of malassigned or underused soldiers were those reputed to be heaviest in drug use. Finally, the survey showed that unit of assignment exerted powerful constraints on associations both during and after normal duty hours.

Phase II: Biochemical and Behavioral Screening

In the spring of 1973, an attempt was made to define the population of drug users on post that could be followed prospectively for the following year. With the cooperation of the Institute's Division of Biochemistry, urine samples were collected under controlled conditions from 80 percent of the lower-ranking enlisted population available for duty. At the time of the urine screen, each participant also filled out a brief questionnaire that inquired as to drug use in the previous month and the preceding 48 hours. Individuals who evidenced recent drug use on either of these measures were considered unconfirmed positives. The unconfirmed positives were then matched with unconfirmed negatives on the basis of rank, race, and unit of assignment. Both the positives and negatives were then interviewed extensively to secure data not only about drug use, but also such demographic and social attributes as religion, work history, arrest record, education, health, and social class.

The results of these efforts were as disconcerting as they were enlightening. First, a double-blind, split-sample study indicated that the thin-layer chromatography technique for detecting drug metabo-

lites was unreliable and that the popular and then standard free radical assay technique was reliable only when comparatively high levels of morphine and its metabolites were being excreted. Second, while the nonanonymous questionnaire on drug use in the preceding 48 hours identified more unconfirmed positives than the biochemical analysis, each measure appeared to detect different persons. Third, the intensive interviews detected more past drug use than had the nonanonymous questionnaire, but again the degree of overlap between those who admitted to past drug use on the questionnaire and in the interview was strikingly low. Fourth, the unconfirmed positives did not differ from their matched negative "controls" in histories of past drug use. Finally, the demographic and social attribute variables uniformly failed to distinguish any drug-positive subset from the total enlisted population. Blacks were disproportionately represented in one of the biochemical tests, but even this difference washed out when education and intelligence were taken into account. The single exceptions were age and marital status—drug users tended to be younger and unmarried.

Thus, depending on the measure used, current drug use ranged from 3 to 12 percent, and past drug use ranged from 40 to 60 percent. The measure that best represented the true prevalence was indeterminant. For purposes of epidemiological study the highest prevalence estimates were achieved by simply asking people about their use of drugs. To implement the intended prospective study, the best course was to devise a composite index of asserted regular drug use that included (1) reported regular past use of illicit drugs other than marijuana, (2) reported regular current use of marijuana, (3) reported intermittent current use of drugs other than marijuana, and (4) extensive and detailed knowledge of the "drug scene."

Three observations from the casefinding phase of the study are important to discuss here. First, the groups at highest risk were the young, unmarried soldiers—the men who lived in company barracks. This seemed the case regardless of the measure used.

The second observation has to do with response to the urine screen activity. There was considerable concern among the researchers that "the word would get out" and increasing numbers of soldiers would evade urine collections. Efforts were made to capitalize on the element of surprise and to locate all soldiers not present. Such concerns proved unnecessary when it became evident that there was virtually no informal communication between companies. A unit screened one day appeared to be just as uninformed about the screening activity as its sister unit screened the previous day. There was simply no evidence of evasions of any sort throughout the month in which the urine screening took place.

The third observation relates to the discovered ambiguity in defining high-risk units. All the measures of drug prevalence, as well as the data from the interview protocols, confirmed previous reports of large differences between units on the post.

No matter which measure of prevalence was used, the companies tended to retain their rank in the distribution. Thus, while the companies did not differ statistically in their absolute levels of reported use, their consistent ranking was congruent with the perceptions of the informants (users, nonusers, and leaders). This led to the premature conclusion that not only were companies with distinctly high or low drug use a reality, but they could be characterized. High-prevalence units were defined as those with varied garrison missions and little opportunity for professional behavior on the part of the men assigned to them; whereas low-prevalence units were thought to be composed of men who were able to exercise their professional skills in garrison, tended to have a professional self-image, were more career-oriented, were slightly older, and were better educated. It turned out that drug use patterns followed less simplistic lines.

Phase III: Intensive Studies

The final phase of the comprehensive research plan involved intensive study and analysis of four areas of interest. This book considers one of these areas—unit studies. The other three are briefly noted to round out the description of the larger research effort.

In one study observers were assigned to the alcohol and drug treatment facilities and charged with documenting the rehabilitation efforts as well as examining how soldiers came to be admitted and discharged from these facilities. A second study focused on the asserted regular drug users and suitable matched controls that had been defined in the previous phase. The aim of this study was to examine the social friendship and acquaintance network structures of users and nonusers to determine interpersonal factors that encouraged the initiation and maintenance of drug use. A third intensive study was a survey of drug and alcohol use, personality measures, and behavioral inventories that employed a probability sample of 700 enlisted people.

The purpose of the unit studies was to determine the organizational and leadership factors that accounted for the "known" differences in drug use prevalence among the companies assigned to Fort Marshall. The task and circumstances represented a multivariate psychologist's dream, for not only were there nearly fifty organizations available for study, but also the successful urine screen experience had demonstrated that if necessary, the entire population of enlisted soldiers could be questioned. All that needed to be done was to specify the dimensions to be measured before proceeding with the correlational design.

The Research Plan

With the foregoing variables in mind, a research plan for the unit studies area was drafted and approved with the confident title, "Drug and Alcohol Usage Patterns as a Function of the Organization, Operations, and Compositions of Companies in the United States Army." This plan proposed two phases of research of six months each. The first phase was to describe life in Army companies from the view of the lower-ranking soldier with the aim of determining those variables and combinations most directly related to drug use as well as providing an interpretive context for subsequently documented relations. The second six months of the study was to involve tests of hypotheses generated in the first phase by means of questionnaires, systematic observations, and conventional inferential statistics.

Two companies were selected for intensive study during the first projected phase of data collection, one estimated to be high in drug use prevalence and the other low. Participant observers were assigned to these units. To assess the generality of the observers' experiences, two other companies comparable in estimated drug use prevalence were also monitored by means of nonparticipant observation and interviews with both individuals and groups.

The four target companies were quite heterogeneous with respect to organizational, operational, and compositional variables. Two of the companies were vastly overstrength with diffuse boundaries and tangled lines of communication between the commander and the various work sections. The other two units were approximately at strength and were organized in the classic pyramid. One unit had relatively little work related to its specific military capability, two units worked intermittently on tasks they were trained to perform, and one unit had both men with nothing to do of military relevance and men working full-time as they had been trained. There were concomitant variations in leadership, experience, and demographic composition.

Army companies are not closed social systems for they receive constant input from higher command that affects their structure and operations. The battalion, as ther next larger military unit, had to be considered; thus the four companies selected for study represented three different battalions assigned to the post.

Data Collection

Army enlisted men worked as the full-time participant observers in two of the companies. The other units of high and low drug use were regularly monitored through observation and through individual and group interviews by an enlisted technician, an Army staff sergeant, and an Army captain (the study director) with the assistance of an Army major with a doctorate in social work. A field manual was developed for the project to provide the sequence of activities and the kinds of information the field workers were expected to collect during the first six months of observation. The field workers were carefully instructed to adhere to specific ethical guidelines in conducting the research. They were then trained in interviewing, observing, and recording techniques before being introduced into the units. The observers averaged two to three days a week in the units, including evenings, weekends, and holidays. Some weeks were more concentrated than others, depending on unit activities, conflicting obligations, and writer's cramp. The study director was in constant touch with the officers in the respective units as he conducted interviews and arranged for groups to be excused from duty for group interviews and discussions.

Every attempt was made to file the field notes with the study director on the day following the observations so that criticism and suggestions could immediately be used to guide the observations and interviews. Each week a copy of the field notes was filed with the project director, who provided additional criticism and guidance. Summaries of the work were presented periodically to the entire research staff for further discussion.

Shattered Illusions

Everything proceeded according to plan through the first four months of observation. The observers were gradually introduced into the units and met with acceptance. Confidence grew in the initial selection of variable sets, and relationships became apparent. The high-use companies definitely evidenced more diffuse organizational boundaries and more ineffective and complicated chains of communication. Leaders in high-use companies seemed to be "paper-pushers" who seldom left the administrative offices; whereas low-use companies were marked by "people-pushers" who frequently left the orderly room to tour the company area and see for themselves how their subordinates were handling their tasks. Finally, first-line supervisors in the low-use units seemed to show a more genuine concern for the welfare of their charges. After two more months of observation, with the observers living in the barracks, questionnaire construction could begin for Phase II.

Two months in the barracks shattered all illusions of a neat, statistically supported research project. First, confidence in a criterion measure was lost completely. The observer assigned to the barracks presumed to be low in drug use reported regular and substantial drug use among the residents, while the observer in the presumably high-use company reported only irregular and inconsequential use. This dramatic reversal in the estimated prevalence of drug use between the companies could not be explained by observer bias, errors in technique, problems of acceptance by the barracks dwellers, or any other known artifact. Not only was drug use unstable for individuals, as the previous interviews indicated, but it also appeared to be unstable within companies. If so, use must be determined by variables other than the organizational ones originally assumed. Since biochemical tests, questionnaires, depth interviews, and participant observation all gave different pictures of drug use, the phenomena to be explained became highly problematic.

Second, assumptions about drug use that were reasonable when the study was conceived were no longer valid. The "Drug Scene" had disappeared. It was no longer possible to think in terms of speed freaks, pot heads, needle freaks, acid heads, and junkies who were organized in militant opposition to the "straights" and "juicers." Multidrug use had become the norm, with only occasional recreational use of heroin. The observers were not better than the computer had been in distinguishing users from nonusers on the basis of demographic characteristics or social attributes. The reason for this seemed to be that users and nonusers were the same people behaving in different ways at different times.

Third, continued observations in the barracks indicated that the hypothesized predictors bore little relation to observed drug use. In the natural course of events, uncaring supervisors were replaced by concerned supervisors; "people-pushers" replaced "paper-pushers"; work group boundaries become comparatively more defined or more diffuse with changes in mission, personnel, and leadership; yet drug use in the barracks was not affected.

In view of these considerations, to continue with the planned multivariate phase could only have resulted in a series of insignificant and largely uninterpretable correlations. There were other, more basic questions to be asked. If not the hypothesized sets of variables, what then did influence drug use in the barracks? How was barracks behavior patterned? What was the role of drug and alcohol use in the observed patterns? What were the contexts in which these substances were used? These questions could only be addressed by continued observation in the barracks themselves.

THE OBSERVERS

Some perspective may be gained for the observations discussed above by taking a closer look at the persons who made them. There were six observers: three lower-ranking enlisted technicians, an Army staff sergeant, an Army major with doctoral training in social work, and the author (an Army captain at the time). Two of the enlisted technicians lived full-time in different barracks. Their ranks precluded two black members of the observer group from living in the barracks.

In participant observation, the rules of the society being studied are not suspended. This held true for the observers of the boys in the barracks. Like all soldiers new to a unit, the observers had first to establish their credibility. They introduced themselves and their institutional affiliation, and they explained that their mission was to learn about drug and alcohol use from the perspective of the common soldier. Ordinarily the soldiers reciprocated with such comments as, "You sure picked the right unit for your study" or "It's about time you guys stopped handing out forms and came to where the action is."

The chief difference between the incorporation of an observer into the barracks social structure and that of any other soldier was time. More time was required for the observers because they were required to abstain from distributing or consuming drugs. Had the observers been permitted to pass the acceptance test of sharing one or two marijuana cigarettes, incorporation into the barracks would have been quicker and smoother. For the observers to have done so, however, would have jeopardized their research roles, which required acceptance from users and nonusers alike.

Soldiers were familiar with undercover narcotics agents, so while admitting the novelty of the medical research ploy, they relied upon their standard social acid tests of acceptability. Did the observer mean what he said about anonymity and confidentiality? That could be easily determined. The observer noted:

> The interview was conducted in our field office. After about an hour, I had to change the cassette tape, and I made the mistake of using the old Army phrase, "All right, gentlemen, take a break. Smoke 'em if you got 'em, but don't smoke mine." To my amazement, they withdrew hand-rolled cigarettes and asked if I really meant it. What could I do? I opened the window and asked them to put their field jackets on the floor in front of the door to keep the smoke in the room. They lit up and then said, "We've got some beer in the car; you want beer? Sergeants like beer, don't they?"

Officer-observers were treated no differently. One way to establish that the officer was as accepting and nonjudgmental as he claimed was to bring beer to group interviews and observe how tense he became. Another way was to inquire, "Sir, have you ever smoked marijuana? Did you like it?" Among the observers, three were recreational marijuana users, one had experimented with marijuana but was not an experienced user, and two had no experience. All observers became equally capable of eliciting comparable data; the critical variable was willingness and ability to present oneself honestly and to listen without evaluating—the first rule of barracks living.

The observers who actually moved into the barracks were, of course, subjected to other tests despite their having worked in the company during the duty day for four months. The principal problems for the observer in the presumed high-use barracks were his own fears and apprehensions. These were no doubt heightened by a recent barracks shooting that was rumored to be related to drugs. The first night after receiving his bunk assignment, he found reason to sleep in the apartment he maintained off the post. On the second night, following some affirmative action counseling by the study director, he got little sleep and noted:

> I lay awake in the dark, listening to every footfall in the corridor, every squeak of the door, and every snore on the bay. Someone came to the bed beside mine, "Hey, Chico, you awake?" the voice whispered. "I was only able to get you a nickle bag; if you got any more money I might be able to get you some more tomorrow. Hey, who's the new guy?" "Some guy from Walter Reed who's studying drug use." "Maybe we should wake him up so he can write this down." They laughed softly, and I prayed they hadn't noticed I had stopped breathing.

On the third night in the barracks, the observer noted marijuana smoking, and the following week he participated in a raucous drinking party. Since he had participated in the drinking spree and since the company leaders were not informed of either the marijuana smoking or the party revelers, the observer was, in consequence, quickly incorporated.

The observer in the presumably low-use barracks had a more difficult time since the elite status of the unit required that the high prevalence of drug use be carefully hidden. The acid test in such situations was to induce the candidate for incorporation to smoke. The observer noted:

> At breakfast, Loveless asked, "Do you smoke weed?" "I've tried it a couple of times." "I've got some real good stuff that's ground down nice." "Is it treated?" "No, it's straight grass, no opium or chemicals." After breakfast, I mentioned I was going to the office to do some work and invited him to come along. "Do you want me to bring some weed?" "No, it might not be a good idea; I'm really not up to smoking right now." "What are you doing tonight, then?" "Nothing planned." "You were going to show me your stereo system at your apartment. We could listen to some music and get high." "Well . . . I'm not so much worried about myself, but the whole drug research project could be compromised." "Oh, well, shit, we can always smoke on the way over there; it's no big thing."

Indeed, it was a very big thing from the view of interpersonal bonding. Marijuana not only confirmed that individuals were who they said they were, but affirmed a commonality between them that transcended the circumstances of the moment. Marijuana use was a statement that the two people saw themselves as alike and united in an important way, and set the stage for further self-disclosure.

That evening, on the way to the observer's apartment, Loveless and his buddy smoked marijuana and took some amphetamine. The observer did not join them, but neither did he inform. Since the buddy was already being court-martialed for assaulting an officer, the situation was low-risk for the barracks residents, but high-risk for the observer.

The men's confidence in the observer grew as he adapted to local appearance and housekeeping standards and as he joined the consensus that Army service was "a bummer." However, he continued to be tormented by one resident who frequently made allusions to his being a narcotics agent. The observer felt well enough accepted in the barracks to test the group's allegiance:

Bunsen began his usual taunts about my being a narc. I was fed up and told him I resented his aspersions on my integrity. I said something like, "I've been around here for five months and nothing has happened. I know who smokes and who doesn't and who buys and who sells. Nothing's happened. Now, either back up your allegations or let's step outside and settle this man-to-man." The group was silent for a moment, then various members began calling out, "Yeah, lay off, Bunsen, he's cool; nothing's happened; shut the fuck up."

After that incident, the observer was not only totally accepted in the barracks, but his chief antagonist became one of his principal informants.

Drug use by the observers was not essential for the conduct of the study, but personal experience with marijuana was sometimes helpful. Respondents were known to comment, "I feel uncomfortable telling you about my drug history while thinking you're straight." In such cases, the observer, in keeping with the general norm of reciprocity and interpersonal honesty, often responded with disclosure of his own history of use.

There was more to barracks living than following abstract rules; there was also positive sentiment that developed in the course of shared experience. The observers sought not only to be accepted in their roles, but to be liked and respected as persons in their own right. On occasion, the role of the observer and the need to feel truly accepted were pitted against each other. Usually, the observer maintained the role, but sometimes he broke set:

When we got in the car, O'Neill said, "We're going to get you high yet," as he offered me some of his bourbon. I reiterated that I was technically still on duty, and that I would like to join them, but I just couldn't. Grady then said, "OK, let's keep the windows rolled up, so that if you get high your Captain will have no complaints." After he lit the first joint and exhaled in the back seat, and as it was passed among the four of us, the Volkswagen quickly filled with smoke. Between O'Neill's bourbon and the smoke in the car, I began to get a little bit high. I began rationalizing on the absurdity of my situation. There I was in a car with three other guys, smoking grass. I was not smoking, but getting high anyway; the chances of getting caught were nil; the guys in the barracks would accuse me of smoking with these guys, anyway. I then thought of my superiors, and their strict instructions regarding my research role, and rationalized my situation again. Marcusi had the "J," but was holding it after he took a hit. I nudged him and said, "Gimme the 'J' and don't look this way; you're not supposed to see this." He smiled, and turned his head. I'm not sure whether anyone even saw me take a quick hit. Nothing was said about it that night or later that I know of. The attitude in the car seemed to be, "Okay, if you want to smoke, fine; if not, OK, it's no big thing," but I felt like I had to take that hit.

The need for observers to demonstrate acceptance and positive sentiment for their barracksmates was reciprocated. The boys continually requested the observer to become a full participant. The observer was chided for talking with a "newbie," but was excused when he reminded them that he was only doing his job. He was asked whether he was mentally taking notes in a request to put aside his research role and be the buddy they affectionately knew him to be; they accepted his extending his tour in the hated Army because they accepted the importance of his work and because they were comfortable in his presence. Outside the barracks, the observers found it particularly difficult not to respond to these demands. One observer noted:

> As I left the barracks, Murphy said, "When are you going to invite us all over to your place for a beer?" "Any time at all." "How about tonight?" "Sure, Gross knows the way." I really didn't expect them to come, since Barker had left his car at home, and it had been five months since Gross had been there. But then Murphy had also said, "Roberts has some good dope. Can we bring it over?" "Sure, why not?" On the drive to the apartment, I started to worry about their smoking dope. I had never tried to present myself as a nonsmoker. In fact, when asked, I had always replied that I smoked occasionally. If they did come over, I felt they were making an overt move toward friendship and trust, a move I didn't want to discourage from a research standpoint. On the other hand, in my own apartment, I would have difficulty convincing them I was on duty, and I also had trouble convincing myself. I knew that no one would mention my smoking to any sergeant or officer, and that all I would be doing is affirming what I had already told them about myself. My not smoking could be interpreted as my lying about myself. When the group arrived, I had no doubts that I would smoke with them if they offered it. Being in my own apartment seemed to be a strong inducement to relax the research stance I had previously taken, for I felt like a host who didn't want to offend his guests.

The final time an observer broke set and joined in smoking marijuana occurred while accompanying one of the men to his hometown during a weekend, where the usual excuses—"I'm on duty" or "I can't because of the research project"—just were not applicable. The observer therefore assumed the role of a houseguest and behaved accordingly.

These three incidents were the only occasions on which the observers broke their pledge to refrain from joining the boys in using drugs. In the course of the study, they bought or were given drugs for the purpose of laboratory analysis, and thus provided another service for their associates in reliably determining what was being consumed. In view of the social pressures exerted on the observers to take part in the life of the barracks, it is reasonable to inquire how they managed to keep in their roles as well as they did.

An important factor was careful and consistent supervision. The observers were in contact with the study director almost daily. Their field notes were under constant review, and they were always encouraged to discuss the significance of their observations and their plans for future notations. In this way their work role was continually made explicit and conscious. When they faced situations that placed them in conflict with the company leaders—such as revealing what they had observed—the study director spoke directly to the leaders. In this way they could negotiate the rank structure by means other than relying on the barracks group. When they drank too much, they were instructed to spend more time counting than in downing rounds. Whenever they were depressed, discouraged, frustrated, or enraged, the study director was available to listen, encourage, cajole, praise, threaten, damn, or promise a better hereafter—whatever was required to get them back into the barracks.

Another important factor was that the primary allegiance of the observers was to the research staff, not to the barracks in which they lived. They were continually included in staff meetings, and they achieved enviable status when they summarized their observations. When not in the barracks, they socialized with the research staff. Moreover, they had outside interests such as classical guitar, tropical fish, white water canoeing, and serious reading that provided alternatives to getting drunk or chasing sweathogs.

The observers had resources that were unavailable to many of the barracks residents. They were also relatively better paid and so could afford to own their own cars and maintain furnished apartments. Transportation gave them not only a means of escape from the barracks, but a desirable service that was useful in barracks bargaining. The apartment provided not only a personal retreat from the barracks, but place for their barracksmates to visit. Finally, the observers had each other. In the apartment they shared and compared feelings and experiences, encouraged each other, bolstered each other in periodic mutiny against the study director, and not infrequently laughed at what they were going through.

2

THE SOLDIER'S WORLD

Constraints of many kinds contend in the behavioral arena and provide background for a description of face-to-face social interaction. The purpose of this chapter is to describe these constraints as they affect the behavior of soldiers in barracks.

SPATIAL ORGANIZATION

The world of the soldier consists of the post itself and the civilian environs beyond. Both offer a variety of things to do, but at the same time both limit access and pattern movements by their spatial and geographical character.

Due to the need for large tracts of land most Army posts are located in rural areas away from major population centers. This means that unless the barracks-dwelling soldier is interested in hunting, fishing, hiking, or communing with nature, there may be little enough to do for recreation. It also means that transactions with the civilian world require a car or bus. Even with a car, soldiers at Fort Marshall seldom ranged more than five miles from the post, judging from the blank, uncomprehending stares of bartenders and shopkeepers when asked whether much of their business came from the post. Only rarely did the boys venture the twenty or thirty miles to either of the two nearest cities.

Most of the transactions observed within a five-mile radius of the post occurred in what is called "Boomtown," "GI Town," or "The Strip." Clusters of small establishments along the major highways leading to the post catered almost exclusively to the needs and interests of soldiers.

The principal business activities in Boomtown involved liquor, food, automobiles, and dry cleaning. Its appearance was tacky, with garish advertising and bright outdoor lighting at night. Because Boomtown had a reputation for fights, robberies, and ripoffs, many soldiers were reluctant to go there unaccompanied. When they did, they chose those establishments located nearest their barracks.

The post itself contained thousands of acres with only a small portion in regular use. In many ways an Army post is much like an American small town, albeit a company town. Its industrial sections include railroad yards, warehouses, motor pools, and repair facilities. Other sections contain office buildings, shopping centers, recreational areas, residential neighborhoods, hotels, apartment buildings, medical facilities, and police, fire, and emergency services. The various sections often are separated from each other by expanses of trimmed meadow bordered by groves of trees. Army posts usually leave much to be desired in the way of conveniences since they have grown up in spurts, with growth of population or changes in function unaccompanied by any development plan. There is no "downtown" or business district; thus it is not unusual to find the commissary distant from the post exchange, or to have the bowling allies, craft shops, and gymnasiums scattered throughout the area.

The barracks are typically located near the industrial sections, which are isolated from other post facilities by distances ranging from several city blocks to a mile or more. Since post regulations forbade hitch-hiking at Fort Marshall, and since the post taxi and shuttle bus services were unreliable, those who wished to use post facilities either had to have an automobile or be willing to walk considerable distances. As in modern cities, walking unaccompanied at night involved the risk of robbery or assault. Thus soldiers without means of transportation tended to stay in the immediate vicinity of their barracks.

SOCIOLOGICAL CONSTRAINTS

One reason that soldiers in barracks have limited contact with the civilian world is that they have limited information about events and activities outside the post. Few of the soldiers read local newspapers, and area television and radio stations covered only selected events. Information about on-post activities was scarcely better. The post newspaper was distributed to the barracks, but it consisted mainly of policy change announcements, reports of intramural athleticsand feature stories of noteworthy people or work groups. The paper seldom gave the operating hours of the various facilities, let alone special events scheduled for the bowling alley, craft shops and gymnasiums. Upon arrival at the post, soldiers were given information packets, describing the facilities and their hours of operation. These packets were oriented toward the older, married soldiers and families and were seldom read carefully or retained. The principal sources of information for barracks residents were announcements made by the company leaders and informal contacts.

Another reason for limited off-post activities was that barracks dwellers felt unwelcome and unwanted in civilian territory. Fort Marshall had enjoyed good military-civilian relations throughout its history. The post commander had regularly attended civilian businessmen's meetings, had invited civilians to the post for major ceremonies, and on occasion had made tents and vehicles available for civilian-sponsored fund-raising events. For the individual soldier, however, the civilian community was not a friendly place.

An elderly resident of the town closest to Fort Marshall noted that soldiers had never had much to do with the townspeople except when walking to and from the railroad station. During World War II, the town sponsored a social club for soldiers stationed at the post, but this was abandoned after the war. The informant also said that soldiers usually kept to themselves "up in Boomtown," a place that had grown up shortly after the post was built where soldiers could buy liquor—even during Prohibition—and could play the slot machines. Boomtown had apparently been considered an eyesore by the local residents, and when asked whether he had ever cautioned his children against going there, the informant replied with incredulity, "Why no, there was no reason for them to go there."

Common soldiers and common citizens apparently have known each other's territory and respected the boundaries since the opening of Fort Marshall. In modern times, when soldiers ventured beyond Boomtown, they chose "neutral" places such as shopping malls, recreation centers, or fast-food restaurants. Near the post they were welcome, but they felt that the merchants were situated there only to take their money.

Nor did the barracks-dwelling soldier feel particularly welcome on the post. After duty hours and on weekends the post was sociologically divided into married and unmarried sectors. Most of the activities involved married soldiers and their families: baseball games, bowling leagues, craft fairs, picnics, and chapel groups. Short of walking in and volunteering—an unlikely event—there was no way for the unmarried soldier to become a coach, scout leader, or committee member. For the single soldier the only available activities were nonterritorial, individual events such as those offered within gymnasiums, service clubs, or post movie theaters. This was true for the single officer or senior NCO as well as the lower-ranking enlisted men.

A further source of isolation derived from the sociological character of the Army itself. Long-standing practice discouraged fraternization among the ranks after duty hours. These rules are enforced by spatial division of the post into segregated housing areas for senior officers, junior officers, senior and junior NCOs, and enlisted people. Unless invited, one had little reason or occasion to enter a residential area different in composition from one's own. The club system was also segregated by rank: a club for officers, another for senior NCOs, a third for junior NCOs, and a "One, Two, Three Club" for the lowest ranks. Attendance at the last named was further constrained by its physical location, for each club was dominated by the enlisted people who were housed nearest to it; thus the medical people went to the club nearest their barracks and seldom frequented the club nearest the artillery units and vice-versa.

The behavior of unmarried soldiers, then, was in large measure determined by their location away from urban centers and from major post recreational facilities. They were further constrained by lack of information about activities and events, by feelings of being unwelcome either in the civilian community or in certain parts of the post, and by Army policies that insured that they associated only with those of their own rank and branch. Given these spatial and sociological facts of life, it is not surprising that barracks-dwelling soldiers organized themselves psychologically to accommodate them.

PSYCHOLOGICAL ORGANIZATION

With the exception of the officer class, the military has never been viewed as a high-status career. One meaning of the verb "to soldier" is "to shirk one's duty, as by making a pretense of working, feigning illness, etc." A career soldier, in the popular view, is one who is too dumb or too lazy to survive in a legitimate civilian occupation. Thus, when enlistees on their first tour of duty say that civilians do not like or respect soldiers, they are often reflecting attitudes and values deeply ingrained in the culture, and which they themselves espoused as civilians only a few months before entering service. The attitude, however, is quite ambivalent. The tremendous respect given the armed services during World War II contrasts sharply with the low opinion of the military that developed during the Vietnam conflict. First-tour soldiers often reported that they wore their uniform home once following basic training, but felt so uncomfortable that they would not do so again.

To understand the feelings of barracks soldiers about being in the Army, one must consider their age, experience, and social skills. Most of the first-tour soldiers were under 21, with limited experience outside their hometowns and with few well-developed social skills or interests. In contrast to the older, better-educated conscript Army, contemporary volunteers were not given to reading for pleasure or pursuing long-term hobbies or projects. Until entry into service, their lives had been dominated by hometown haunts, interests, and social connections. As a consequence, they felt uncomfortable negotiating their way in a strange city, becoming acquainted with women, or asserting themselves to join a camera club, chorale society, or youth activities center. Thus, instead of attributing their discomfort with the civilian community to ambivalent feelings about military service, or their uneasiness to lack of experience and social skills, many enlistees seized upon their short haircuts and the less than enthusiastic reception of their hometowns to conclude, "Civilians don't like soldiers; all they want is our money."

Between 1941 and the end of the draft, military service was a part of growing up for large segments of the American male population, and a distinction has developed between a single tour of service—to acquire skills or as a patriotic duty—and a military career, with negative connotations of occupational incompetence. Many single soldiers made such a distinction and categorized their world psychologically into those who were "in the Army" and the careerist "lifers." Most of the barracks residents saw themselves as "in the Army" for a short time for the purpose of acquiring skills or simply "getting it over with." Assuming the status "in the Army" allowed enlistees to dissociate themselves from the negative connotations of being "a soldier," and they tended to view themselves in terms of occupational specialties: medical technicians, truck drivers, policemen, or mechanics. "Soldiers," in contrast, were those who endorsed the Army as a way of life and who accepted and promoted military values and standards of dress and deportment. The result of this psychological distinction was that the barracks dwellers attributed their lack of participation in on-post activities to avoidance of the "lifers" and their families rather than to the external constraints of the physical space and sociological organization on the post. Before the draft ended this distinction even extended into the organization of the barracks, with the regular Army volunteers being set apart from the draftees.

TEMPORAL ORGANIZATION

The final important factor of behavioral organization concerns the temporal constraints imposed upon the soldier by membership in an Army unit. Soldiers may see themselves principally as policemen or truck drivers, but their activities are not organized in the same ways as those of law enforcement officers or teamsters. From the point of view of the formal organization, they are first and foremost persons with general military obligations which may incidentally include certain occupational specialty duties. This fact was recognized by the soldiers in their often repeated statement, "The one thing different about the Army is that you can't quit." The structure and character of soldiers' duty hours must be understood in order to comprehend the structure of the nonduty hours in the barracks.

When soldiers were asked to recall their Army experiences, they recounted places of assignment rather than specific months or years: "When I was at Fort Polk . . ." or "On my second tour in Germany. . . ." This organization of time was a typical of first-tour soldiers as of thirty-year careerists. Since much of the work in Army field units takes place outdoors, season is the next most salient recall category. Soldiers often remembered whether it was cold, wet, muggy, dusty, or sweltering. Months, weeks, and days had little recall value unless some dramatic event happened, such as "during the Cuban missile crisis . . ." or "the day President Kennedy was shot. . . ."

These recall tendencies are quite understandable. The natural cycle of any Army company in garrison is one year, at the end of which events begin repeating themselves. In a year the unit has prepared for the annual general inspection, has been to the field for training, and has met the annual operational readiness test. The company picnic has been held; Christmas and Thanksgiving have been duly celebrated. In the summer the unit may have seen temporary duty in support of reserve or national guard training, and, most likely the company commander was replaced after 12 to 14 months "command time" by a more junior captain who needed command experience. The events may not occur in the same order each year, but the same major events recur in each 12-month period. In garrison these cycles are generally marked in memory by the name of the company commander: "When Captain Dow had the company . . ." or "Shortly after Captain Smith took over. . . ." But with the exception of comments on the commander's personality or policies, the yearly cycle is low-keyed and largely uneventful for the individuals involved.

Months, weeks, and days were scarcely any more varied. The principal activity was preparation for the next yearly event, be it the annual general inspection or the operational readiness test. Between the highpoints the company busied itself by maintaining equipment and training to use it. Except for important inspections, the pace of activity was slow and easy; what was not done one day could be completed the next. The schedule was therefore quite flexible, so that a battalion scheduled to be the honor unit during retreat ceremony could spend 20,000 to 30,000 man-hours practicing drill and ceremony routines. The end of the month was signaled by traditional "payday activities" when soldiers assembled in formation to be paid and were then dismissed for the rest of the day to transact personal business. Few soldiers are paid in cash anymore, and few businesses still extend credit with the understanding that a cash payment will be made in person at the end of the month. Nevertheless the Army traditions of a payday formation and payday activities live on.

The casual, largely uneventful pace of garrison duty should not be confused with monotony and boredom, for the individual soldier experiences variety in his daily assignments and has considerable freedom to structure his duty time when compared, for example, to an industrial worker on an assembly line. For the barracks resident the duty day began when he was awakened between 5:30 and 6:00 A.M.. He attended to his morning toilet, performed minor housekeeping in his area, went to breakfast in the dining hall, and then reported to the morning formation at 7:00. After formation he went to his duty section, where he worked until noon. After a leisurely meal of an hour or more he attended formation or reported directly back to his duty section, where he worked until 4:00 P.M., when he returned to the barracks for the afternoon formation.

The structure seems rather rigid, with two and sometimes three formations each day at which attendance was taken and announcements made, but actually the content of the day was often varied. The company might not report directly to the duty sections after morning formation, but might have an hour or so of physical training or a classroom talk by the company commander. In inclement weather activities were adjusted accordingly unless the unit was in the field on a training exercise. The company also had a number of special duty commitments to perform; selected individuals were thus detailed for vehicle driving, trash collecting, painting, lawn care, or flower gardening instead of their normal duties. From time to time temporary duty away from the post was necessary, and work teams were dispatched for up to 90 days to meet these commitments. None of these activities was particularly dramatic, exciting, or even noteworthy, save as they provided variety within the basic duty structure.

The individual could introduce his own variations and exceptions to the basic pattern as well. Soldiers working on high school equivalency diplomas reported directly to the education center rather than attending the formations; those who worked in offices outside the company did not attend formations; those who were about to leave the service and who were participating in transition job-training programs could waive formations. Even individuals assigned to the company might be excused from duty to attend to personal business. As long as the first-line supervisor knew where the individual was and his reason for being absent, he was accounted for in the formation. Since the work pace was really not all that hectic or demanding, supervisors could be most lenient in excepting individuals from the duty sections. Moreover, because of the limited work demands in garrison, individuals could often exercise control of their time by "shamming," "ghosting," or otherwise "getting over the system." Thus a task like checking the water level in the radiator of a truck could take two or three hours if a nap was taken in the course of the job. So long as a person's presence was not required by his supervisor and so long as he was accounted for at the next formation, little was said about occasional absences unless they became too frequent or flagrant.

The typical duty day ended at 4:30 in the afternoon, Monday through Friday. The only official responsibilities after hours and on weekends were guard duty and charge of quarters (CQ) duty, both of which were rotated among the company members. Guard duty involved walking around the battalion area and motor pool, dressed in combat gear, carrying an unloaded rifle on a schedule of two hours on and four hours off. CQ duty involved taking messages, turning on fire lights, and responding to emergencies. Even these chores could be avoided if a soldier paid another to take his place.

The stereotypic vision of the Army as a "yes-sir, no-sir, jump-to" institution ruled by martinets is easily dispelled by the following observer's description of morning wake-up in the barracks:

> I entered the bay at 5:00 A.M. and went to the far end opposite the door. No one seemed to notice the squeaking hinge, rattling chain, and slam of the door when I entered. The bay is quiet except for the sounds of

heavy breathing and an occasional snore. A radio is playing quiet music from a station in Atlanta, and I sit and listen to Franky Lane and then Frank Sinatra croon through the static.

5:15. At the far end of the hall a soldier begins banging loudly on one of the doors of the individual rooms. "Hey, Charlie in there?" He goes to another door and repeats the process with full forearm blows, but no one on the bay stirs. Later the assistant CQ begins knocking at one of the doors in the hall; "Is this Smith's room? Do you know where the cook's room is?" He goes to the next room and repeats the process, but nobody seems to notice.

At 5:30 a buck sergeant comes onto the floor with a broom. He moves down the hall, rapping on each door with the broom handle. He enters the bay and begins turning on lights while constantly chattering, "Oh, you beautiful people, it's morning." He calls two men by name, ane pokes them gently with his broom handle, then continues with his chatter. "Come on, get up, time to rise and shine." A man groans, "Aw, what the fuck time is it?" The CQ continues to chatter, "got some good chow for you over at the mess hall," and leaves the bay.

One man at the far end gets up and wobbles to the latrine in his underwear. Everyone else continues to sleep. Shortly thereafter, a second man in his underwear sleepily makes his way to the latrine. The two men nearest me have pulled the covers over their heads.

5:40. There are sounds of wall lockers being opened and banged closed. A man walks toward the latrine dressed in the fatigue duty uniform (olive-drab cotton work clothes), black jump boots, and an olive-drab baseball cap. Another man returns from the latrine dressed in his boots, fatigue trousers, and a T-shirt. Two area mates are dressing and talking casually. "What time did you get in last night?" "12:15." "Did you have to work all night?" "Yeah, from about six to midnight. They had me on the grill, but I kept getting the buns in upside down, so I asked to be transferred." "Well, I had to go to class last night. Imagine, nine two-hour classes on how to run a hamburger joint" "I'm going over to the mess hall, see you later." "Ok, see you."

6:00. There is systematic knocking on the door from the other end of the hall, and the first sergeant makes his way through the billets. "Morning . . . good morning . . . this one over here I wish I had a big icicle . . . morning, sleeping beauty [kicks bed] . . . this one over here I usually don't have any trouble with . . . hey, you left your radio on all night and it's burned itself out . . . must have gotten to bed late last night . . . oh, what a beautiful morning; not too hot and not too cold . . . get up, we miss your smiling face." He leaves the bay.

Smith gets up. He has no sheets on his bunk. Johnson says, "You don't use any sheets? When was the last time you changed that mattress cover? That thing's filthy. I should talk, though, I've never changed my cover, but I change the sheets every week. I couldn't sleep on something that dirty." Smith ignores him and goes to his locker. Cressey is also sleeping without sheets in his fatigues and boots.

Murphy and his area mate get up and open their wall lockers with a clatter. Murphy: "Fuck! It feels like buffalo shit in my mouth. He just stood over me and dumped right in my mouth. Buffalo shit in my teeth and under my tongue. I sure didn't have any trouble getting to sleep last night; I was feeling no pain at all."

Sergeant Martin comes into the bay and wanders around looking at the areas and talking with the men who are standing around or are sweeping out their areas. Martin notices the two soldiers sleeping, shakes them gently by the shoulder, and calls them by name. Neither responds. Several men have gone to the closet in the hall to get dust mops, brooms, and the electric buffer.

Williams sits on his bunk and polishes his boots. When he finishes, he starts to iron his fatigues on his area-mate's bunk. Johnson comes from the latrine with his hair slicked back to hide its length under his cap. Bonner asks Hart for the buffer when he is finished. Peterson quickly leaves the bay and returns with a broom. Johnson bums a cigarette from Bonner and stands watching him buff the floor.

6:50. Platoon Sergeant Ragland comes in and asks the sleeping soldiers, "What you doin' in that bed?" The soldiers get up immediately, open their lockers, and turn up the radio to drown out effectively all other sounds on the bay. They dress quickly as the electric buffer is passed in a zig-zag line down the center aisle. The platoon sergeant later comes back and says to them, "Hey when you gonna sweep out your area?" One hastily picks up an empty cigarette package from under his bed as the other makes the beds and locks his radio in his wall locker. At this point the first sergeant blows his whistle to signal the morning formation. The brooms and mops are returned to the closet, and the men leave for the first official function of the day.

This description introduces the character of the interpersonal relations in the barracks. The men did not wait on each other for breakfast, tended to restrict their conversation to bunkmates, and readily cooperated in tidying up the barracks. Of particular note is the behavior of the four sergeants who were informal and relaxed. Leadership at the platoon level is intensely personal and face-to-face, with very little of the "and-that's-an-order" character; instead, first-line supervisors rely on reasoning, cajoling, or moral persuasion. An example of the latter is the platoon sergeant in the foregoing description who at least once a week put his platoon "at ease" in formation and lectured on the condition of the barracks:

> "We got a pretty sorry and miserable bunch of people in this platoon. A bunch of pigs with no more self-respect than to go to bed with their clothing on. The god-damned barracks is filthy and it stinks. You sorry-assed people who can't take a shower or brush your teeth or sleep on sheets like civilized people are nothin' but animals. Now, when I was coming up we took pride in ourselves and our unit; we took care of each other, and when we found a pig who wouldn't take a shower, we saw to it that he did. But not today. You miserable menses just don't care about yourself or each other. I never, in all my days, seen more sorry-assed excuses for soldiers. Now, I want that goddamned bay cleaned up and cleaned up right. If you guys don't have enough pride to do it on your own, then we'll just have to have a GI party on Thursday night, and I'll just stand over you until you do it." The harangue was invariably the same. He always promised the clean-up party, but never was seen after 4:30. The men fidgeted in the ranks, and snickered as he was talking.

During the duty day a work group often had time to interact informally. The following observation was made in a transportation company that was assigned to support a summer training exercise. The drivers had transported the trainees to the ranges and then had several hours to kill before their services were again required. The first hour they napped in the cabs, read the morning paper, listened to radio music, and talked quietly in groups of two or three. The platoon sergeant then brought out a bag of tools and requested that first-line maintenance be performed on the trucks to include batteries, oil, water and lights. In short order the men were behaving as a group:

> Six men work on a truck with junior sergeants making notations on the maintenance tickets. The talk is animated if somewhat forced: "Goddamn, where's the clutch in this motherfucker? Turn the motherfucking radio on . . . Give it here; I'll put in on the fucking truck . . . What did Sergeant Tweed do with them wrenches? You drive it, get up in the mother . . . This truck ain't got no spare tire . . . Tell the second echelon mechanics this fucker ain't got no transmission . . . Gimme my wrenches . . . Still ain't no transmission . . . Did he say anything to you about working nights? We usually rotate that job around the second platoon . .– Twenty fucking hours of duty is a lot of extra work . . . You got a leak there . . . where? Intermediate axle . . . Shit, it's just up from the differential gasket . . . Who the fuck pulled this truck into the mud?

Bobinger, check the axle flange bolts. A man comes into the area lug-
ging the black tool bag and says that he is Dr. Kildare, and another yells
to him that he has a sucking chest wound. There is some kidding about
Bobinger's age [about 30], and he retorts, "Get fucked, you goddamn
ignorant hillbilly."

The language used is not the most elegant and the topics of
discourse are not the most profound, but such episodes were part
and parcel of working out a system of informal, interpersonal relations in the work group. The one who cursed most eloquently, the
one who responded quickest with a verbal retort, the one who sat in
the cab reading the mileage, and the one who lay in the mud checking
the seals—all were indications of status among the group members.
The platoon sergeant noted that the degree and volume of chatter
were his best sign of morale, and that he only begun to worry when
the group was silent. The lieutenant commented that much of the
maintenance the men were doing was unnecessary, but that he had
to keep the men busy because "The brass don't like to see them
sleeping in the trucks; but after they're finished here I'll just let them
go into the woods to joke and smoke until we're ready to move out."

STRUCTURE OF THE DUTY DAY

Stretches of idle time were not restricted to temporary duty assignments, but were characteristic of most work days in garrison. The
explicit mission of the garrison Army is to maintain readiness for
deployment. This is usually interpreted in the narrow sense of maintaining equipment and being trained in its proper use, but in the
broader sense, readiness also implies an established, stable pattern of
informal relationships that enable the work groups to function
efficiently. The fact that, in the words of a senior sergeant, "in garrison there really isn't that much to do," should not obscure the equally
important fact that what got done—including cursing, joking, and
smoking—was critical to the establishment and maintenance of work
group performance capability. It was during the informal banter and
horseplay that each member of the work group came to know his
place as well as his rights and obligations. This was essential for
reducing interpersonal conflict and effecting an informal system of
dominance and subordination that enabled the formal chain of command to operate. The character of the work day and the nature and
quality of interpersonal relationships are best illustrated with an extended description of a single day in the life of a single soldier.

The soldier chosen for illustration is PFC Charles Lohman, a black who worked as a surveyor's assistant in an engineering unit, was pretty much excluded from the black social groups in the unit, and existed in a peripheral, low-status position in his work group. The observer found Lohman snoring quietly at 5:30 A.M.; he was sleeping in his fatigue trousers on the mattress cover, with only a blanket wrapped around him. Twenty minutes after the first call to get up, he got up, dressed, folded his blanket, and placed it under his pillow. His first verbal interchange of the day was with his white bunk mate, Frank Bousman. The observer could tell that their relationship was close because they used first names:

> Bousman rolls over. "You know what time it is, Charles?" "No, but I know it's time for you to get up." Bousman rolls over and goes back to sleep. As Lohman locks his locker and leaves for breakfast, he says, "Get your lazy ass up, Frank." "Shit. This place will be clean when you get back." "I'm going to breakfast and I want to be able to buff the floor when I return."

At 6:25 they left the dining hall and returned to the barracks. On the way they passed a group of blacks:

> One of the blacks says to Lohman, "What's happenin', man?" Lohman fumbles for a reply and finally manages "Hi" after the group had passed. The other blacks looked up, saw Lohmam, and then looked down again.

Back in the barracks the area mates had worked out a division of labor for housekeeping; Lohman immediately took the broom from Bousman, swept the area, and ran the buffer on the floor. He then polished his boots. The observer noted:

> Bousman looks at me, smiles, and shakes his head. "Look at this guy. He jumps out of bed, rushes through breakfast, then cleans the area and shines his boots. Usually I have to drag him out of bed. At least he didn't make his bunk; that's typical. He's the only guy who does that. Every time he makes his bunk they send him on temporary duty." Lohman listened quietly, looked up and smiled, but continued to work on his boots.

Lohman's bed-making habits might have been superstitious, but more likely he had learned that every time he used sheets, they got stolen. He was not, however, a total outcast:

Lohman wanders down the center aisle where Hardy, Heinz, and the new man are talking. As Lohman approaches, the group opened a place for him to join by moving from a triangular configuration to a square. They break up with loud, prolonged laughter, apparently at the new man's expense. He smiles and looks sheepish while the other laugh, and Lohman says, "Hardy really got over on that one."

At 7:00 the men were milling around outside waiting for the morning formation. Lohman sat on the step, seemingly inattentive to the conversation about the bridge project that was going on behind him, but later got up and joined the group. When the whistle blew, he took a place in the formation:

Lohman falls in at the end of the line in the squad leader's place. In a surly tone Sergeant Eickor says, "You're in my place; move down to the end of the line." Lohman steps to the side, forcing everyone in the line to move down one place. After formation he walks with Bousman during police call as they pick up papers around the area.

The interchange with the squad leader which could have been avoided was the first interaction with a sergeant during the day. In the main the men knew what to do and assumed their responsibilities without being told. The observer noted:

After police call I join Lohman, Bousman, and Gilman who are deciding what to do first that day. Bousman tells Lohman to come with them, but Lohman says, "No, I got to go to the motor pool." "That's where we're going; you might as well ride with us; it's better than walking." We go to Gilman's car and ride the three blocks to the motor pool. Gilman complains and worries about the upcoming IG inspection. Bousman says, "Don't sweat it. We never have to work weekends preparing for one of them. All we do is clean the barracks. They don't expect the soil lab to be clean."

In the motor pool at 7:45 they proceeded with their work directly but deliberately:

Lohman checks the battery fluid and then tears up some rags. "You gonna grease your battery cables?" "What for?" "No, mine's OK." Lohman takes a rag and picks up a gob of grease from a barrel in the shop. He uses a stick to apply the grease in a thick coat around the terminals. He works slowly but does a thorough job. Bousman then says, "You gonna wash yours?" "Yeah, I guess so; meet you at the wash point."

To this point Lohman and his buddy Bousman have been behaving as co-equals. Lohman has suggested greasing the battery cables, and Bousman has suggested washing the trucks. The subsequent scene at the wash rack, though all in good fun between friends, demonstrated Bousman's superior status in the relationship. The observer noted:

> They wash the trucks inside and out with rags, brushes, and plain water. Bousman has managed to get himself thoroughy wet from the waist down. As he turns his truck around to get to the other side, Lohman sprays water at the closed driver's window; Bousman laughs and ducks involuntarily. Later Bousman sprays water over his truck onto Lohman, laughs and says, "Sorry, Charles, I didn't see you standing there." Lohman is now soaked all over. There is no retaliation as he moves with his hose around his truck, spraying water on the ground in front of Bousman, who looks up and smiles. "Sorry, I didn't try to get you." "I wouldn't blame you if you did."

Lohman and his buddy parked their trucks in the prescribed places and walked to the shop, joking about how wet they were without any mention of Bousman's dousing of Lohman. At the shop they filled out the equipment inspection and maintenance worksheet that told what they did and what needed to be done. By 8:35 they had completed their formal military duties for the morning and could be about the business of sorting out status relations in the work group:

> As we left the shop, Bousman said, "Is Gabby still over there?" Lohman snickers as we walk to Gilman's car for the ride back to the operations office. On the way back, Bousman comments, "You can tell Gilman hasn't been at Marshall long; he kept saying, "Aren't you through washing the truck yet? We gotta get to work." You know he hasn't been around long; I was enjoying killing some time." Gilman does not respond.

In Bousman's view, Gilman was slow in assuming a proper attitude in the work group and required some sensitivity training to heighten an awareness of his position in the pecking order. In the office the observer continued:

> Bousman interjects, "Hey, have you guys seen Gabby's picture in the soil office?" "No." "He brought in an eight-by-ten glossy black-and-white picture of his mother." "Really? You're shitting me." "No lie. He has it on his desk." "I won't believe it until I see it." "Let's go then; I think I'll get a big *Playboy* foldout to hang beside it. Try not to look too

surprised." We walk to the soil lab and sure enough it's there. Gilman leaves the room when we enter. Lohman looks around and comments, "When are you and Gilman going to clean this dump?" Bousman snaps back, "That better be the last time you mention those two names in the same sentence." Dunham asks, "Where is old Gabby, anyway?" Bousman sarcastically replies, "Oh, he went to wash some dirt," Dunham: "I think I'll find some pink titties in *Playboy* to paste over that picture; then the old lady wouldn't look too bad." The group breaks up in laughter.

At this point the sergeant entered the room, unmindful of the business at hand, and immediately referred to the predominant status hierarchy of the group:

Sergeant Eickor comes in and says, "Lohman, aren't you sleeping yet?" "No, what time is it?" "Nine o'clock. You've already missed half an hour already." "True, true," Lohman mumbles as he sits down and listens to the group return to cutting down Gilman and each other.

For the next hour and a half the group engaged in small talk and horseplay in which the verbal and physical jostling accurately reflected the competition for status position in the group. Verbal facility and physical agility were essential for establishing and maintaining position in the group. Lohman, though not unintelligent, was not verbally facile and thus became the butt of the other's remarks:

Lohman sits back on the couch and listens to the small talk. Every once in a while he tries to enter the conversation, but usually doesn't make it, and at times there is difficulty hearing and understanding him. Bousman and Herdon kid him about the black music and dance show on television, "Soul Train." Lohman seizes the opportunity to talk about the show. Bousman interrupts, "Hey, Charles, do that high-stepping dance you were showing me last night." "No man, I gotta be motivated for that."

The small talk was mostly a never-ending series of put-downs that were often forced and sometimes failed miserably:

Bousman says, "Hey Dunham, you know what your girlfriend told last night? She said if I dropped by on Saturday night she would give me your paycheck." "Oh yeah. Yours said the same thing to me." "I don't have a girlfriend." "In that case, neither do I."

There is a fight in the corner. Dunham is trying to insert his moistened finger into Herdon's ear, which is called "giving a wet Willie." He finally gets Herdon after wrestling him down into a chair. Herdon gets up and chases Dunham out of the room, returning to give a wet Willie to Bousman. He then threatens Lohman, who leaves the room with Herdon chasing. They scuffle in the corridor, and Lohman chases Herdon back through the room and then outside. They return laughing. Lohman sits on the couch and Dunham and Herdon go to the photo lab.

Horse-play and continual banter were standard routines in Army work groups, but on this particular morning the principal business was shaping Gilman:

Later Gilman came into the room and said very seriously, "Well, I guess I'd better get my moisture test run." Dunham says, "Oh, goodie-goodie; I want to see this." Bousman and Gilman disagree on how the test should be run, and Bousman explodes, "You go ahead and run the fuckin' test if you know so much; I'll watch." Lohman, Dunham, and Herdon laugh at them. Bousman then gets angry and accuses Gilman of taking a short cut on the test that will produce an unrepresentative sample. Gilman finally gives in and does it Bousman's way.

Once Gilman seemed to get the word that Bousman was in charge of the soil lab, the activity returned to the standard routines. Herdon did not manage to give Lohman a wet Willie earlier, so he returned to the attack:

Herdon sits next to Lohman and gooses him in the ribs, mumbling, "Motherfucker." Lohman gooses him back and they wrestle on the couch until Lohman finally runs away. He returns laughing and sits next to Herdon as he starts looking through Gilman's tapes. "Oh, the OJ's!" Herdon growls, "Shit. You put that on and I'll stomp that tape player in the ground. By the way, how'd you get so wet?" "Dirt man over there sprayed me while we were washing trucks." Herdon laughs and leaves the room.

In this episode Herdon has not only managed to pre-empt space occupied by Lohman, but has also followed up his victory by making a disparaging, threatening remark about his choice of music, and, as a final insult, has forced Lohman to acknowledge his inferior position to Bousman by explaining his spoiled appearance.

The room was then quiet as Lohman read the paper and hummed along with the music on the tape recorder, and Gilman worked on the soil sample using Bousman's procedures. Gilman asked about Bousman's whereabouts, and Lohman took the opportunity to put down the already battered Gilman:

> Gilman asked, "Where's Bousman?" Lohman replied, "How the hell should I know? I'm not his mother. He might be in survey, or in drafting, or the photo lab, or in S-2, or in G-3, or he might be in the latrine." Gilman returns quietly to his work.

Lohman's victory, however, is short-lived:

> Bousman said as he came into the room, "Hey, Charles, we got another vehicle to clean. Mendez said you could wash his car." Lohman seems to grope for an appropriate response but comes up with nothing. "I have to drive Chilly Willy [the company commander] today," Bousman continues, and both he and Lohman laugh at the prospect. Bousman then sits next to Lohman on the couch and reads the post paper.

It was now 10:30 and Lohman announced to his buddy that he was leaving the survey office and would return at 2:30. If questions are asked, he could count on Bousman to cover for him in offering a reasonable explanation for his absence. His departure provided an opportunity to observe his relations with other members of the unit outside his immediate work group as well as to see how other soldiers were spending their duty time:

> We walk over to the communications office where Packard, a black, is trying to start a lawn mower. Lohman says, "If that came from S-4 it won't start; take it back." Packard asks me what I'm doing and I explain. "Well, take some notes on this shit. This guy is a slave driver and is asking me to take this mower back after he brought it over." Lohman smiles broadly as walk into the guard shack where Heinz, Lyon, and Smith are shooting pool. Smith says, "Brother Lohman, give me a cigarette," and then asks me what I'm doing, "Man, I see you around here writing all the time." I explain. "Man I can tell you what's wrong here. This place is all fucked up; that's all. There's too many chiefs around here. Everyone wants to be a boss." As we turn to leave, Smith calls out, "Hey, Lohman, don't leave; I'll whip your ass at pool when these chumps get done practicing." Outside Packard is now cutting grass with a swing blade. Lohman says, "Man, they got you doin' that shit?" "This isn't so bad; it's cool today so I don't mind; gives me something to do and keeps my mind occupied. Haste makes waste, or something like that." Then they launch into a discussion of cars. Lohman wants a Road Runner, jacked up in the rear with wide tires, a four-speed, and about 23 carbs. Packard disagrees and argues for a Riviera or a Grand Prix.

The men in the communications office were as busy as those in the survey section. The conversation with Packard about cars was the first serious, sustained conversation observed this morning on the part of Lohman or anyone else; they conversed easily since they were from nearby towns in the same state. As they talked, Lohman demonstrated why he was not well accepted among the blacks in the unit; he simply did not know the language:

Packard says, "Hey, you're getting one of my home in the survey shop." "A what?" "A home; you know, a guy from my hometown is coming in the Army and he chose Fort Marshall and survey. He'll be here next month." "You didn't tell him not to come here?" "Yeah, I told him, but it was too late." "Man, I'd never let a friend of mine come in here. I go home and tell them not to join the Army." "Yeah, I wish I would have gone Air Force or Navy. Those guys have it good; they live in good barracks and have good jobs." [Pause] "How's everyone at home?"

Lohman was unfamiliar with the meaning of "home," but recovered by sliding into the "GI blues." At the pause he did not respond with the standard acknowledgment of agreement, "Dig it," so Packard changed the subject.

Lohman then went to check his mail, asked the barracks orderly about another black friend, and sat on the barracks step where the observer was better accepted among the blacks than was Lohman:

We sit on the steps until four blacks from B company come up to us. One is Hildebrand, whom I had tried to follow during inprocessing. Hildebrand ignores Lohman, but greets me, "Hey, what's happenin'?" I explained why I was not tagging along with him that day. "Here's a good man you can follow; maybe you can commit him to Walter Reed." [Laughter] "He isn't crazy enough; if I committed him, I'd have to commit the whole battalion, myself included." [Laughter] "Dig it." The blacks say they have been on the crate detail that morning which apparently involves building wooden crates for missile parts. They don't know anything about it except they don't like the detail and wish they were working on the bridge. They then switch to put-down routines. Lohman leaves in the middle of a story and I follow, saying, "Catch you guys later." "Yeah, man, later."

After the noon meal Lohman and his buddy, Bousman, went to the barracks to take a nap. Buck Sergeant Eickor played cards with Bousman while Lohman dozed. Unable to achieve acceptance among the black soldiers, Lohman maintained his precarious position in the white work group by vigorously endorsing the dominant norms. One of these norms was never to appear by word or deed to be very enthusiastic about the Army, the post, the unit, or one's duties. The observer noted:

> During the card game Eickor asks me what I am doing and I explain. "Are you going to the bridge with us this afternoon?" "If Lohman goes." Lohman rolls over in distress, "Why you bring news like that in here when I'm sleeping?" "You should be glad to do some work in your MOS [military occupation speciality]; that's what the Army trained you for." "The Army didn't train me. The men in survey did. I don't have no Army training. I'm no gung-ho Army man like the new dirt man [Gilman]." "He'll get his soon. Your deal, Bousman."

The function of buddies in the Army—they were called "P's" (for partners) in Vietnam—is to take care of one another, to cover each other when under fire by the enemy in combat or by the sergeants and officers in garrison. Lohman alerted his buddy of the time to get up that morning, and Bousman returned the favor, following an hour's nap:

> Bousman tugs gently on Lohman's boot. "Hey, Charles, you want to go to the section?" Lohman yawns, stretches, and sits on the edge of his bunk. "You notice I said section, not work; there's a fine distinction there." They smile at each other and leave the barracks. Outside on the steps the group of blacks from B company has grown to eight or ten. Lohman walks through them and is ignored.

The consequence of the banter and rough-housing between Lohman and Herdon earlier in the day now becomes clear. They are both of the same rank; Lohman has a little more seniority in the section. The problem is to load a vehicle without interpersonal friction or recourse to a sergeant. Who will take the less preferred tasks? Lohman, of course. The observer noted:

> As we enter the building, Lohman calls out, "Hey, Lohman! We got a job to do this afternoon. Come on; you can help me load the jeep." Lohman follows Herdon into the office and returns carrying the tripod; Herdon carries the transit, rulers, and paper. Lohman then returns to fetch the rod. At the bridge Lohman carries the rod to where they are excavating while Herdon sets up the tripod and transit for Dunham, the chief surveyor. Dunham explains to Lohman the shots he wants to take, positions him, takes the readings, and waves him away. Lohman sits alone, waiting for further instructions.

The fact that Lohman loaded the tripod and then returned for his rod while Herdon attended to the transit is revealing. Had Lohman held a status in the work group equal to Herdon, they might have squabbled about who carried what, and Lohman could have argued that the tripod was not his responsibility since he was the rod man, not the assistant surveyor. Dunham, the chief surveyor, was equal in rank to both Lohman and Herdon but took no responsibility for either loading or unloading; he gave instructions and took the readings, for he earlier claimed dominance over Herdon by initiating the "wet Willie" frolic. At the building site, however, the chief surveyor and his assistant continued to jockey for position:

> Dunham decides that the reading taken by Herdon is a foot low, and signals the dozer operator to raise his blade by that much. Until the dirt is filled in there is nothing for the survey crew to do. Dunham and Herdon begin giving wet Willies to each other again. Bousman drives up with the company commander and a lieutenant; while they review the construction, Eickor slips Bousman a muddy wet Willie. Bousman comes over and gives it to Lohman who then chases Herdon, who manages to plant one in Dunham's ear as he passes him. Dunham chases Herdon, yelling, "Retribution is hell! I'll get you, you low-down share-croppin', dirt-eatin' bastard." Another reading is called for, and everyone assumes his prescribed place.

After an hour at the site, the survey crew finished their work. They watched the bridge construction for another hour until rain threatened, and returned to the survey office. At the office they watched the rain and waited for the end of the duty day.

For Private Lohman the duty day ended where it began—in bed. The afternoon formation was canceled when it rained, and the duty day closed as undramatically as it began:

> Lohman says, "It's four o'clock; time to go." "Yeah, let's get out of here." We pick up our hats and walk to the barracks. Lohman speaks to no one, but goes directly to his bunk where he lies with his eyes closed. There is no one else in the barracks. Lamsen enters and wakes Lohman as the door slams shut. "What time is it?" "Four twenty-five." "Lohman gets up and stretches, "I guess it's time for supper." "You going to the mess hall?" "Yeah, I guess," "OK, I think I'll call it a day. Thanks for helping me." "OK." He walks out alone.

Several major points should be noted from this extended description of a single duty day. First, the interpersonal interactions during the day were almost exclusively among members of the work group within the unit; the only exceptions were brief interchanges with others over the noon hour. Second, the soldiers did not have much "work" to accomplish; the major duties consisted of an hour devoted to washing a truck and another hour of surveying at a building site. Third, most of the day was spent in banter and horse-play to establish and maintain status positions among the work group members; this enabled the group to function with minimal interpersonal conflict when it was required to perform. Finally, status assertion and maintenance in the work group required verbal facility and physical agility; without these, particularly the former, the individual was consigned to a low status, not only in the work group, but also (as in this particular case) in the racial group as well.

Is Private Charles Lohman typical or representative of soldiers in general? In so far as his day evokes those principles which govern life in the Army, he *is* typical. He may not be typical in the particulars of what he does or the style in which he behaves, but Private Lohman, like all soldiers, structured his duty time and interacted with his peers within a distinct arena, most of which was constructed for him. As Chapter 3 will illustrate, the interactions during the duty day exert considerable influence on the character and structure of interactions after duty hours in the barracks.

STRUCTURE OF EVENING ACTIVITIES

The duty day ended at 4:30 P.M., and the men returned to the barracks to prepare for the evening meal and activities. The observer noted the following sequence:

4:20. I enter the empty bay and notice from the window that the battalion is marching across the road to the parade field. Johnson comes in dressed in jeans, a flannel shirt, blue cord jacket, and tennis shoes. "Didn't you have to work today?" "Yeah, I got off at four o'clock, but by the time I got back here the formation had already started. They didn't tell me anything about it, so I didn't go down." Johnson points to a cartoon taped to a locker, and we laugh at it.

We return to the window to watch the retreat. Johnson says he took some snapshots from the window in the other bay as they marched back. Williams comes in dressed in off-white cord slacks, a purple dress shirt, and a green pilot's jacket. "How'd you get out of the retreat?" "I've got guard duty, but I sold it for $5.00 to Watson, and still got out of formation." Look at that crazy fucker smiling like a cat from ear to ear." "He'll be up in a few minutes and we can go eat." Johnson points out the cartoon again.

Smith comes into the bay, and is greeted by, "It's about time; where the hell you been, playing Army? Hurry up and change so we can eat." "Where are we going?" "To the mess hall. It's the end of the month, dummy, I'm broke." Smith changes into brown slacks, a brown shirt, loafers, and a tan windbreaker, and they leave together.

I am again alone on the bay. Most of the guys must have gone directly to the mess hall. The bay is filthy; the floor is scuffed and dirty, beds are unmade with cigarette butts and papers under them. Cressey comes in, says "Hi," changes into jeans, a fur jacket, and a knit cap, and then leaves. The new guy in fatigues comes in, goes to his locker, and then leaves with a mattress cover.

Murphy walks in and asks me to loan him $6.50 for snapshots that are ready at the PX. "OK, I guess so, it sounds like a worthy cause." "You've got it! I've been looking all day for someone with money. I'll pay you back on Friday. Let's go." "Let's go where? You mean I not only have to lend you money, but I also have to take you to the PX?" "If I walk they'll be closed when I get there." "OK, but I think I've just been conned." We take my car to the PX.

When we return to the bay, Lohman is watching the television that he keeps chained to his bunk with a plastic coated cable. Three other men are playing cards on a bunk, and two others are lying down resting. Everyone but Lohman has changed into civilian attire.

The men went to the dining hall in groups of two, three, or four, largely depending upon who was around the barracks at the time and was ready to eat. The quality of food varied directly with the rank of those eating. Breakfast and lunch were typically good because the senior sergeants and the colonel were likely to drop by. In the evening the mess sergeant and every other appointed leader left the area, so the junior cooks and barracks dwellers fended for themselves. Toward the end of the month, when money was short, soldiers were more inclined to eat in the mess hall rather than at fast food restaurants near the post. The observer noted:

We arrive at the mess hall; the doors are open and there is a short line. The menu includes pork steak, potatoes, beets, asparagus, rolls, salad and dessert. I get steak, potatoes and rolls. We follow Gross to the back of the dining room where more than four can sit together. The pork defies my most vigorous attempts to cut it; the potatoes are hard, uncooked, and tasteless; the rolls are soggy; even the cola is flat. Amid complaints from all sides about the food—"What a plate of shit!" "What do they think we are, anyway, hogs?" "Yeah, this slop is really bad tonight!"—I dine on the raisin carrot salad that is at least edible.

The quality of the meals also varies according to the number who normally eat in the mess hall. The meal just described took place at the end of the month when there is maximum attendance; at the beginning of the month the menu could be more limited:

Gross and Johnson have already left the bay, so I go to the mess hall alone. I pay and enter the line. The dining area is practically deserted, and I soon found out why. I got two cold, limp hot dogs and two stale buns. That's all there was. No vegetables. No potatoes. Soggy cherry cobbler on the dessert table. I took a piece and went for some milk; there was no milk. I went for soda; there was no soda. I went for coffee, there was no coffee. I settled for water. I joined Gross and Johnson, who were both very disgusted. "How do you like this shit?" "Will you write a report on this in your book?" "I paid 90¢ for this. You're damned right I'll write a report." Johnson turns toward the kitchen and yells, "This isn't food, it's shit." Several people looked around and laughed; there were no other reactions. I remembered that the battalion had recently won the top mess hall award on post, and wondered what the other soldiers were eating tonight.

The men finished their evening meal by 5:30 or 6:00 at the latest. Some left the area to be with girlfriends; others left for evening college classes; others were off to do laundry, work out at the gym, or simply drive their cars around the post and the immediate area. The men who remain in the barracks entertained themselves. Weather permitting, informal athletics were popular:

After supper I stop by the bay. Bezoni is sleeping and Peters is reading a book at the desk. Peters says everybody is out front playing ball. From the window I see Murphy hitting a softball to Cressey who is playing short for pop-ups and grounders, and Smith is playing deep for line drives and flies. I go down to the field and join Smith at Murphy and Cressey's invitation. Murphy bats for a while, and a new guy joins us. Murphy tires and Cressey bats. We cheer and boo each other on good and bad plays until it gets too dark to play. On the way to the shower, Murphy asks about the new guy and Cressey says, "Never seen him before; he's probably from another company."

Traditionally each company had a recreation area called a day room. The day room was furnished with pool tables, card tables, magazines, vending machines, and a television set. With the advent of small portable televisions, tape recorders, and increasing Army pay, the day rooms were not much used. The observer noted:

> The day room is big, open, and empty. It is the size of a bay, but had been divided into three areas by partitions. There are two pool tables, a soda machine, and a candy machine on the right side, with iron, straight-back chairs against the walls. The pool tables are not in bad shape, probably because there are no balls or pool cues. There are no curtains or shades on the windows that run the full length of the room. There are two large, old paintings on the walls, a seascape and a mountain scene. There are also a few reenlistment posters taped about the room.

> The second area is about one-fourth of the total area, and is the reading and card room. It contains several card tables and checkerboards printed on the tops. There is music playing from the radio in the his-fi console, but the tone arm has been torn off the turntable. The magazine rack contains mostly Army publications on how to buy a car or shop for a loan. There are a few copies of *U.S. News, Golf, Tennis* and *Time* magazines. The most recent is eight months old, and the oldest dates back 18 months. The paperback book titles are unknown to me; they appear to be little used, with unbroken spines and clean pages.

> The third area is furnished with easy chairs of wrought iron and cushions that face the black-and-white television. There are curtains at the windows to reduce the reflections on the television screen. The curtains are old, tattered, and sagging from their hooks in several places. They are too small for the windows and do not meet when they are closed. Two soldiers are watching the "Mike Douglas Show."

Shortly after this observation was made, the television set gave out and was neither repaired nor replaced in the subsequent year. The day room was mostly used as a classroom, and no evening activities were ever recorded.

To watch soldiers watching television, the observer had to return to the barracks:

> Watson lies on his bunk, watching TV with Murphy. I ask what the show is about; Murphy says, "The Killer Bees." "Sounds good." "It isn't. The lady is the queen of the bees. They kill on her command, supposedly, but they've only killed once and they seemed to do it on their own." We watch the program in silence for a moment, then Murphy says "Hey, I bought a really good camera today." "What kind?" "A Canon SLR. I got it at the PX. I'll take it home next time I go; I'll be sure to lose it here." We return to the program and watch in silence; the commercials are watched as attentively as the movie. Murphy falls

asleep mumbling, "Wake me when the bees kill again." I ask Watson what Murphy did to get so tired, but he could think of nothing special.

I go for a drink of water. When I return the movie is still on, and Murphy is asleep. "Did the bees kill again?" "Yeah, they got a lineman on top of a telephone pole. They came out of the transformer box." "Did you wake Frank?" "Naw, I let him sleep; the movie's not that good anyway." Murphy says, "I'm not asleep; I saw what happened." We watch quietly again. Then Murphy says, "Have you read the book *Death of an Army?*" "No. What's it about?" "It's good, written by a retired lieutenant colonel. He tells why the Army is a dying institution, and talks about the confusion of procedures that used to be straightforward, and says that's why the Army can't change with the times." "Do you agree?" "Yeah, all the way. It's a good book. My father gave it to me. I'll bring it back next time I go home.

The favorite television programs were the network movies, reruns of "Hogan's Heroes" and "Star Trek," police stories, and athletic contests.

As a rule somebody went for food sometime during the evening:

"Since the meal was so bad tonight I think the 9:00 run will have to be moved up to 7:00, but the 11:00 run will be on schedule," Tucker said as six of us stood in his room. Shortly thereafter we piled into his car and drove to the 7-11 store for ice cream, pastries, and sodas. Even though a 9:00 and 11:00 run does not occur every night on schedule, at least once a night someone makes a run to either 7-11, Burger King, or MacDonald's. The person going usually makes a public announcement, and the others will either go or give him a list of items and money. The people who go are the ones with cars, which usually means Tucker or Dennis. Sometimes Richards and myself. At least one run is made every night, no matter what the quality of the evening meal.

By midnight most have returned to the barracks. Many slept with the ceiling lights on, and those awake talked quietly in their areas before retiring. By 1:00 A.M. all was quiet save for the sounds of deep breathing, snoring, and a couple of radios playing softly in the night.

STRUCTURE OF WEEKEND ACTIVITIES

With the exception of occasional weekend guard duty, soldiers in the garrison Army worked a five-day week. At every possible opportunity—on weekends, holidays, and days off—they went home to their families and hometown friends. It was not uncommon for soldiers to drive 250 miles on a day off in the middle of the week, and up to 700 miles on the weekend. On a three-day weekend the observer found eight of 30 men in the barracks and asked their reasons for staying:

Williams: no car and restricted to the company for disciplinary reasons.

Rogers: no car because someone stole the battery.

Gino: has walking guard and car needs new tires.

Grady: has duty; recently paid $1800 for a Buick, but it is knocking badly.

Sessions: lives in Colorado—too far to drive alone.

Loveless: has walking guard and car is in the shop after a recent accident.

Benedict: has walking guard duty.

Warner: no car.

It was usually possible to pay another man to pull evening or weekend duty. The standard charge was $10 during the week and $20 on weekends. Thus the principal reasons for remaining in the barracks were lack of transportation, money, or both.

If it was impossible to get home on weekends, the next best alternative was to go sight-seeing. Two men reported driving 100 miles north of the post to a well-known amusement area, returning to the barracks the same night, and driving 75 miles west of the post to a national historic site the next day. Both excursions were "just to look around." Sometimes the men attended major league baseball games or visited museums in the nearest large city. The following observations were made on a quiet Sunday in the barracks:

Williams comes in and asks Daniels what is on television; Daniels throws him a guide. Williams scans the guide and turns to leave. "Hey, where you going with my guide? That's got to last me all week." Barker has left to make a hamburger run, and Watson and Firestone have joined the football group. Edmonds leaves the bay, and Lohman joins Daniels watching the movie.

Soldiers with money and the necessary social skills also used the weekends to interact with women. Soldiers classified women as either "nice girls" or "sweathogs." Nice girls were suitable for marriage or a serious relationship. Dating of nice girls was mostly a hometown activity, but it was also possible to meet them at clubs and dance halls near the post. The following description of a Saturday night out of the barracks illustrates the process of such interactions:

> Warner comes into my room very stylishly dressed in slacks, a dress shirt, and a vest. He has a date with Vivian tonight, a girl he met at the Tip-Top Club. When they first met he told her he was dating a girl at home and had to remain faithful to her, but that relationship has some problems now, and he can date Vivian. He is ready an hour and a half early, and he asks me if I have any talcum powder because he is beginning to sweat. Spitz drops by my room on the way to the shower, and invites me to go to the German-American Club with him. Sure, why not.
>
> The club is about a mile from post, set back from the highway on a winding road. It is a large, old building that seems to have living quarters on the second floor. Inside an elderly man asks us for 75¢ as the cover charge. A younger woman in her thirties asks if we had table reservations. Spitz says no, and show points to a table with two chairs. Spitz says we are waiting for two other guys, and would like to wait, if she didn't mind. The room is large, paneled in dark oak, with exposed beams and supporting posts. There is a large wooden dance floor surrounded by tables and benches. The band is setting up at the far end, and the eight band members range from teenage to at least sixty. Spitz says the band plays mostly polkas alternated with slow, contemporary music.
>
> The hall is about half full when we get there. Spitz tells me that a lot of older people come here to dance every week. He points out a table of four marines who are regulars, and another table with two soldiers. "The two girls over there are with their mother. They're Portuguese. I've danced with the younger one before." [He nods a hello and they reciprocate.] More couples come in, some in their 20's and some in their 40's. The younger men wear contemporary slacks, but most of the older men wear suits. A few of the older women wear elaborately embroidered peasant blouses, and some of the waitresses are dressed in complete traditional costumes. The band begins to play a polka, and the floor quickly fills; first two older couples, then a few younger, and the halls comes to life with people laughing, turning, and whooping to the music.
>
> Two girls come in, one about 17 and the other maybe 19. Spitz begins talking freely with them. He explains that we are waiting for Rogers and Collins. Nancy, the younger one, asks if we've seen Randall. The girls then pay the cover charge and sit at the small table near the service bar. Spitz explains that Nancy used to date Randall, and Diane formerly

dated Collins. "They come here pretty often. I like to come here because everyone is friendly. The girls are here for just a good time, and don't mind dancing with GIs. They don't think you're here just to pick them up and get into their pants."

After 20 minutes Roger and Collins have not arrived, so Spitz suggests we go check out the Tip-Top which is just down the highway. Spitz says the atmosphere at the Tip-Top is completely different, for it's a "night club." Actually, it's a large cocktail lounge with two bars and a small dance floor. The carpeting, paneling, mirrors, and subdued lighting are contrived to make the place appear more plush than it really is. Inside a man in a dark suit and bow tie is asking everyone for $1 as the cover charge, and is requesting the people to please check their coats. Spitz suggests we leave our jackets in the car to avoid the checking fee.

The crowd is much younger here. Single men sit at the bar, and the tables are occupied with couples and foursomes. The band is playing contemporary rock music, and we have to shout to be heard. The dance floor is about half-filled as we make our way to the second bar in the back of the room. Most of the men have long, contemporary hair styles, and the servicemen are immediately obvious with their shorter haircuts. Spitz again amazes me with his knowledge of the regular crowd. "See that young girl dancing with the GI? She's only 16. Not bad, uh? Her mother brings her here and sits at that table while she dances with the guys." The dance was over, and the GI escorts the girl back to a table where a very obese woman sat nursing a drink. He nods, smiles, and walks over to a table where three other soldiers are drinking. "See those three girls that just came in? I strain to see through the smoke and darkness, "They're real bitches. I asked them to dance last week and found out they won't dance with soldiers."

We spot Warner and Vivian to our right, and make our way to their table. Warner introduces us to Vivian, we comment on the band, smile goodbye, and make our way back toward the bar. Spitz says, "She's not that bad. Warner really did all right."

The band takes a break, and a second group of musicians takes over. I notice a really cute girl dancing with a GI and point her out to Spitz. He says she comes here regularly, but he has never danced with her. He challenges me to check her out. When she returns to her table occupied by her rather chunky girlfriend, I approach just as another guy is sitting down at the table. "Excuse me, I was just going to ask you to dance, but didn't realize you were talking." "Oh, you're not interrupting at all," and we push our way to the crowded dance floor.

After the dance I asked if she would mind if I got my drink and talked with her for awhile. She immediately said thanks, but no thanks, maybe some other time. Spitz returned from the dance floor to ask how

I had made out. I said she was pretty nice, but didn't want me to sit with her. Spitz explained, "Well, I should hope not. You went at it too fast. First you dance with her a few fast dances, then some slow ones, and if she continues accepting your invitations, then you get to sit with her." [Sorry, I didn't know the house rules.] Spitz comments about the scarcity of single girls tonight, and suggests we return to the German-American.

We spot Rogers and Collins with the girls and join them at the table. Spitz tells Collins that he met Diane at the Tip-Top. I introduce myself to the girls, and learn they are first cousins who live near the post. One works as a receptionist at the electric company and the other is still in high school. They have dated at least six men in the platoon at one time or another.

Suddenly a whistle blows. Spitz says it's time for a whistle dance, and says I have to get in this dance because it's a good way to meet some cute chicks. All of the girls parade in a circle surrounded by a circle of men moving the other way. When the whistle blows, you dance with the girl in front of you. Since I don't know how to polka, I sit and watch.

At midnight Nancy says she is ready to leave, and offers to drive Rogers to the Tip-Top so that he can get his car from Collins. Since the last dance is at 12:30, Spitz suggests we also go back to the Tip-Top. Spitz introduces me to a civilian, mid-30's, who is sitting at the bar. The civilian seems to know a lot of people in the place, and tells Spitz how he picked up the hat-check girl the other night after work as she was hitchhiking home. He also talks about the new barmaid who is single and advises Spitz to get acquainted with her. Spitz says he is ready to leave, but will definitely get to know the barmaid next week.

On the drive back to the post, Spitz says, "See how the GI image really hurts? Some girls won't even dance with you if they think you're a soldier. The civilians have a much better chance of getting a date with a girl." He also says that a lot of guys do not go to clubs because you're supposed to be 21 to get in. He is only 20, but has a fake ID card. At 1:00 the barracks is dark. We enter quietly and go to bed.

This episode illustrates several points worthy of emphasis. First, Spitz was acutely sensitive to his GI image when among civilians, although there was little evidence during the evening that he was discriminated against. Given the predominance of soldiers at these clubs it was unlikely that the two girls would not dance with soldiers, but assuming such is more comforting than the alternative thought, "They won't dance with me personally." Second, the evening was structured by other members of the work group, the platoon. Platoon members changed clubs in search of their Army buddies, and the girls they knew also knew other members of their platoon. Third, Spitz, with some college experience, was comparatively sophisticated in approaching women. He demonstrated his social skills when he instructed the observer on the etiquette of inviting oneself to sit at the table of an attractive dance partner. Earlier in the evening he instructed the observer on how to go about meeting women at the women's barracks:

> Spitz wants to check the WAC shack [barracks] to see if a particular girl is in. I offer to take my own car and meet him at the club, but he says he is not sure she is in or whether he really wants to take her out tonight. At the barracks he tells me that the way to meet girls is to ask the charge of quarters for someone you know is not in. "Then you just start talking with the CQ; if she seems nice, you just ask her for a date."

Knowing how to strike up a conversation with a strange woman may not seem like so much of a social skill that it requires instruction, but for people with little experience outside of high school settings, an experienced instructor was much appreciated.

Not all soldiers were as sophisticated as Spitz, or as anxious to have women believe they are interested in more than "getting into their pants." For the latter goal instruction was also available:

> Wilkins said, "You wanna know how to pick up chicks. I'll tell you. First you ask her for a fast dance. If she seems to like you, you ask her for a slow dance. If she likes that, you ask her to the car for a drink. Then you say, 'You wanna fuck?' "

"Sweathogs," on the other hand, provided sexual gratification with no implication that the relationship was, or ever could be, serious. "Sweathogs" were not whores, but were exploited even more viciously. The following observation was made at a bachelor apartment off post:

> Six of us were sitting around the wooden cable spool that served as the dining room table. Gross began telling about his personal sweathog, Cindy. "I met her at the shopping center one day, asked her to go swimming in the quarry, and then fucked her. Christ, she's the best lay I've ever had. When I introduced her to Copley, he just out and says, "Suck my dick or I'll punch your teeth down your throat." Yeah, he really said it, just like that. Cindy looks at me, I shrug and say he's my best friend, and she blows him right there. God, can she do a job with her tongue. I'd never kiss her though—all the cocks she's had in her

mouth." Gross then decides he will bring Cindy to the apartment, and leaves.

Gross returns with a short, stocky girl who has a badly scarred face from acne. He introduces her to the guys as "my cunt, Cindy," and goes to the refrigerator for a beer. Cindy looks a little embarrassed and sits quietly at the table. When Gross returns, she asks him for something to drink. He returns to the kitchen, and takes one of the dirty glasses from the sink for her. Murphy comes from the bedroom stark naked except for his shoes and socks. He streaks through the apartment, runs up to Cindy, and flicks his penis near her face. She turns away without expression, and sips her soda. Gross exclaims to the group, "See what I mean? Isn't she outa sight?" The laughter is nervous and subdued.

SUMMARY

This chapter examined the organization of the behavior of soldiers by utilizing four sets of inevitable constraints. Geographically, the soldiers in the barracks were isolated from the civilian surroundings and from many activity centers on the post; therefore behavior outside the company area is heavily dependent upon access to transportation. Sociologically, the barracks dwellers have little information about events and possibilities for recreation either in the civilian community or on the post; after duty hours the post is largely segmented into activities for the married and for the unmarried, with the former being more numerous. Psychologically, the barracks dwellers accommodate to these realities by rationalizing that civilians do not like soldiers and that they are only "in the Army," unlike the careerist "lifers." The primary allegiance of most first-tour soldiers remains the family and their hometown friends and relatives. Temporally, garrison duty is not terribly demanding and provides considerable latitude in the structuring of duty time. The principal constraint on affiliation imposed by the temporal arrangements of the duty day is the restriction of associates to the small work group, where the chief activities are banter and horse-play, which serve to establish and maintain status relations. Social interactions in the evenings and on weekends are an ever-shifting kaleidoscope of dyads and triads that assemble for brief times, break up, and then recombine in different patterns. A soldier's associates during leisure times are almost always his own barracks mates.

3

"ON MY OWN TIME"

Soldiers who live in company barracks are the population at highest risk for drug use in the Army. Drugs are used mainly after duty hours or on weekends, and consumption is usually adjunctive to other on-going leisure time activities. To understand drug use it is necessary first to understand the structure and dynamics of life in the barracks.

For the barracks dweller, the day is divided into two distinct segments. The period fromabout 7:00 A.M. to 4:30 P.M. is acknowledged as Army time, during which the soldier subordinates himself to those with legitimate authority to give orders and directives. After 4:30 P.M., unless there is some special duty, the individual considers himself "on my own time." Claim to off-duty time represents a kind of declaration of independence from the formal authority structure and military organization, and is invoked whenever there are attempts to place "illegitimate" demands on the individual after duty hours. In fact, "on my own time" is a cognitive fiction akin to the rationale that "I am not really a soldier; I am just in the Army as a truck driver (policeman, medical technician, heavy equipment operator, etc.) who happens to wear a funny scout suit to work."

Technically, all of the soldier's time belongs to the formal organization. The 30 days of annual leave granted every soldier is an outgrowth of the traditional notion that every soldier is available for duty seven days a week, 24 hours a day. The rotated roster duties of guard, charge of quarters, and duty officer's driver are, more than anything else, explicit reminders that all time belongs to the organization; thus the time left to the individual for his own private concerns is accorded at the discretion of the company commander. In practice, however, the commanders and their subordinates concur that the individual is on his own time unless he is required for duty. After 4:30 P.M., officers and sergeants leave the company area to join their families or to take up their part-time employment. The barracks dwellers remain in the company area, and military rank and authority become largely irrelevant.

Formal authority for maintaining order and safety rests with junior sergeants who rotate the responsibility of being in charge of the quarters. The responsibility of the CQ, as he is called, is to answer the telephone, secure the doors and windows, check for fire hazards, turn off the lights, and monitor the activities in the barracks. These junior sergeants are usually only a few years older than the majority of the privates, and they do not usually attempt to exert their authority after duty hours. In the rare event that a CQ breaks away from his television programs to wander through the barracks, he is more likely to join in activities than to restrain them.

Formal authority after duty hours is focused upon the battalion staff duty officer and noncommissioned officer, who are responsible for answering the battalion telephone, monitoring the walking guards, assisting the company CQs, and handling emergencies that arise from time to time. These responsibilities are rotated among the junior officers and senior sergeants in the battalion, who seldom visit the barracks.

Thus, on their own time and in the absence of effectual authority and structured activities, the barracks dwellers are left to evolve around their own codes and sanctions. The purpose of this chapter is to describe the social structure of barracks living. This includes the range of possible alternative affiliative choices, the organization of social behavior by means of dyads, triads, and cliques, the nature and function of larger social categories that exert social power, and the barracks norms that determine whether and how a given individual will be incorporated into the ongoing structure and group activities. None of the descriptions refer to drug or alcohol use, for these are only templates that overlay the basic structure and design; these will be appropriately dealt with in separate chapters.

A PHYSICAL DESCRIPTION OF THE BARRACKS

Before discussing the social structure of the barracks it may be helpful to describe its physical organization. This is important not only to provide a picture of the setting in which the behavioral data were collected, but also to serve as a reminder that the organization of physical space contributes to the behavior occurring therein. The placement of walls, doors, and furniture determines not only the possible activities and number of participants in a social group, but also the probability of interaction and the degree of privacy afforded.

There are two kinds of barracks: those characterized by open bays (traditional) and those divided into individual rooms (modern). With the advent of the volunteer Army, traditional barracks were renovated by partitioning the bay into rooms to increase privacy; modern barracks were built at some posts. Some of the observations at Fort Marshall were made in the traditional barracks, in which only the sergeants are accorded private rooms while the privates share a single large bay.

The bays at each end of the building measured 30 by 60 feet. Each bay accommodated a platoon of up to 50 soldiers when bunk beds were carefully arranged. The rooms opening on to the connecting corridor were reserved for sergeants with the exception of one room occupied by the cooks who kept irregular hours.

The ambience of an open bay was more like that of an institution than a home or residence. There were no curtains at the windows that began five feet off the floor and ran the length of the bay, and the globe lamps, before fluorescent lighting, hung on their chains from the exposed steel beams that supported the concrete ceiling. The room was furnished with iron bunk beds, metal wardrobes (wall lockers), three or four desks, and a few straight-back iron chairs. The monotony of the brown tiled floor, murky green painted walls, and battleship gray furniture was relieved only by an occasional area rug or art poster taped to a wall or wall locker.

The placement of the wall lockers and beds divided the large room into smaller two-, three-, and four-man living areas. To discourage theft, all personal possessions were kept in the wall lockers equipped with hasps and heavy padlocks.

The increasing number of married soldiers served to reduce the need for barracks space. The trend, therefore, was to remodel existing barracks and partition them into individual rooms affording single soldiers greater privacy. Each room was approximately 12 feet square, and the ambience was more like a college dormitory. Fluorescent fixtures hung in suspended ceilings, and the light reflected pleasantly from the pastel painted walls. Each room contained a bed, desk, chair, and wall locker, and many rooms had carpets on the floor. The furniture was still iron, painted gray, but the curtains at the windows and the art posters, fish netting, trophies, pictures, and personal possessions on display provided some diversion. The soldiers were allowed to arrange and decorate as they chose within rather broad limits. Because the barracks often were included in tours given to visiting dignitaries, the display of Confederate flags, swastikas, and certain pictures of nude women ("tits and ass are OK, but no hair") was actively discouraged. Remodeled barracks frequently had recreation and laundry rooms for the convenience of the residents.

DETERMINANTS OF SOCIAL AFFILIATION: THE BIG FOUR

It would seem that a soldier assigned to an Army post with 30,000 others of the same age would have an enormous range of potential associates. In fact the barracks dweller was restricted to only a couple dozen associates. The four major determinants of his affiliative choices were his work group, rank, residence, and race.

Work Group

By far the most potent determinant of social choice was the company of assignment. Merely being assigned to a company set the 200 or so members apart from the rest of the post by psychological boundaries that were just as effective as any steel fence or concrete wall. Individuals were practically powerless against these forces, which not only prevented them from moving away from the company, but actively oriented them to other soldiers who shared membership in the organization.

The company in one observed barracks occupied the third floor, while a sister company in the same battalion occupied the second. In fourteen months of observation absolutely no informal interaction or visiting back and forth between the barracks members of the two companies was recorded. One reason was the rarity of opportunities for the soldiers to meet and talk. A stranger in a barracks area was immediately suspect as a thief unless he could demonstrate a legitimate reason for being there; a plea for companionship was not a valid excuse.

Even when there were occasions for meeting, no extension of the relationship was ever implied. Members of the study company played on the battalion football team with players from the other four companies. They practiced and scrimmaged together for three months. After the final game of the season, two players from another company were invited to a party on the bay, but the relationship ended there despite the fact that they lived in the same building and ate in the same dining hall.

An informal touch football game after supper likewise implied no potential for future interaction. The observer noted:

> 1700. Murphy is changing his clothes at his locker and invites me to play football. We go to the front of the building where ten other men are waiting. Four of the men are from B Company, so Gross decides we should team up by companies, but no one volunteers to play on the other team so the sides will be even. Finally, Gross says, "Come on Barker, let's play over here." It gets dark in about an hour with my team leading by two touchdowns. After the usual "nice game," we return to our bay, and the guys from B Company went to theirs on the floor below.

The same pattern holds for dyads on the golf course. In one case, the observer and his companion overtook a player on the second hole who asked to join them. They played the next eight holes together; the stranger thanked them and left. The situation is no different at the field house:

> I went to the field house where I shot baskets for about 15 minutes when I was asked to join seven other guys in a game. We shot free-throws to determine the teams, and they played about 5 games to 15 points each. The teams were evenly matched, so we kept the same teams for the two hours we played. I, along with everyone else, was beat. No one seemed to know anyone else; we showered in silence and then left.

Even the activities intended to facilitate acquaintance were not enjoyable if the individual had to go alone. The observer recounted his experience one night before he became well acquainted:

> 2000 [8 P.M.]. I go to the dayroom, but it is empty and all the lights are off. I pass five men sitting on the steps, smoking and talking. They do not speak to me, and no one else is in sight. I wander to the service club and am surprised to see casino night in progress.

> At the first table, three men are playing poker. The chips are different colors but seem to have the same value. Two men come in and watch with me until one of the players goes broke and the game breaks up. The blackjack dealer is reading a photography magazine. One of the winners at poker sits at the table and arranges his chips into neat piles. The dealer looks up, then returns to his magazine. The man gathers his chips almost apologetically, and goes to the dice table where four men and a woman are playing. One man has his fatigue cap on backwards, smiles broadly and calls, "Come to me, sweet baby." The others watch

quietly without much enthusiasm, occasionally calling a number and putting their chips on the table. On the roulette table a baby is sleeping in a carrier. The woman checks the baby and returns to the crap table.

The liveliest game is Chuck-a-Luck, where the pit man keeps up a constant string of banter with eight men betting. "Place your bets, suckers . . . the winners are five, three and one." The players respond as loudly, "Give me five on three." "I'm a winner on one."

Soul music is playing softly on the console. A man near me counts his chips, and I ask to get some. He explains that the cashier gives everyone 20 to start out, and the chips can be cashed in for lucky bucks. "When you save up enough lucky bucks, you can turn them in for prizes." At the counter such prizes as cigarettes, after shave lotion, an instamatic camera, and a lemon squeezer are on display. I ask the cashier for some chips, but it is 9:30, time for the casino to close. The dozen or so players are cashing in their chips, and I'm alone writing my notes beside the sleeping baby.

Thus the soldiers would join with strangers in an athletic contest in a public area, but could not seek out partners in any barracks but their own. They could play poker for "lucky bucks" at the service club, but could not seek out a card game in another company. They could go to the craft shop, bowling alley, stables, or swimming pool, but always returned to the barracks alone. There were many recreational facilities on post, but few friends outside the company.

Even so, a company of 200 men should offer a considerable range of affiliative possibilities. A company, however, is not a work group. If the company is a "line" unit, with four platoons, each is a separate work group. If the company is a "support" unit, there are multiple work groups, some as small as three or four men. As noted previously, most of the duty day was spent with the work group, and, since the barracks are assigned by work section, leisure time was restricted to the same people. The psychological boundary separating platoons was almost as rigid as that separating companies. The observer queried a soldier about his best friend in the Army:

> "I'd have to say that, in the Army, I'm the closest to O'Keefe. He used to be in the third platoon, but got transferred to the second. I haven't seen him in a couple of months. He sometimes comes over here [50 feet between the buildings], but I've never been over there to visit him."

In a company with large work groups like platoons, which may contain up to 50 soldiers, the individual had more choice than in a barracks that housed multiple small work units. In such a barracks the motor pool people tended to hang together, as did the administrative personnel and those assigned to the supply office. The boundaries were more permeable than between platoons that resided in separate buildings, but this advantage was offset by another factor: the time of arrival in the company. In a barracks where all work in the same group or platoon, new men are assimilated into the existing structure. In a barracks that housed multiple segmented work groups, a new soldier was left to his own devices to integrate into an existing group or wait for the emergence of a new group:

> Cressey, Smith, Johnson, and Eagleton have together left the Army or have been reassigned. Edmonds and Miller put two bunks together and move into the Murphy-Barker area with Peters and Watson. By rearranging the bunks and wall lockers, they have a six-man area with a desk and refrigerator. The seven new men on the bay share the two areas nearest the door and the hallway.

Subsequent observations confirmed the pattern of oldtimers drifting to the back of the bay and rearranging the furniture to establish their enclaves, leaving the new men in the company to work out their own relationships at the front of the bay. Thus the affiliative choices of the soldier are constrained not only by his company of assignment, but also by the work group within the company and, in certain companies, by his time of arrival in the unit.

There are only two ways to surmount the psychological boundaries within the company. The first is to change work groups, but since soldiers are assigned by the military occupational specialties and since work groups are designed around these specialties, the only way to get reassigned is to get branded as a troublemaker, a gross incompetent, or both:

> Gino is always hanging around the third platoon, although he is assigned to the first. I asked why, and he said, "I used to be in the third platoon, but the lieutenant said I was a 'bad influence,' and he transferred me to the first. He even gave me a direct order to stay out of the barracks over here."

Gino kept most of his informal social ties with his old work group, but he had a few other relationships in his new work group and thus provided a bridge to facilitate interaction between the groups. Incompetent soldiers provided even better bridges because they experienced more frequent reassignments.

Despite making technological progress, the Army remains in

many ways a labor-intensive organization. There are many jobs to do that require little more than the ability to report for work at the appointed time and place. A clerk typist who cannot type is transferred to a job that requires only filing skills; if he can't master filing, he is transferred to the mail room or is given the job of running errands; if all else fails, he becomes a duty soldier who cuts grass and rakes leaves. The Army gives up only when the individual refuses to come to work anymore. As the incompetents bounce from work group to work group, they acquire associates along the way and thus provide a complete network between the different work groups in the company.

The second way to surmount intracompany boundaries is to occupy a position in the organization that encourages contact with soldiers in different work groups. Company clerks are good examples because they handle all of the company records, speak to nearly everyone who comes to the orderly room, and are "in the know" by virtue of their daily contact with the first sergeant and company commander. In the same ways, but to lesser degrees, the cooks, supply clerks, and mechanics have daily transactions with soldiers who are not assigned to their work group. The interactions during the duty day often provide the basis for developing more extensive, intracompany social ties after duty hours:

> Barns, a cook from headquarters platoon, seems to know everybody. He is on the battalion football team where he met Casey, and he knows Foxx, the mechanic, because he drives the mess truck on food runs. He usually has time during the meals to drink coffee and talk with the guys as they eat.

In summary, surmounting work group boundaries within the company was possible, but not very typical. The most intense social interaction occurs within the work group and then diffuses rapidly among other members of the company.

Rank

After the work group, the most potent determinant of affiliation was military rank. Almost without exception, private soldiers did not socialize with their officers after duty hours. The senior sergeants who lived in the barracks did not socialize with the privates, and the sergeants who lived with their families were never around the barracks to permit informal interaction. Sergeants who supervised work groups invited soldiers from the barracks to their homes for a meal and television, but these invitations were decidedly special occasions for special people in the work group. On Thanksgiving Day the observer recorded:

> I talked with Sergeant Murdock in front of the mess hall. He introduced me to his wife and explained that this is the first time in three years that they have had a holiday meal in the mess hall. His wife says that when they were in Germany she used to roast three turkeys on Thanksgiving and invite all of the guys to their home. The apartment on post, however, is too small, so they are dining out this year. She says she misses the men in her home on the holiday.

Since military rank is highly correlated with age, the barracks dweller has only his age-mates in his duty section as potential friends.

Residence

The third major determinant of social affiliation was residence. As a rule, soldiers who were married or lived with girlfriends in apartments did not spend much leisure time with barracks dwellers. After normal duty hours, married soldiers concentrated on their wives, children, neighbors, and community concerns. As one married man expressed it in a group interview, "After 4:30, I just want to get as far away from the fucking Army as I can; I don't even want military people as my friends." Others in the group affirmed his sentiments.

There were only two occasions when a married soldier invited a barracks dweller to his home. The first was a special event, like a going-away party, where members of the work group were invited. Typically the host was also the guest of honor or had a particularly close tie with the guest of honor. Other occasions were special invitations, structurally identical to being invited to the platoon sergeant's house. The observer noted:

> Winston, who is married, has driver of the guard today. He invites me to meet his wife and have dinner at his house some time. "My wife works in a state hospital for the insane and would be interested in someone like you. I mean, she knows about psychology and could probably understand what you're doing better than I could." I told him I would welcome an invitation for a decent meal any time.

Such special events imply guest behaviors rather than those of a friend who is welcome to stop by any time for however long.

The second set of circumstances in which a married soldier invited barracks dwellers to his home was the case of a troubled marriage where the male needed buffers between him and his wife to restrain arguments and squabbling:

> Morton goes on duty at midnight and is waiting in the barracks. He mentions that his wife has left him. Loveless says, "You two are always splitting up, not that it's any of my business, but isn't this the third or fourth time?" Cranston says she left because he went over to the apartment and got a little drunk and rowdy. Morton says, "That wasn't the only reason; in fact, the party really didn't get going until after you passed out." Later, Morton complained that Cranston is the only one he can count on to come to the apartment when he is invited: "All the others say they'll come, but they never show up."

Thus the individual soldier is constrained to make affiliative choices within his work group among those who share his rank and residence—inevitably other barracks dwellers. Even this very limited set of choices is further restricted by race.

Race

The Army is racially integrated in every area of military life governed by the rules and statutes of the formal organization and the directives of those in legitimate authority. Formal rules and legitimate authority do not apply when soldiers are on their own time. Army regulations, for example, require that all soldiers, regardless of race, be admitted to the dining hall, but no regulation requires soldiers of different races to eat at the same table. When soldiers are on their own time, the Army is quite rigidly segregated.

In the dining hall individuals have considerable freedom to define relationships to other people by where they choose to sit. In the barracks, however, there was almost no choice, for bunks were assigned on a first-come, first-placed basis as space became available. Hence a diagram of the barracks would show greater racial integration than the mess halls, but behaviorally the barracks were every bit as segregated. Under no conditions was a white ever incorporated into an informal group of blacks. Only under very special conditions was a black incorporated in an informal group of whites in the barracks.

Life in the barracks after duty hours was controlled by the majority group, and blacks were not in the majority. While blacks maintained formal, day-to-day business relations with their white barracks-mates, they typically changed clothes immediately after duty and left the barracks to associate with other blacks. To meet other blacks they had to cross intra- and intercompany boundaries; hence race provided a notable exception to the impermeability of these boundaries. A similar exception to this rule involved Spanish-speaking soldiers, who commonly segregated themselves from both the blacks and the whites, and had to cross organizational boundaries to do so. The means of scaling work-group barriers was provided in the dining halls and the ethnic bars on or near the post; the motive was the tension between the majority and minority groups.

The reasons for interracial tension are woven into the fabric of American society, and the same threads simply assume different configurations in that section of the tapestry that is the Army.

The following excerpts come from two different group interviews, one with all white members and the other with all black. The excerpts are juxtaposed to demonstrate that the two groups hold essentially the same views toward each other with respect to the three central issues of Army life: work, discipline, and food.

White: "You're damned right there's discrimination against us. The blacks are always coming up with some phony excuse and getting over on the sergeants; 'course we all do that [laughter], but the blacks definitely sham [loaf on the job] more than the whites, which means we have to do all the work."

Black: "I wouldn't call it discrimination, but there's sure as hell a lot of prejudice. Who does all the shamming? Right, the whites. Whenever there's a dirty, stinky job to do, you don't see no whites around. No, let the nigger do it."

White: "The thing that really burns my ass is the two standards of discipline in the Army. Whenever an NCO or officer jumps on a brother, they scream "prejudice" all the way to the colonel. Us whites just get slapped with fines, extra duty, and restrictions."

Black: "There's definitely two standards of discipline in the Army. Sir, you just check the company records. Blacks always get more Article 15's [punishments], and whitey just gets off with a warning. The blacks get heavier punishments, too. Check it out."

White: "They think the world owes them something special all the time. Y'know what we had in the mess hall last week? Pig guts and tomato sauce. Yeah, man, no kidding. Soul food, special

for them; I'm Italian and I don't see no cooks making ravioli for
me."

Black: "Sometimes I just get so hungry for chitlins, beans, and rice,
and a side of greens. What do we get in the mess hall? Spaghetti
at least three times a week. The man just won't even let us eat
right."

What are the facts? Fact: Greens and black-eyed peas were served
as frequently as brussels sprouts and stewed tomatoes. They may not
have been prepared like mother's, but a variety of ethnic food was
available in the mess halls. Fact: An examination of disciplinary records over a 12-month period revealed no significant relationship between race and either the frequency or severity of punishment in the
four companies studied. Fact: In work assignment, sergeants were
scrupulous to the point of obsession in avoiding any hint of discrimination.

The tensions between blacks and whites, then, had little to do
with the Army as an institution per se. The Army simply provided yet
another setting for the definition and testing of majority-minority
power differentials rooted in the larger society. In the barracks the
power edge was maintained and honed through repeated interpersonal assaults that made it practically impossible for the barracks
dweller to cross racial lines to select leisure time associates.

Early in the study one white observer received explicit instructions on how to go about his work and how to get along with the
blacks:

Copley says I should hang around the motor pool because it contains
most of the white group in the barracks. "The blacks usually stay away
from the barracks, but you won't have trouble with them if you just act
natural and let them call the shots. Y'know, don't get uptight when
you're called 'honkey' and 'cracker,' but just join in the 'game' and call
them 'niggers' or 'black SOB's.'" I was skeptical, but he continued,
"You'll have to learn to tell when 'honkey' is serious and when they're
joking, but don't let them get away with anything or they'll walk all
over you."

The tone was invariably "joking," but the intent of maintaining
the power edge was always serious. Whites in the barracks repeatedly cracked the tired old joke, "Smile, man, so I can see you in
the dark," and blacks responded by smiling as if the line were original. If offense was taken, the aggressor always fell back to, "Hey,
man, cool it; I was only joking. Don't take it personally."

Indeed there was seldom any personal meaning intended, for they worked together during the day and had some contact at night. The observer noted:

> Murphy, Gross, and Cox [who is black] are watching television and eating pizza when I enter the bay. Murphy says he is going to play golf before it gets dark. Cox asks if he is going to leave his television out while he is gone with the clear implication that he would like to continue watching it. Murphy says, "With you around? No way." "Why not?" "Because a cocksucking spook like you would steal it and have it pawned in Boomtown before I got back." "How do you know that?" "Because you're a cocksucking spook, and I know you're a spook because you have a gold tooth." Cox laughs, but Murphy locks up the television in his locker.

A slightly more subtle way of maintaining the power edge was the content of the conversation. Whites often believed that blacks did not like oral sex and were repelled by descriptions of it. Therefore, explicit, detailed descriptions were sometimes used to "keep them in their place":

> Four men are loafing on the steps before the formation. Sergeant Wilson approaches, and Oster shifts the conversation to "eating pussy." Wilson jumps on Oster for having his hair too long (it was clearly within the hair length regulation). As he leaves, the men make sounds like "mmmmmm" and "slurp." Payne explains that Wilson can't stand to hear about "eating someone out" and was kidded so much about it one time that he got sick and threw up.

In view of the continual stream of racial slurs and banter there is little wonder why the blacks tended to leave the barracks and never invited a white to join them. The familiar epithets were so predominant in the verbal repertoires of the whites that they often just slipped out unintentionally through the gossamer restraints of polite, proper behavior:

> Sergeant Kenny [who is black] had invited five of the men in the platoon to his apartment to watch the bowl game. Mrs. Kenny has fixed a plate of snacks, and the guys compliment her on how comfortably the rooms are arranged. We are alternately laughing, talking, and getting serious about the game. Billins watches a black player fumble for the second time and explodes, "They ought to kill that fucking nig-ger." The room is quiet. Sergeant Kenny looks at the floor, then goes to the kitchen for more refreshments.

The only blacks to be incorporated into white barracks groups were those willing to endure the continual banter and accept subordinate status. Such blacks were typically from rural parts of the country and often did not have the money, clothes, language, or social skills to be accepted among the urban blacks. The case of Private Lohman, whose duty was described in the previous chapter, is illustrative:

Charles Lohman is a 20-year-old black from Cypressville, Alabama. His father is a farmer who owns his own land. He says he never has had any trouble getting along with whites because his play groups always included both blacks and whites, and he attended integrated schools.

He arrived in the platoon at the same time as Hanson, Holmes, Marshall, and Lamb, and he spends most of his evenings with them. They consider him part of their "newbie group" in the barracks and distinguish themselves from the "old timers" at the far end.

When I picked them up for a group interview, it was necessary for one man to ride in the luggage area of my VW station wagon. Holmes jokingly said, "To the back of the bus, Charles," and Lohman immediately went to open the door of the trunk.

At the group interview, the men were boisterous as usual, but during the introductions, Lamb said, ". . . and this is our boy, Charles. He don't talk English so good, so I'll translate for him." Lohman looked down, but clearly said, "I can speak for myself if I have anything to say."

Lohman bought a used television that he keeps chained to his bunk, but anybody can watch it whether he is there or not. Whenever the group is watching television and a white joins them, he gets up from his bed or chair and offers it to the white. He usually says that he is just leaving anyway, and then goes for a drink of water before returning to the group.

He seldom leaves the barracks at night, and I have never seen him in civilian clothes. He neither drinks nor uses drugs, but complained at the end of my interview with him that he "just feels depressed and nervous all the time."

After the constraints of work group, rank, residence, and race have taken their toll, the barracks dweller has very little choice in the selection of his social companions. Judging from the tendency of men who have been transferred out of a unit to return to it after duty hours, it appears that the process of becoming incorporated into a barracks group is sufficiently aversive that the individual will maintain existing ties, whenever possible, rather than submit to initiation into a new barracks group.

The only way to escape the major determinants of affiliation was to be lucky enough to have existing ties. A few soldiers were stationed close enough to their homes that, although they lived in the barracks, they continued to maintain social contacts in the civilian community. A few other soldiers had contacts from previous assignments and reconstituted the group from Korea or Germany at the new post, despite the fact that the members were assigned to different companies widely dispersed throughout the post. Most barracks dwellers, however, were trapped by the restrictions imposed by work group, rank, residence, and race, and had no choice but to join the group or go it alone.

BARRACKS SOCIAL STRUCTURE

The existential truth that each person is alone in the universe does not contradict the equally true proposition that each person is committed to a social existence with others. The individual is born into a pre-existing social unit, the family, and is nurtured and sustained in the pre-existing social order of the community. He learns of his existential alienation when separated from his social unit; he learns how their presence dispels loneliness; and he learns how their acceptance can banish it completely. Military life serves to accent both of these existential truths.

Part of the soldier's sense of social isolation stems from an unwillingness to make extensive personal commitments to other soldiers. In the effort to recruit and maintain an all-volunteer force, the Army attempted to assign personnel as close to their homes as possible. The recruits typically had every expectation of returning to hometown, family, and friends when they completed a three-year tour; hence they went home as often as possible to maintain their place in the social network. For the barracks dweller, the Army post was not a community, but a place to work; their community was the hometown to which they had to return each weekend. The barracks was viewed simply as a dormitory.

Personal relationships in the Army were not made with the expectation that they would extend beyond the time the parties were stationed together. Army companies experienced continual personnel turnover as soldiers were recruited, discharged, and reassigned to other posts. All personal relationships were bounded by the brief time that the individuals were together—typically no more than 12 months, and often less.

The fundamental social unit in the barracks was the dyad—two soldiers who consider themselves buddies or partners. Their relationship generally was established and maintained more by circumstance than choice, and typically emerged from proximal bunk assignments in the barracks and being forced to work together during the duty day. The dyad is the most intimate of all barracks relationships, but is commonly acknowledged as only temporary. The Army buddy who remains a lifetime personal friend may emerge from shared combat experience, but this is highly unlikely in the garrison Army. The silliest question to ask a soldier is to name friends in the unit, because the answer is always, "I have no friends in the Army." The observer noted:

> I asked Wolfson whom he considered as his best friend in the barracks. "All of my friends are at home. I have no friend in the Army, and never will. You see, there are two types of friends, best friends and Army buddies. Like, I have some best friends at home who I trust and respect and do lots of different things with them. I know I can count on them to be there if I ever needed them. Army buddies are people you know you have to work with and live with, so to avoid hassles, you try to be friendly with them. If you do things with them, it's usually because of common interests; like, when Rogers and I go to the gym to work out. You trust and respect Army buddies to a certain degree, but you can't rely on them to make a personal sacrifice for you. Hell, with guys always moving and getting transferred all the time, you can't even be sure your buddy will even be in the unit tomorrow."

Having a real friend in the Army was found to be more a measure of the depth of individual alienation and impoverished social relations than a mark of adjustment:

> Barker said he has to go to Chicago this weekend to be the best man in a wedding. "Is he a good friend of yours?" "No, I hardly know the guy. We spent eight weeks together in basic training, and now I get this letter telling me I'm the best friend he's ever had, and would I please be his best man. I guess I'll have to go; if I'm his best friend, he probably doesn't have anybody else to ask."

Barker showed singular compassion, for the more typical response was to avoid personal involvements with other soldiers. The observer noted:

Wilson told me that Cranston had invited him to usher at his wedding. "Now the guy has the nerve to tell me I have to buy a bow tie. Piss on him. If I have to buy a tie, he can just find somebody else. I thought I was doing him a favor."

Thus the soldiers accepted the temporal reality of their military existence by creating a new category—somewhat more than an acquaintance but less than a friend—called the "Army buddy," and they built a social structure in the barracks to met their social needs.

While the buddy is taken to be "someone you can count on," in point of fact he is not. Leave, special duties, and personal business insure that there will be many times when one's buddy is unavailable for companionship. The tendency of soldiers to run in threes provided stability and continuity in social relationships at Fort Marshall. Each barracks resident assumed the position of a partner in a dyadic relationship, but also functioned as the third in numerous other relationships. In this way, when one's buddy was absent, he could turn to other affiliative sets.

Since barracks residents were members of multiple triads it was not uncommon for two or three sets of relationships to come regularly together to form loosely bounded cliques. Membership in a clique at a given time—and membership could change from day to day or hour to hour—was typically limited to five or six. The size of a clique seemed to be determined by the number of people who could fit comfortably into a single automobile or who could participate in a common conversation around a table in a bar.

The social structure of the barracks was not a rigidly structured, tightly bounded group, nor a series of such groups with mutually exclusive memberships. Instead the social structure was a series of loosely bounded cliques with overlapping memberships. The cliques formed on the basis of propinquity in space, membership in work groups, time in the company, race, and common interests. The patterns of interaction observed were like an ever-shifting kaleidoscope in which the elements joined in discernible repeating forms but then dispersed to recombine in still different repeating forms. After a week in the barracks, the observer tried to capture this stable yet unstable pattern:

The barracks seems to be organized by dyads and triads. There seem to be definite groups and subgroups, but at the next moment, everybody is mixed up in a new combination. For example, Gross, Barker, and Murphy spend a good deal of time together and will wait on each other for breakfast and supper, yet last night Barker spent the entire evening watching television with Cressey. Cressey hangs around with Watson most of the time, and they both work in the motor pool. Another strong dyad is Miller and Edwards, who used to share an area until Miller got transferred to another company. When Miller isn't in the barracks, Edwards hangs with the Gross-Murphy-Barker group. At the far end of the bay, Riley, Kinney, and Roberts share an area and usually hang there together. Roberts and Kinney work together in the operations office. Riley sometimes hangs with the motor pool group around Cressey and Watson. The dyads sometimes fuse around Gross, Murphy, and Barker in interaction marked by continual banter with ever-shifting alliances in the put-down routines.

Black groups never mingle with white groups, although black individuals are sometimes incorporated. Prescott, Peterson, and Perry share an area, but are usually not around the barracks. When they are there, they are with other blacks that I have not seen before. Cable is seldom in the barracks, although I have seen him in the mess hall with other blacks from C Company. Connors works in the orderly room with Murphy and plays on the football team with Barker and Gross. He spends little time in the barracks, but when he is present, he is part of the Gross-Murphy-Barker circle. The only interracial dyad I've observed is Clifton and Morgan, who went to a rock concert together last weekend and to the post movie theater last night; they do not spend much time together in the barracks, however.

The dyads, triads, and cliques functioned to provide the individuals with interpersonal bonding and a sense of stability in the essentially unstable interpersonal environment of the Army. It is from these face-to-face encounters that the individuals derived a sense of belonging and social worth. The arrangement of triads and cliques also insured that there were always others with whom the individual felt comfortable when primary contacts were temporarily unavailable or permanently severed.

In addition to the face-to-face aggregates that may loosely be considered groups, there were larger social categories to which the individuals belonged. The function of the larger categories was not so much to promote interpersonal bonding, but to provide ways for diverse cliques to unite in asserting social power when all of them were faced with a common threat. The social categories derived from social norms that specified who was to behave how toward whom. Thus, for example, when the first sergeant or company commander exerted pressure to clean up the barracks or to control rowdy parties, the cliques were likely to coalesce under the banner of "privates against the lifers." At other times, when new soldiers did not conform to established barracks standards, an "old timers versus the newbies" norm might be invoked to bring the older cliques together to exert conformity pressures. On still other occasions, the category of "heads" or drug users could be invoked against the out-group of "straights." In the first case, "privates" included everyone, irrespective of time in the company or drug of choice; the second case divided the barracks on the basis of time in the company; and the third ignored the seniority dimension. The primary function of these categories was to mobilize the effect of social power; but in some instances category membership could provide avenues for affiliative alternatives, as when one drug user approached another with whom he otherwise was unacquainted and invoked category membership as justification for the interaction. When a soldier asked another where he could buy drugs, he was invoking a common social category that carried with it an obligation to respond to the request in a friendly way.

The social structure of the barracks, then, was one of dyads, triads, and cliques that provide the primary sources of face-to-face interpersonal bonding and a series of superordinate social categories into which the cliques could be incorporated to marshall and exert social power. The most intimate relationship was the dyad—two partners or buddies—but like all Army relationships, it was time-bound with minimal interpersonal commitment. Given the social structure of the barracks and the quality of the resultant relationships, it is not surprising that these unions were forged and maintained with a modicum of social skill. That is to say, to become part of the social structure and to partake of the leisure time activities required only a modest sensitivity to the rules of conduct and a willingness to engage in those activities preferred by young, unsophisticated, largely working-class people.

INCORPORATION INTO THE SOCIAL STRUCTURE

At Fort Marshall the process of social affiliation was complex, remarkably efficient, but not particularly difficult. At the end of about three days, everyone in the barracks "knew" whether the new man would fit in. Whether a new man could be incorporated into the barracks group was almost totally dependent on endorsing the values and behavior patterns of the residents; that is, whether the newcomer presented himself as a "regular guy" or appeared in some way a "jerk." This determination was made during the acquaintance proc-

ess through face-to-face discussions and—equally important—
through casual observation.

The "Regular Guy" Norm

The first requirement was that the new soldier be approachable. This
meant spending some time in the barracks waiting to get acquainted
with area-mates. Not to do so was to risk being judged "stuck-up" or
a "snob." The newcomer might facilitate approach simply by sitting
on his bunk, nodding to those who passed, and otherwise appearing
friendly. He might also read magazines that others might seek to
borrow, or play solitaire, or study a chess board in the hope that
someone would ask to join him. When approached, the new man was
expected to enter the acquaintance ritual with elaboration rather than
give simple and direct answers to questions.

Getting acquainted was always a search for commonalities, an
exploration of the potential for future interactions. In the Army there
are three inevitable probes that support the fragile web of interpersonal similarity: Where are you from? Where have you been? What do
you do? A ten-minute introductory interchange was sufficient to establish the new soldier's home state and hometown, whether or not
he played athletics in high school, why he joined the Army, whether
he had an automobile on post, whether he served overseas, his occupational specialty, his experience in that specialty, and his feelings
about his current assignment.

In view of the time-bounded nature of military acquaintance it is
significant that most of the information exchanged was based on
military experience—the here-and-now. It is also significant that personal names were of little interest. Soldiers wear their surnames on all
of their uniforms and are invariably addressed by that name alone. In
the barracks it was not uncommon to find soldiers who had worked
together daily for six months or more who did not know each other's
first names. In fact the use of first names signaled an unusual degree
of intimacy between two soldiers and was usually observed only
between buddies or members of very cohesive work groups.

Observations were equally important in determining whether
newcomers were to be incorporated into barracks groups. A soldier
who sat on his bunk reading religious tracts was apt to be labeled a
"Jesus freak" and either shunned or derided for having a holier-than-
thou attitude. The reader of car or sex magazines, however, was
accorded greater potential for incorporation. A soldier turning a radio
to a country-western station ran the risk of being considered a "red-

neck," whereas a rock, soul, or top-forty station implied commonality with the majority of the barracks residents. Wearing a pressed shirt, sweater, casual slacks, and Army oxfords carried the implication of straight-laced, "square," or even sissy; whereas the more typical sneakers, faded jeans, and grubby sweatshirt signaled acceptability. A picture of a nude woman taken from a magazine was more acceptable than a photograph of home and family. By the same token tough, manly actions were preferred to timid, effeminate responses. Nothing so formal as a vote determined whether a new person would be incorporated into barracks groups, but from in numerable conversations, innuendos, and asides a consensus emerged as binding as any parliamentary action. The observer noted:

> Loveless was talking about the new man in the barracks over breakfast. "Well, it looks like we have a real Jesus freak on our floor. He's got trophies on one wall, his boxing gloves on another, and a picture of Jesus Christ on the third. God, I just can't stand those bastards always trying to shove their religion down your throat. And did you see his yellow pajamas?" [laughter]

As a general rule, no information was passed on if the newcomer was a "regular guy," but if he tended to be different, he was the talk of the group. Recall Private Gilman, in the preceding chapter, who dared to place a picture of his mother in his work area. The essential point is that regular guys do not "come down on" or negatively evaluate others, but accept the proposition that everybody should be allowed to "do his own thing."

There were limits, however, to the doctrine of doing one's thing, particularly when that thing had major implications for the behavior of other members of the barracks groups. In order to be accepted into the groups, the newcomer had to accept and abide by several other behavioral rules or norms. Failure to conform met with swift and certain censure.

First, the newcomer had to accommodate himself to the standards of military appearance and deportment acceptable to the barracks dwellers. Army units differ in the degree of spit and polish expected. Medical units were regarded as the least military in haircut uniformity, dress standards, and the use of military courtesies. Support units such as engineering, transportation, and signal companies came closer to the popular image of soldiers, but the nature of their work insured that a goodly percentage would have scuffed boots and soiled clothing. Elite units such as the airborne infantry and military police were routinely inspected by visiting dignitaries and shown off on the parade ground; hence they maintained higher standards of dress and deportment. Within all units, however, there was a diversity of acceptable appearance as, for instance, the cooks, mechanics, and clerks in the headquarters platoon, who were usually not held to the same standards as others in the unit. Also within every unit, whether engineers or military police, there existed minimally acceptable standards that had been informally negotiated between leaders and subordinates. The negotiated settlement emerged from the perpetual conflict between leaders who persistently strove for higher standards and subordinates who believed that no matter how much they did or how hard they tried, their efforts would not be appreciated or deemed sufficient.

The tensions between "desirable" and "acceptable" were nowhere more passionately evident than on the issue of haircuts. While the Army was more liberal than the Marine Corps, which maintained the close-cropped "white-wall" style, it was decidedly more conservative than the Navy, which permitted beards and bushy, albeit well-trimmed, hair styles. Despite regulations dictating when a moustache was too long, and despite the posters in every unit showing pictures of acceptable hair lengths, the question of when a soldier needed a haircut was usually a judgment call. In a really impassioned haircut squabble it was possible to find sergeants with rulers measuring forelocks to the nearest quarter of an inch. The issue was actually not hair length, but the domain of legitimate authority over the affairs of the individual soldier. The leaders claimed the right to set appearance standards, and common soldiers disputed this right as an infringement of their private affairs. Until the crux of the matter is recognized, the regulations appear trivial and the enforcement stupid and intolerant. The observer recorded the following interchange involving a private and his first sergeant:

> The first sergeant read from the regulations, " 'The moustache shall not extend beyond the corner of the mouth.' Now, isn't that clear, and isn't your moustache way beyond the corner of your mouth?" "Yes, First Sergeant, but read the rest of the sentence where it says, 'below a line parallel with the line extending from the bottom of the lower lip.' My moustache is clearly within the regulations." They continued to argue until the private became insistent. The first sergeant than positioned himself within two inches of the private's face, ordered him to shave his moustache, and extracted a subdued, "Yes, First Sergeant, I understand."
>
> When the private had left, the commander said, "Top, you're wrong." The first sergeant exploded that the alternative reading would permit

hair all over the face, save below the line parallel with the lower lip. He then slumped into his chair, cursing, "Goddammit, I wish we could go back to the real Army where standards were clear, orders were obeyed, and if you didn't like it, you could just get the hell out." To placate the first sergeant, the commander referred the matter to the Inspector General for a definitive ruling, but the private trimmed his moustache.

In the barracks, the soldier was under continual pressure to push the acceptable standards to the limit. In one unit the observer was required to get a haircut by the battalion commander before beginning work lest as a medic he provide an undesirable influence. The jesting response of the men in no way detracted from the import of their message:

Wilson came back to my work area in the orderly room, chuckled and said, "What are you trying to do, create a lot of hassles for us? Hey, Diamond, come back here and look at the strac troop. With that skinhead, you're going to make it rough on all of us when the first sergeant sees you. Maybe we'll have to rearrange your face a little to fit your new haircut." [laughter] Diamond says, "Someday you'll learn to just push your hair up under your hat like I do; they'll never notice."

After haircuts, shoe shines were the biggest bone of contention between the leaders and the men. Again there were definite cues for appropriate behavior:

On the bay three of the new guys were polishing their boots. They had several different rags, burned wax, and water. I had not seen such intensive boot polishing since basic training. Murphy and Gross stopped and watched with disgusted scowls on their faces. Gross said, "You fucking newbies don't know how things run around here; you believe everything they tell you at formation. You'll learn you can never do enough, and what you do nobody gives a shit for anyhow." The fourth new man was lying on his bunk watching television, and said, "Hey, man, I ain't polishing nothing; fuck 'em." Murphy and Gross ignored him, harumphed again about the crazy newbies, and left the bay together.

Housekeeping provided another area in which there are definite pressures to conform to the standards of the barracks group rather than to those in formal authority. The pressures were particularly acute on the open bays where comparisons could easily be made between areas. Those who were slow in taking up verbal cues on how to behave received more explicit guides:

Last night someone poured lighter fluid on the highly waxed floor of the new man, Simpson, and ignited it. Murphy had been riding Simpson on how his floor would set an unnecessarily high standard for the bay, and had gone so far as to kick his wax can the length of the room. Cressey admitted later that he set the fire to teach the new guy a lesson.

The Anti-Army Norm

Before entering the service, the boys learned about Army life and its problems from movies and stories told by fathers, uncles, brothers, and friends. To be accepted in the barracks required maintaining these images of an ensnarled bureaucracy, incompetent leaders, unnecessary rules, and miles of paperwork. Army life is filled with more than enough instances to support the stereotypes, but the barracks dweller had to go the additional mile, disapproving of everything "military." Admission to movie theaters on post was far less than that charged in town, but the soldiers felt it was worth the extra money "to get away from the goddamned Army." The post had many recreational opportunities, ranging from craft shops to bowling alleys, yet they were largely shunned because of the predominance of "lifers and punk dependents." The observer noted:

> I asked Bunsen and some others if they were interested in going to the rock concert in the field house. They had not heard about it, but Bunsen spoke for the group, "Naw, who'd want to go to an Army concert anyway? With all those lifers and dependents, you couldn't have any fun."

Even when bored, soldiers often preferred doing nothing to attending an Army-sponsored activity:

> I was driving around post with Marshall and Stevens and noticed the battalion softball team playing at the north field. I suggested we stop and watch, but Marshall said, "Forget it. You show up at those things and the lifers think you like the place; no way, I'd just get sick talking to them in the stands."

The worst name to call a fellow soldier was "lifer"—a person who talked and acted as if he liked the Army and was willing to emulate the leaders. On a field training exercise the observer noted:

> Several men told me to watch Osterhagen making a fool of himself. He is considered so "gung-ho" that if the lieutenant tripped, he'd have to

extract Osterhagen from his ass. Osterhagen is the only man beside the lieutenant to paint his face with camouflage grease. He is extremely energetic and inevitably volunteers to ambush or raid the command post. When on an assignment he acts like John Wayne playing Sergeant Rock, and then returns to the platoon telling how he was the hero of the encounter. The lieutenant later told me he thought Osterhagen was one of his better troops because he was always there, ready to help, and showed some determination to get the job done.

"Lifer" was an attitude, a generally positive orientation toward the Army that was so despised among the barracks dwellers that few dared be as blatant as Osterhagen. Even the individual who willingly joined in barracks bitching about the follies and frustrations of being in the Army was not immune from the slur if he saw a future in the Army and admitted to having career aspirations. Warner was just such a soldier. He was one of the boys, yet he worked to insure his promotion. He sought advanced schooling and dared to comb his hair differently:

Three of the guys were sitting in my room talking when Warner stopped by, his hair slicked straight back over his head. Bunsen immediately began to taunt, "Look at Warner the lifer; what are you, trying to project the NCO image? Or did you get your hair mashed down walking into trees like the rest of the lifers?" The two others took up the teasing and began pulling at Warner's hair until it stood straight up on his head. Later in the evening I noticed Warner had combed his hair in his accustomed fashion.

Even holiday meals merited only grudging approval. On Thanksgiving the dining hall was decorated with placemats, holiday napkins, printed menus, and streamers. At the front was an ice sculpture with fresh shrimp banked on either side and cornucopias filled with apples, oranges, bananas, and nuts. The menu included turkey or ham, two kinds of potatoes, greens, beans, beets and black-eyed peas, tossed salad, a complete relish tray, and pumpkin pie or cake with ice cream for dessert. The Army custom is for officers, sergeants, and their families to share the Thanksgiving and Christmas meals with the troops in the dining hall. The observer noted:

Tompkins was lying on his bunk, watching a football game. He said he wasn't going to the mess hall because there were "too many lifers over there and the food would be rotten anyway." Wilson, returning from the mess hall, said, "The food was okay, I guess; about the usual."

Thus one important commandment for getting on in the barracks was: If you can't say something bad about the Army, then don't say anything at all.

The Squealing Norm

Another requirement for acceptance in the barracks was not to inform the authorities about who did what, when, or where. On their own time, barracks residents insisted on handling disputes in their own way. The most common complaints were rowdy behavior, loud music at late hours, and destruction of property. Word quickly got out if anyone dared compalin to the sergeants or officers. There were three ways of dealing with deviants from the norm.

The mildest form of norm enforcement was verbal abuse. Stage whispers and asides were made in the presence of a "rat," a "squealer," or a "dime dropper." A direct verbal assault was also not uncommon. The observer noted:

> I was sitting on the steps outside the barracks when Burns and Creswell walked in from the parking lot. they stopped outside Keel's window and Burns yelled, "Hey, Keel, you low-down, sharecropping, dirt-eating sheep-fucker. It's eleven o'clock, and I'm Burns, and I want you to get the time and name right when you go squealing to the orderly room in the morning. You hear me, you squealing pig-fucker?"

The second level of norm enforcement was anonymous harassment. Techniques included knocking on the door of a "rat" and quickly moving on, or bolting the door from the outside while the "fink" slept, saturating the door jamb with lighter fluid and igniting it.

In cases where informing might result in official disciplinary action, a third level of enforcement, physical assault, was used:

> Gross told the group that the new man had stopped him in the hall and said he didn't appreciate his sleep being interrupted by Gross and his buddies carousing. "I told him to go fuck himself if he didn't like it. He said he was going to see the company commander. I just shrugged, turned away, and then reeled around and doubled him with a fist in the gut."

Whether Gross's story was true or not is irrelevant, for it is very unlikely that anyone who heard it could fail to get the message.

The Stealing Norm

Theft is a major problem in military life, and barracks members at Fort Marshall were frequently enjoined not to steal from each other. Larceny was not uncommon, but barracks thieves were seldom apprehended in the act or with stolen goods in their possession. Much of the petty larceny involved tent pegs, entrenching tools, ponchos, and other items of equipment that must either be replaced or paid for by the responsible individual. Enforcement of the theft norm was accomplished mostly on the basis of circumstantial evidence: who had the opportunity, the motive, or too many pieces of extra equipment? If there was clear evidence, the preferred way of dealing with the thief was to report him to the company commander for formal disciplinary action. This was a notable exception to the general prohibition against informing. More typically the suspected barracks thief was carefully regarded and shunned by all residents.

The ethics of theft in the Army involved more than adherence to the biblical commandment. Theft from other barracks members was always condemned, but theft from a soldier in another barracks was acceptable so long as one did not get caught. The observer recorded a complex transfer of three car batteries:

> Bunsen came into the barracks, swearing because his car battery had died and he had had to walk several miles; he had a date, so Gino lent him his car. Bunsen's girl was not there when he arrived, and on the way back, Gino's car stopped because the battery was dead. When Bunsen returned to the barracks, he said he had stolen a battery from a parking lot of C Company, but needed help transporting it. Since I had the only other working vehicle, I agreed to assist. We drove to the C Company lot where Bunsen calmly walked to a battery sitting on the ground and carried it to my car. We then drove to his car and exchanged the good battery for his dead one. Then I followed Bunsen to our parking lot where he lifted another battery from Wilson's car without asking permission. We then drove to Gino's car, exchanged Wilson's battery for Gino's, and drove back to our parking lot. Bunsen then exchanged Wilson's battery with Gino's dead battery. I asked why he bothered to replace Gino's dead battery. He was not sure, but felt Gino would appreciate having his original battery back. We did not replace a battery in the car in C Company lot, but simply discarded the dead battery in a ditch.

The ethics of stealing from other soldiers also bears witness to the tenuous, fragile quality of social relations among barracks dwellers. It was wrong to steal from buddies so long as they were present in the barracks. When a soldier went home for a weekend, he entrusted his television set or tape deck to a buddy, but when he went on extended leave, he was more likely to lock all of his possessions in the supply room for safekeeping. When a soldier went AWOL for more than a few days, it was as though he were a complete stranger. The observer noted:

> Ransom had been AWOL for over a week. Creswell and I were stripping his room and taking everything to the supply room. I was packing and Creswell was preparing the inventory report. He asked, "See anything that you want?" "What about the inventory?" "I never entered it." "What if Ransom comes back." "Tough shit, man."

Theft from fellow soldiers was stealing only under well-defined circumstances. Theft from the Army, however, was never stealing, but merely exacting one's just due. Army field jackets, boots, and wool blankets were popular items. Stealing from the Army usually required the cooperation of the person responsible for the equipment, but since such petty theft was "not really stealing," finding an accomplice was relatively easy:

> Cressey is leaving the Army and is checking his gear into supply. He casually mentions tht he wouldn't mind taking his field jacket with him for hunting trips. Waller, the supply clerk, winks and says, "It just so happens that I can't find any record of you ever being issued a field jacket." Cressey picks up the jacket, wishes Waller good luck, and leaves. Waller says he doesn't mind helping the guys out whenever he gets a chance.

Fitting In

To be incorporated into the barracks a new man had to present himself as an approachable "regular guy" and he had to abide by the commandments of barracks living: he had to be willing to let everyone do his thing; he had to accommodate himself to the dress and housekeeping standards of the barracks; he had to verbally scorn the Army at every opportunity; he could not invoke formal military authority or squeal on his buddies; and he could not steal from his comrades. Those who were not regular guys or who could not live by the commandments had to go it alone. They were perpetually subjected to snide remarks that encouraged them to change clothes quickly after work, leave the barracks, and return after most had gone to sleep. The loners often found part-time jobs to fill their leisure time, or simply wandered alone through the post facilities. They have appeared previously in these pages at casino night in the service club, watching television alone in a stifling day room, reading in the library, or shooting pool in bars near the post.

Marconi, a morning report clerk, was a loner. He had fairly delicate features and spoke in a whine. He had been a music major in college and often talked about classical guitar. He frequently went about his work within earshot of the first sergeant, complaining about how the noise in the barracks had robbed him of sleep. No one in the barracks knew or cared much about him. The observer noted:

> I asked Marconi how his weekend had gone. He said he had a great time. "I went to the Holiday Inn, sat by the pool and drank vodka collins. There was a MacDonald's right next door." [nervous laughter] "Did you go alone." "Sure, why not?"

Whether a new man will fit into the barracks social structure was usually determined in his first week in the company. Where he fit depended largely on the ways work groups were organized and to some extent on the number of other new people in the barracks. If the company consisted of a few large work groups, the newcomers initially sought out others who were new to the unit, but were rapidly incorporated into the mainstream of barracks social life. If, however, the unit was structured by multiple, segmented work groups sharing the same barracks, an "oldtimer syndrome" often prevented entry into any group but one made up of newcomers. Physical barriers were often used to exclude potential new members:

> Cressey was being transferred to Korea. Roberts said that he was moving to the ghetto and gestured toward the Barker-Murphy area. Barker held seniority, so Murphy was not consulted in the move or the arrangement of the furniture. Barker and Roberts rearranged the wall lockers and managed to appropriate about a third of the floor space of the new man's area next to them. They had an extra bunk and simply shoved it into the new man's area for him to dispose of. When they had finished, they had barricaded into the corner with only a small opening between the lockers as an entry.

The oldtimers also exerted psychological pressure to avoid contact with newcomers:

> I commented to the new man that it didn't look like Roberts and Barker had done him any favors, and we began talking. Barker, Murphy, and

Gross walked by several times, scowling, but I continued to maintain eye contact with the new man. Later, Barker said, "Hey, why are you hanging around with the newbie? You can move into our area if you want." "It's just part of my job." "Oh, yeah, I forgot."

How a newcomer fit into the confederation of cliques depended upon the goods or services that he could exchange for inclusion. Social relations in the barracks were based on the exchange of commodities and services in short supply. Not everyone owned an automobile, thus the individual who provided transportation had little difficulty making friends and influencing people. Not everyone owned a television or a tape deck, and those who did shared access with their barracks mates. Similarly, a deck of cards, chess set, or collection of magazines provided a means of extending and maintaining relationships. Barracks life was not exciting, and any new diversion was welcomed and paid for by transferring social power to the innovator:

> Gino bought an electric football game that he has set up in his room. Many of the guys have stopped by to play, and he is now talking about setting up a league in the barracks with a schedule, play-offs, and bowl games.

The debts were never figured in any conscious, calculating way. Soldiers never offered to chip in on gasoline expenses, and the owner of the car never thought to suggest it. The television viewer shared his pizza with the television owner, and neither saw this as a direct pay-back. Yet the trade-offs were continuous and determined the position the soldier occupied in the social structure. All goods and services were pooled from each according to ability to pay and were awarded to each according to ability to extract.

Tangible goods and services were necessary but not sufficient to maintain a position in the barracks social structure. Equally important was verbal ability. The storyteller was always in demand, and tales of sexual adventure and conquest were always appreciated. If the soldier could not tell stories, he had at least to have the ability to conceal naivete if he was to hold his own:

> Patton, Morton, and Wilson are discussing girls. Morton says, "I bet you'd like to bust her hymen, wouldn't you?" Patton asks in a puzzled tone, "What's a hymen?" Morton laughs and says, "Hey, Wilson, I think we have a virgin on our hands. How old are you, Patton?" "Nineteen." "A nineteen-year-old virgin, eh? Well, look, the hymen in a girl

tells you whether or not she's a virgin; if it's broken, she's not, see?" "Where's it at?" "Oh, I don't believe this; it's in her cunt, where else?" "Oh, I don't know these biological terms; why didn't you just say cunt?" Wilson says the biological name is vagina and asks Patton if he knows what a clitoris is, and the sex education class continues.

Verbal put-downs and mockery in a social group were other ways of establishing and maintaining a favorable position. The individual who could initiate and top put-downs and barbs achieved prestige in the group. He who could hold his own maintained his position; he who could not reply quickly or in kind became low man in the pecking order. The volleys of banter were invariably sexual or scatological in theme, and the winner always had the last word:

> Prescott, Peterson, and four others are discussing the upcoming three-day weekend. Prescott tells Peterson not to make plans because he will probably have guard duty. "Bullshit, I'm going to be sticking my chick all weekend." "Bullshit, you're so dumb, you think screwing is sticking your finger in a cunt." "If that's what you think then I've been screwing since I was four years old."

The verbally slow soldier, or one who used dated retorts, became the "ugly duckling" and the butt of many remarks. Such individuals, however, could pay their way in the group by absorbing the banter hurled at them. Private Lohman, mentioned earlier, was a case in point. As a black from the rural South he lacked the social skills to make points among urban blacks. In response to the standard greeting, "Hey, man, what's happ'nin'?" he regularly fumbled with a lame, "Hi, how're you." When another black would tell a joke and then extend the palm of his hand to be slapped in appreciation, Lohman usually just looked at the proferred hand and smiled weakly. Although he did not have money for civilian clothing, he purchased a used television and chained it to his bunk so that anyone could watch it. Despite the television and his willingness to endure racial barbs and slurs from his comrades, he still felt it necessary to pay more. The observer noted:

> I was in the operations office with Lohman and Bousman. Lohman said he needed a credit statement for the money he loaned him. Bousman parried, "Not me, Watson's the one you want. How much does he owe you?" "Thirty-five dollars." "Christ, I wouldn't loan anybody in the Army over $10 without their old lady's bra as collateral. Who else owes you?" "Cressey owes me seven, Herdon five, Winston five, and Smith ten." "What are you, a loan shark?" "No, a bank."

Private Waller provided a striking contrast to Lohman. As Lohman worked desperately to maintain his hold on the lower rung of the social hierarchy, Waller worked just as hard to organize a clique with himself as the prime mover. Waller was married, but had moved back into the barracks to save money. He quickly invested in an electric coffee maker from the PX, and with cups, spoons, coffee, cream, and sugar from the mess hall, he set up a coffee bar in his wall locker. The coffee was free to anyone who spent a few minutes talking to him, and he soon had a regular clientele. Waller had more than the usual tales of Army woe. He had waited eight months for a pair of false teeth and was currently caught between the first sergeant's suspicion that he was a shirker and the hospital's inconclusive tests that he was epileptic. His trailer house had recently burned to the ground; his wife could not get an insurance settlement; and the commander would not let him go home on excess leave. Just hearing about Waller's predicaments, with his teeth sitting on the table because they did not fit, provided hours of entertainment for his listeners.

Waller could also tell stories. He claimed that his wife and he were swingers and readily produced snapshots as proof. He had also met a girl in the neighboring state, and their weekend encounters provided a serial of entertainment:

Waller told about his weekend with the girl he had been writing to last week. "We were in the Holiday Inn right off post, see, and we were just watching TV. I started finger-fucking her with this finger." He held up the middle finger of his right hand and pantomimed. We chuckled and Bousman looked at me as if to say, "I can't believe this guy." Fredericks exclaimed, "Finger fucking. Why didn't you just go on and screw her?" "I was building up to it." Fredericks looks to the ceiling and says, "Shit." Waller continued, "Anyway, after I had that one in there for a while, she says, 'Is that all? Try another finger.' So I put these two in there." [He holds up two fingers and pantomimes.] Again, Bousman and Fredericks express their disbelief. "Then, after another little while, she says, 'Put another one in.' So I put these three in, and then I stuck in these four fingers." Bousman interrupts, "Aw, come on, man, there's no cunt that big." "I swear to God it happened, and that's not all." I commented, "Now, he's going to tell us he stuck his whole hand in," and the others laugh. "That's right. There was still room, so I stuck my whole hand in there. I swear, it was the biggest cunt I've ever seen." Waller draws a line about an inch above his wrist; Bousman says, "Impossible. Next you put your foot in." "No, my tongue." He looks to the ceiling and runs his tongue in and out of his mouth, and breaks us into laughter because he has his teeth out. "She was a little large, but I have a big tongue. When I finally fucked her, though, I had to put both hands around my dick before she could feel anything. She must have screwed every man in Missouri one at a time." Fredericks reaches in the air and opens an imaginary cunt and pantomimes head-fucking it. The group breaks up in laughter again.

Because Waller had so many personal and medical problems, the first sergeant finally declared him "excess" and assigned him to help out in the supply room where he did indeed help out all of his buddies with any equipment they needed, thus further securing his position in the group.

The confederacy of cliques was bound together by the exchange of goods and services, and ordered by physical and verbal aggression and defense. Once the pecking order of social dominance was established, those high in the order could enforce their will on those below with very little effort:

There had been no heat or hot water in the barracks for three days, and the room was freezing cold. Gross and Smith sat in their area with the window open. Smith got up to close the window, and Gross growled, "Leave the goddamn window alone." "But it's cold in here." "I like fresh air; if it's too cold for you, get the hell out." Smith said, "Well, it's not that cold," and crawled under his blanket with his clothes on.

This example is quite telling. Indeed, cold and cruel as barracks life might appear, the thought of going it alone was a worse chill for most soldiers. The barracks members endured day by day and week by week in a world in which time was measured only by the period remaining on one's current enlistment, and social stability existed only in the structure and dynamics of the informal social groups that are the same in Army companies the world over.

SUMMARY

This chapter has shown how the barracks resident was limited in his choice of leisure time associates to other members of his work group, his rank, his residence, and his race. The only way he could escape these constraints was to be fortunate enough to have previously established social ties, to have well-developed skills and interests, or to have learned to exist as an isolate outside the social structure of dyads, triads, and cliques. Whether an individual was incorporated into the existing structure depended upon his willingness to abide by the central norms of barracks living regarding expressions of disapproval of other soldiers, military standards, or the Army as a way of life, squealing to those in formal authority, and stealing from barracks mates. Where the individual fit in depended on the work group structure of the company and the physical layout of the barracks. How he fit in was largely determined by the social skills, goods, and services he could exchange for inclusion. With this understanding of barracks life as background, the next chapter considers the place of alcohol in social interaction.

4

DRINKING WITH THE BOYS

Soldiering and alcohol have been almost synonymous since the invention of armies. The image from ancient times of drunken soldiers looting and pillaging conquered cities lives today in movies and fiction: soldiers leaving the base for the nearest town for a night of drinking, whoring, and brawling. All armies in all times have faced health and performance deficiencies stemming from the excessive use of alcohol, yet there has remained a singular attraction regarding its use. Alcohol use has been encouraged as a means of promoting camaraderie, cohesion, and group solidarity; on the other hand the high incidence of ensuing fights, property destruction, and inability to function effectively has always been lamented. The ancient ambivalent pattern is no less true in the contemporary garrison Army, which encourages drinking on some occasions, discourages drinking on others, and is fundamentally indifferent to drinking in still other circumstances. This chapter describes the drinking patterns and practices of lower-ranking enlisted soldiers, considers the major norms that govern these practices, and provides an analysis of the function of alcohol for the barracks dwellers.

OCCASIONS FOR DRINKING

Sanctioned Drinking

The first type of sanctioned drinking is associated with battalion "organization days" and with company parties and picnics. The annual "organization day" is designed to foster unity and cohesion within the companies and pride within the battalion. This ceremonial event descends from the old regimental field days when the enlisted men in the companies competed with each other before the admiring eyes of the colonel and his officers and guests. Competition included military skills like marching and marksmanship as well as boxing, baseball, and track and field events. The guests included girlfriends, wives, and families as well as townspeople who joined in with food, drink, music, and dancing at the end of the day. In an age without radio, television, or rapid transportation, and in an organization in which enlisted soldiers may have served with each other under the same officers for five years or more, the field day was one of the highlights of the year and was well attended and eagerly anticipated. Times and organizations have changed, however, and the observer noted little enthusiasm for the present-day battalion picnic:

> I mentioned to Corwin that I was going to the battalion picnic tomorrow. He said I was wasting my time, since no one would be there but the lifers. He then yelled out, "There's nobody here going to the lifer picnic, is there?" He then snapped out the names of the men in turn. "Conner, you're not going, are you? Johnson? Eggers?" No one said that he was going.

The enlisted men viewed attendance at the picnic as positive sentiment toward the Army, thus in a battalion of over 900 men, less than 200 went to the "organization day." The observer noted:

> Most of the people congregated around the beer truck. They seemed to segregate themselves by companies, and the overwhelming majority were sergeants and officers. Someone tried to initiate a tug-of-war between my company and another unit, but there weren't enough interested to form a team.

The result was scarcely different with required attendance. In one battalion the men assembled in formation in the morning, marched to the athletic field, were addressed by the colonel, and were encouraged to join in the tent pitching, pie eating, and greased pole climbing contests.

> Most of the men sit in groups of two or three clustered by platoons within companies and by companies. They drink their beer and grumble about the day being a waste of time, evidence little enthusiasm for the competition, and grudgingly "volunteer" to participate when the lieutenant encourages them. As the sergeants and officers become more drunk and more involved, the men quietly slip away to their cars or to the barracks to sleep.

Company parties and picnics were also scheduled. Voluntary attendance was greater than for battalion functions, and participation in the activities was a bit more spirited, although anti-Army sentiments continued to run high.

The first sergeant announced at the formation this morning, "You all know about the company picnic today. It doesn't mean you have the whole day off; you work as usual until 11:00, then you're off for the rest of the day. Just remember that you're off to go to the picnic. This is your company and you've paid for the food. Now I happen to know that Sergeant Ragland has bought enough chicken, ribs, steak and beer to feed two companies, so you should at least go over there for some good food and beer. You don't have to hang around if you don't want to, but at least help us eat the food. OK, now I want a good police call this morning, and then I want to see you all at the picnic."

The men stood passively in the ranks with only a few guarded glances and smiles at having to work until 11:00. As the formation broke up for police call there was a lot of chatter. "Hey, are you going to the picnic?" "Damn right I am; I paid for the food." "Not me, I don't dig hanging with the lifers." "You don't have to hang, just eat the free food and split." "Naw, I'd rather eat off-post and take the afternoon off."

Throughout the morning a detail of men set up tables and barbecue racks made from 500-gallon oil drums split lengthwise and welded to metal frames. Three kegs of beer and cases of soda were put on ice in garbage cans, and the trays of beans, salad, relishes, and potato chips were brought from the dining hall. The men arrived in two's and three's, got their food, and ate in small work-group clusters. The observer noted:

When I went through the line, Waller was cooking ribs with a pair of tongs in one hand and a mug of beer in the other. "Hi, Pappy, you look in good spirits." "Yeah, I've already had nine cups of beer and two of these mugs. Don't take that one, here's one that's better." I ate on the fender of a jeep along with five other men from the second platoon. There is little talk except for comments about the food. "These ribs are good." "So's the chicken. Did you get any beans?" "What kind of beer is this?" The company commander ate quickly, and then took the bag of athletic equipment to the ball diamond, followed by several men who had also finished eating.

Many people left the area after eating. The observer continued:

I talked with Sergeant Banks, who said he had sergeant of the guard today, and had gotten off just long enough to eat. "Then you're not

hanging around?" "No, I don't like these things anyway. No one really
has much fun; they all isolate themselves into their regular gorups and
never talk to each other." "Are all picnics like that, or just this company?" "All I've ever been to. The EM don't want to talk to the NCOs
and officers, so they just talk to each other or split. This should be a
time when everyone gets together to have fun and get to know each
other better. I'll eat the food I paid for and leave; if they charged for the
food, I wouldn't be here at all."

Those who remained played volleyball, softball, horseshoes, or cards,
or talked with friends while drinking beer.

About half of the company had shown up at some time or another. By
one o'clock there were about thirty people at the ball diamond, and the
same number around the eating area. The ball games were between
work groups, and there was good-natured shouting and kidding between the teams and from the stands. One of the sergeants volunteered
to umpire, and is endured the usual taunts about his eyesight. The
company commander also took a good deal of razzing: "It's Ron
Sloboda, the slowest ball player alive; come on, Ron, beat out the
bunt." "OK, Shorty, let's get a hit." "Boo, go back to the desk; who told
you you could play baseball?" The CO laughed and seemed to enjoy
the games, as do most of the others.

The ball game continued throughout the afternoon. The beer and
soda trailer was brought to the ball field, and the team at bat drank
beer on the bench. Eventually the party wound down to a dozen or so
die-hards who endeavored to empty the keg:

The few that remained were all drunk. Walker got in his car and drove
about 100 feet from the group. He then began cutting doughnuts in the
sand with numerous fast starts and sudden breaks. Sergeant Ragland
commented to the company commander that he hoped Walker
wouldn't run the car into one of the nearby trees. Finally, a rear wheel
became lodged in a deep rut, and Walker came stumbling back to the
group. Ragland tried to talk him into going to the barracks to sleep, but
he protested that he wanted to go home and beat the shit out of his old
lady. They moved out of earshot and sat talking quietly on the ground.

Curiously, the two men most disenchanted with the Army stayed to
the end, arguing with Sergeant Cassidy. "Twenty-five more fucking
days left in this goddamned Army, and then I'm through with you
dumb-fucking lifers." "Murdock, you won't find it any different on the
outside; you were a dud before you came into the Army, a dud in the
Army, and you will be a dud after you get out of the Army."

Sergeant Wilkins was very drunk and could hardly stand. Several men tried to get him to join a chugging contest, but Wilkins just smiled, weaved on his feet, and slurred, "I'd better not; you can get in real trouble drinking beer too fast." They persisted until he accepted a cup of beer, tried to drink it in one motion, and then fell back on the ground, giggling amid the laughter of the others.

A second sanctioned use of alcohol is to ease interpersonal tensions.

Murphy and the new clerk in the orderly room have not been getting along well at all. Today the first sergeant gave Murphy five dollars and told him to take the new man to the 500 Club and drink beer until they resolved their differences. Murphy said, "It'll take more than five dollars worth of beer for me to like that son of a bitch, but we took top's money anyway."

When a unit returns from field training, all of the vehicles are dusty and mud-caked. The field equipment is unpacked, and the vehicles are washed off. Sometimes there is a keg of beer waiting when the clean-up is finished. On other occasions a leader may arrange for beer when in the field as a reward:

Sergeant Macke announces that the lieutenant is pleased with the training and is going to be lenient about beer tonight. Everyone could have three beers, and Macke was taking money orders for different brands. The men grumbled about the three-beer limit, and when the beer came, we had to go individually to pick it up to prevent hoarding. No one was particuarly enthusiastic. Henderson said, "The lieutenant must be finally coming around. We've given him so much shit out here about drinking that he must have given up on us."

A third sanctioned use of alochol is at outdoor athletic contests, where the spectators bring beer to drink during the game. The observer noted:

The scene at the stadium reminded me of a small-town football game. There were maybe 100 people in the stands on each side of the field. Someone handed me a mimeographed list of the player line-ups. Children were playing touch football behind the bleachers or playing at cheerleading while their parents sat talking and drinking beer before the game. One sergeant had a cooler in front of him and wore a baseball cap in the battalion colors. The officers and sergeants were congregated in one area, married men and their wives in another, and the single men seemed to cluster by work groups with the exception of the blacks who were from all companies in the battalion. I sat down by Williams, and he immediately offered me a beer.

The interactions at an athletic contest were as segmented as those during the duty day and those at night. Sometimes, however, alcohol on special occasions permitted a momentary lifting of the barriers of rank and residence.

Tonight the company won the post slow-pitch softball championship. Sergeant Cowly collected a dollar from everyone in the stands, and brought back several cases of beer in the last inning. The men were drinking and joking with an occasional blast from the air horn. Someone suggested they gang up on the first sergeant, who grabbed his wife and said, "If I go, she goes too." The group then turned to the company commander, who took off running, but tripped over third base. He got up laughing, and asked for another beer.

The fourth sanctioned use of alcohol involves beer in the barracks. Although units studied did not have beer available in vending machines, the men were free to bring in quarts and six-packs to drink during the evenings.

Eight men are watching television. Watson and Cressey have six-packs that they share with the others, while Smith and Gerard have quart bottles. When I join the group, Gerard passes his bottle to me. Simpson brings in a pizza and offers it to Watson, who takes a piece and passes it on. Everyone takes a piece until the empty cardboard is returned to Simpson. Watson laughs and gives him a beer.

Beer drinking was so prevalent that there was scarcely a time when someone was not having a "brew" somewhere in the barracks. Unless the men became heavily intoxicated it is doubtful that they would even consider such consumption "real drinking." Beer was an accepted beverage almost anywhere, anytime, and with any activity, including driving. The observer recounted:

Murphy invited Johnson and me to come home with him for the weekend. Just after we drive off post, Murphy suggests we stop at the 500 Club for beer. Each of us chips in $2, and he buys a case of premium plus some chips. Four hours later we buy another six-pack that we drink in the remaining hour of the drive. When we entered the house, Mrs. Murphy said, "You must be thirsty after that long drive. How about a beer?" We all accepted her gracious offer.

The leaders were also unconcerned about quiet parties that took place in the barracks. The following description of a barracks party illustrates many of the points discussed earlier regarding interpersonal affiliation in the barracks. The party was organized by Pappy Waller, who bought a case and a half of beer, and talked up the party to the people who regularly used the coffee bar in his wall locker. Waller played the role of host and organized the party on payday "just so we could have something to do." The observer noted:

> When I enter the barracks, the party has just started in Waller's area, and he immediately offers me a beer. The overhead lights are dimmed, and six men are sitting on the bunks and in two straight-back chairs. The radio is tuned to a Top Forty station. Two men are talking about arranging a ride home for the weekend, and Waller is teasing Johnson about being afraid to introduce him to his girl. Simpson and Biddle sit quietly drinking their beers.

A man on the fringe of the group saw an opportunity to contribute to the success of the party.

> Simpson stands up and says, "Hey, want me to break out my eight-track?" "You've got an eight-track? How come we've never seen it before?" "I keep it in my locker; there's been no occasion to use it till now." Simpson gets his tape equipment and Johnson says, "All right. Now we can really party. Let's see those tapes . . . Country Gold 1965? Country Love Songs? Is this the only stuff you have? Don't you have any good Rock 1974?" "What you see is what I got." "Geez. Put on Rock & Roll 1967." Johnson looks around in disgust while Simpson starts the music. I volunteer that I have some cassettes in the car, but no one has a cassette player. Simpson turns up the sound, saying, "Listen up, guys, this is really a good song." But Johnson turns it down, saying, "Fuck off, Simpson, it stinks."

The idle conversation continued and Waller told about the April Fool's jokes he had pulled that day. A junior sergeant who occupied another room joined the group, was offered a beer, and the discussion turned to his fractured ankle. The topics of conversation accurately reflected the dimensions of interpersonal relations in that they were almost exclusively concerned with the present or the immediate past.

> Benson throws a bottle into a box. Johnson says, "Careful, man, I have to clean up this area in the morning." "So what?" "So up your ass. You're not going to destroy my area like the last party." "Shit, that was

nothing. In Korea we tore up the hootch every night. Of course, we had Koreans who cleaned up in the morning." "Really?" "Yeah, they cleaned, made the bunks, washed clothes, polished shoes. Ah, that was the life." Parks interjects, "You haven't seen the parties until you've been stationed in Alaska. That place was wild every night, especially during the winter."

The junior sergeant left the party after one beer. Waller continued to play the genial host, insuring that no one had an empty can of beer. Two other men joined the group and were immediately offered beer, but after an hour the party was dying.

Barnes is pretty drunk. He goes to the center aisle with a boot, and with a full wind-up, hurls it against the door. "Damn, that chicken-wire glass is hard to break." "You mean the glass in the door?" [The lockers obscured our view of the throw.] "Yeah, I just wanted to see if it would break." No one picks up the challenge, and there is a lull in the conversation.

To be successful a party in the barracks required that something "unusual" happen; so far this party was just like every other night in the barracks except that no one watched television. The observer then noted:

Murphy comes in, takes a beer, and says, "Where did that shit music come from?" "It's Simpson's." "Christ, don't you have anything else?" He goes through the stack of tapes, reading the titles and requesting votes that are invariably thumbs down. "All right, the critics have spoken; I'll have to get some music." He returns, saying, "OK, critics, how about Hendrix and Joplin's greatest hits? That's what I thought— gentlemen with class. Get that garbage off." Waller changes the tape, and Johnson turns the volume on full.

Whether it was Murphy exchanging his banter and tapes for inclusion or simply the loud music, the party began to come to life.

Waller says, "Now that we have some good music, I'll bring out my strobe light." "You've got a strobe?" "Yeah, bought it last week for $15, but haven't gotten a chance to use it." As he is connecting the light, Murphy and Johnson begin pantomiming the guitar players. With the strobe working, they really try hard, and Johnson's expressions are very funny as he reaches for the high notes. Murphy deadpans the bass after someone shouts that there couldn't be two lead players in the band.

When I return from the latrine, I walk past Murphy, who throws a punch at me in slow motion. I fall back against the wall in slow motion, and suddenly we have a lively group with everyone up, wrestling and shadow-boxing in the strobe light. Someone hits Murphy in the face with a pillow, and a general pillow fight breaks out. Waller is clearly the loudest, but Murphy is the center of attention.

The horseplay ceased for more beer, whereupon the group was ready for something different. Johnson challenged Murphy to catch a bottle cap in the flashing light, and Murphy repeatedly failed. Murphy moved around the group, challenging each in turn, and then challenged them to catch a beer can that he held in his hand. The can appeared and disappeared at different positions in the light, and no one was successful.

Bensen just looks at the can, closes his eyes, and lies on his bunk. Murphy says, "Oh, we have a good one here," and begins making whammy motions with his hands in front of Bensen's face. Bensen watches, mesmerized, and finally shrinks back onto the bed. Murphy continues the hand movement while everyone watches quietly, not wanting to break the spell.

Murphy was clearly the life of the party at this point. When he tired of the hypnotism routine, he changed activity.

Murphy went to the open window, leaned far out, and threw his beer bottle. "Direct hit, right on the sidewalk. Come on, Johnson, let's see you try." "We're not going for distance tonight?" "No, just accuracy." Johnson throws his bottle, but it is short. No one else takes up the challenge.

Bensen again goes to the aisle and begins throwing the boot at the door. He returns, saying, "Damn, that chicken wire is really tough." Waller picks up the boot and hurls it at the window. There is a resounding crash of glass and Waller returns, looking mean and tough. Bensen is doubled on his bunk, laughing. "April Fool, you son of a bitch. I was just throwing at the door, hoping somebody would be stupid enough to try to break the glass." Everybody laughs as Waller gets a broom and sweeps up the glass so no one will get cut. The incident seems to put a damper on the roughhousing.

A few minutes later, someone mentions we are out of beer. "Anybody want to go for more?" No one volunteers, so Waller unplugs his strobe light, the lights are turned on, and everyone disperses to their bunks to prepare for bed.

Drinking that was sanctioned at athletic events and organization picnics, as a reward for performance, and as a form of relaxation in the barracks was a comparatively benign activity. There were a few arguments, fights, and incidents of reckless driving, but on the whole there was little to justify the three-inch steel pipes surrounding the urinals to prevent their being ripped from the wall. The legendary brawls and vandalism must therefore occur consequent to episodes of unsanctioned drinking.

Unsanctioned Drinking

The authorities at Fort Marshall did not sanction the use of alcohol when on duty, the drinking of wine or hard liquor in the barracks, or any drinking that resulted in property destruction or vandalism. Enlisted soldiers routinely ignored all of these prohibitions, but were cautious in overstepping the limits.

Standing guard at night was the most eligible occasion for drinking on duty. Guard duty consisted of walking around the perimeter of a motor pool or patroling parts of the battalion area. Soldiers served on guard patrol for two hours and then had four hours off before returning to their posts. No one ever did much talking while on guard duty, so between shifts the guards returned to the barracks and their buddies.

> Four men on guard duty were in the Murphy-Barker area drinking beer and debating the merits of *Playboy* vs. *Penthouse*. Because of their duty status, their drinking was moderate, averaging only two or three cans each. The guards are required to be in the barracks when not on patrol, so someone who does not have duty usually goes for beer. Cressey told me that on cold nights they sit in automobiles and drink whiskey, but they have to be very careful because the officer of the guard drives around periodically. Whenever they see car lights approaching, they jump out of the car and begin walking; they haven't been caught yet, so they think their system is pretty good.

Walking guards worked from 4:00 in the afternoon until 6:00 the following morning during the work week, and pulled a 24-hour shift on weekends and holidays. Tower guards in the stockade worked 8-hour shifts without breaks and sometimes used alcohol in the towers. The observer noted:

> Loveless and Wilson started telling me about guard duty. "I don't see why we pull that duty at all. They have television cameras in all the

towers anyway." "Loveless and I split a pack of beer and a pint of rum tonight, and we still didn't get high." "Yeah, it's so boring, you can't even get drunk." They finished off a quarter of a fifth of whiskey while we talked, and Loveless then announced, "I've reached my goal for the evening—finally I'm high. Goodnight, world."

The most popular drink on duty, however, was beer because the effects could be more closely monitored and controlled; also, beer was by far the drink of preference among the enlisted men.

I walked back from the motor pool with Hansen. He said, "Damn, it's hot. Let's see if Waller has any cold beer in the refrigerator down at supply." Waller had none, but recommended we see Bousman at the Operations office. On the way to Operations, we stopped at the sandwich shop where Hansen said, "We usually drink our lunch, but some sandwiches would taste good with the beer in that air conditioned office." We entered the Operations office and Hansen sang out, "I've got the eats, if you've got the beer." Bousman was sitting at his desk and pulled a cold can of beer from the drawer for each of us. Whenever the lieutenant or one of the sergeants entered the room, Hansen and Bousman put their beers into a desk drawer and quietly continued eating and talking.

A final instance of drinking on duty was observed during field training. Most soldiers did not look forward to going to the field because of the work involved in loading the trucks, pitching the tents, digging foxholes, and running through exercises with limited blank ammunition. In the field there were long stretches of inactivity, punctuated with drinking.

On the first night after the base camp was set up and the evening maneuvers were cancelled, the men sat around in small groups, talking and drinking sodas they had brought with them. Wilson had filled his canteen with daiquiris; Jones had a fifth of bourbon; and Lemsen had a pint of vodka. Several men had brought six-packs of beer along, and the motor pool crew managed to stash three cases in among their gear. The sergeants stayed to themselves, and didn't bother us the entire evening.

The second category of unsanctioned drinking was wine or hard liquor in the barracks. The proscription on drinking hard liquor in the barracks could be more safely ignored in the barracks than on duty, since there was almost no possibility of detection. The observer noted:

I was watching the electric football competition in Gino's room, when Loveless offered me some scotch. I needed ice, but there was none in the refrigerator. Loveless took my glass, poured two jiggers from a half-gallon bottle, drank it straight, and followed with a sip of Pepsi. Shortly after this, Wilson came in and drank the same amount in the same fashion. We then returned to watch the football game.

Distilled spirits, however, were not as popular as the pop wines which were also prohibited in the barracks.

The commander announced in formation this morning that he was enforcing the no-wine-or-liquor rule in the barracks, and he would ban beer, too, if there were any more wild parties. The restriction, if enforced, will hit Gunderson hardest, for he simply lives for his bottle of Annie Greensprings Cherry Wine. Almost every evening, he and Roberts pass a bottle between them as they lie on their bunks, listening to music.

In summary, liquor and wine were common in the barracks, although care was taken to hide their presence and consumption seldom exceeded a bottle of wine or a couple of shots. In the evening it was not uncommon for someone to make a trip to the liquor store, which was analogous to the evening runs for food.

Bunsen could not drink scotch with neither ice nor a mix other than cola, so he decided to go to the liquor store. He went down the hall, announcing his intention and collecting orders and money. He returned with a six-pack of beer, a bottle of sangria, two bottles of apple wine, and two half pints of bourbon.

A final form of unsanctioned drinking involved physical assault, property destruction, and creating public disturbances. Surprisingly few incidents of assault occurred in the barracks during the Fort Marshall Study. The form of drinking that provoked the greatest ire from leaders were rowdy parties. The observer noted:

Following the last game of football season, Barker and Gross invited the whole team to the barracks for a party. When I got to the barracks, Cressy and I were elected to go for beer, since we were the only ones not wearing football uniforms. Barker collected $1 or $2 from everyone. We bought two cases, but when we returned, the party was already in full swing. Six bottles of wine were circulating, and I was offered one from each direction when I sat the beer down.

Murphy had his stereo on full blast; the sound could be heard from the far end of the building, where we came up the stairs. People generally just sat around bullshitting, but Murphy tended to be the center of attention. He pantomimed the lead guitar player and sang along so loudly that the voice on the record could not be heard. Sometimes he improvised crude sexual songs or variations of the GI Blues to the merriment of everyone. After about an hour we were out of beer, and three of us went for another case.

At its height, the party numbered about 13 people. Gunderson and Rogers joined since they lived in the barracks, and Brighten came from his room with a pint of blackberry brandy. Barker and Murphy got into a quick wrestling match that Barker won, to the cheers of us watching. The football team members who did not live on our bay left about midnight, and others slowly drifted away thereafter, leaving about eight of us to the bitter end.

Cressey's "thing" for the evening was squirting lighter fluid on the floor and on wall lockers, and then igniting it. At one point he took Murphy's saucer cap, put fluid inside, lighted it, and did a Mexican hat dance. Murphy seemed pissed that his hat was chosen, but he smiled lamely while it burned, and then reverently replaced the remains in his locker "for inspection."

When Cressey finished his torch routine, Murphy and Gross attacked him and tore his T-shirt and jockey shorts to shreds. Gross then began attacking others, and Murphy and Roberts were quickly stripped. I went to change to an old pair of shorts just in case, but Murphy and Cressey saved me the trouble. At the end, everyone still at the party was wearing only shreds of clothing that had been salvaged from the attacks.

By 1:30, everyone was running down. Murphy, Barker, and I began cleaning up the bay while Gross threw the three cases of beer bottles out the window. Barker and I swept the torn, shredded underclothing into a pile in the middle of the room and went to sleep.

In the morning Sargeant Ragland came in to wake us up. He simply stared at the pile of clothing and stirred it around with the broom handle he was carrying. The commander was upset about the beer bottles on the lawn, and threatened to ban beer in the barracks. Ragland threatened midnight GI parties in place of beer parties, but the only consequence was that Murphy spent the entire day getting the bay in shape.

As a rule property damage involved broken windows, dented furniture, and beer-soaked mattresses. Sometimes damage could be concealed with a little ingenuity:

Paulson came in drunk last night and ran his fist through the plaster-
board wall at the top of the stairs. The guys taped a recruiting poster
over the hole, and the platoon sergeant expressed great satisfaction in
the improved spirit and attitude of the men.

While the Army officially frowns on alcohol consumption on
duty, on the use of wine and liquor in the barracks, and on drinking
that leads to property destruction or complaints, enlisted men dis-
creetly ignore all of these proscriptions. But whether sanctioned or
unsanctioned, alcohol consumption seems inextricably woven into
the fabric of Army life.

Drinking Off Post

While it is safe to say that someone is drinking somewhere in any
given barracks on any given night, most of the drinking done by
common soldiers took place outside of the barracks and off the post.
Whenever money and transportation were available, soldiers at Fort
Marshall preferred to go to a bar or club. Unless such drinking resulted in arrests, an automobile accident, or property destruction
upon returning to the barracks, drinking off post was of no concern to
the leaders.

An understanding of off-post drinking patterns begins with a
description of the places chosen, for the ambience and recreational
opportunities in various bars determine what soldiers do while drinking. Places to drink off post were both numerous and convenient.
Outside the gate lay Boomtown—a block or two of bars, pawn shops,
used car dealers, massage parlors, and the like. In addition there
were bars and liquor stores along the major highways leading to the
post. An automobile made it possible to reach many other bars and
clubs in the area. Thus the question to be resolved is how favorite
bars were chosen from the tremendous number available.

Where Soldiers Drink

Soldiers classified bars into four types: "redneck places," "nice
places," "rough places," and "dives." Their choice of bar depended
upon money, transportation, social background, social aspirations,
and, most important, the status of relations in the barracks.

A "redneck place" was described as one where only country-
western music was played and where customers were not very
friendly. Music was hardly the major criterion in this judgment, given

the prevailing popularity of the country-western sound among all social classes. The men routinely complained about civilians mistreating soldiers, regardless of the context, thus rejection per se was not a distinguishing feature of "redneck" bars. Everyone at these bars turned whenever the door opened. If a regular entered, they hailed him and resumed their conversation, but when a stranger appeared, they stared briefly, then returned to subdued conversation. In essence a "redneck place" was a territorial bar with a regular, largely local civilian clientele, some of whom had southern accents and many of whom preferred country music. Sometimes active attempts were made to exclude strangers.

> Franklin needed cigarettes so we walked to the El Rancho. As we approach he assumes a rolling, swaggering gait and says, "This here is redneck heaven," in a heavy hillbilly accent. The bar falls quiet as we enter. A man at the bar in an accent heavier than Franklin's put-on says, "Any of you boys shoot pool? No, huh, not a pool player in the bunch." Franklin asks if we want a beer, and Johnson agrees to a quick one. As we order, Fredericks asks the barmaid if she has any water. "Of course we have water. What are you, some kind of wise guy?" She is joking, but we laugh tensely as she goes to the back room. She takes a long time and Johnson comments, "They have water, but not for you."
>
> The pool player yells for the barmaid to bring him a plate of jalapeno peppers, and she returns with about five on a plate. The man eats one whole and comments, "These must be pretty old; they aren't hot like the ones in Texas. Any of you boys ever been to Texas? Well, then, I know you like Texas peppers even if these are too old." Franklin takes a pepper, pretends to eat it whole, and palms it under the bar. He chews slowly, swallows, and says, "You're right, they must be old." Tex watches with a sneer that turns to slack-jawed incredulity. When his jaw reaches its low point, Franklin pulls the pepper from under the bar, examines it carefully, and then eats it without a murmur. Tex laughs uncomfortably and retreats to his bar stool. The other men at the bar snicker as Johnson eats his pepper in obvious pain.

"Nice places" were physically no different than "redneck places." Both had juke boxes, pool tables, pinball machines, and other amusements. Both were scaled by the extent of paneling, carpeting, vinyl upholstery, and dim lighting, which created an ambience ranging from dumpy to classy. The principal distinguishing feature of "nice places" was their friendliness. In "nice places" no one paid much attention to new patrons and the conversation at the bar was between companions or with the bartender. Many such places employed oriental barmaids who welcomed the few words of Japanese, Korean, or Thai spoken by soldiers who had served in Asia. The music on the juke box tended to more mixed than in "redneck places", and included rock, soul, and top-40 tunes in addition to country-western.

A regular patron of a "nice place" could be advanced a beer when short of money, and it was possible to establish ongoing relations with the proprietors and other regulars. On a slow night the observer found a degree of intimacy unusual for an Army environment:

> As I was drinking at the Three Aces, Mary Jane, one of the regulars, tapped me on the shoulder and sat down. She unwrapped an aluminum foil package that contained steaming rice and barbecued chicken. She had some chopsticks and invited me to try the food that Kim, the bartender, had prepared. Kim came over and dished out more rice, as two other regulars joined us at the table. As we ate and talked about the food, the bar took on a nice, friendly, congenial, good-time air.

"Rough places," on the other hand, were notorious for robbery, arguments, and fighting. Although the physical ambience may have been little different than a "nice place," the lights were not apt to be as dim. "Rough places" tended to be favored by barracks loners or those whose socialization included survival training environments marked by belligerent drunkenness. The observer noted:

> At the Screaming Eagle, Koko, the barmaid, was having trouble with a very drunk soldier, whom she had escorted to the door twice. I went to the cigarette machine, and when I turned around the drunk was back, blocking my path. I excused myself to get by, but he said, "You've got just fifteen seconds to drink your beer and get the hell out of here." I said, "Hey, man, cool it. What's your problem?" "Now you've got five seconds to get out or I'll cut your fucking throat." I left without finishing my beer. In the barracks I described the incident to Solomon, who often drinks there. He explained, "Yeah, that's Little Richard from the med battalion. He pulled that shit on me once, but I decked him, and I haven't had any trouble since. In those places if you ever let them push you around, you can never go back."

"Dives" were frequent only after other amusements had been exhausted; they were not places in which to spend an entire evening. A "dive" was marked by broken furniture, cracked linoleum floors, filthy toilets, and alcoholic patrons. The chief feature of "dives" was an aura of dirt and stale air. A broken-down railroad hotel in a town near the post was one "dive" where soldiers sometimes ended a night of making the rounds:

> About 11:30, at our third stop of the night, the guys decided to check out the 40-year-old go-go dancer in ripped leotards at the Crossroads Hotel. On the way they joked that I would really get a kick out of this place, "It's a real rat hole."
>
> The building itself is an old wooden structure with a sagging front porch. The hotel has not been painted in years. Inside, the bar was small, dark, dingy and dirty. The patrons around the bar looked like Bowery applicants who just stared at their drinks. When we entered, a young girl was dancing on the elevated platform to last year's music on the juke box. She wore only a bathing suit bottom and panty hose. Although she was not particularly attractive, she acted as if she were, as she went through her junior high cheerleading and majorette routines that were only remotely in time with the music.
>
> When she finished, someone ordered another round, and Martin said he'd prefer to drink from the can rather than touch one of the beer mugs. We were laughing and joking when Maddrix said, "Uh-oh, now for the main attraction." A woman approached the bar, wearing plastic knee boots, dark panty hose, and a three-piece pink chiffon night gown. Struggling with the help of a man at the end of the bar who pushed on her butt, she stood on the bar and looked over the crowd. Her hair was ratted, her make-up running, and her stomach distended through the nightie. Her smile revealed a missing tooth that induced howls of laughter from our group. She then attempted to work her way to the circular bar, trying to get her clothes off without upsetting any beers. By the time she reached us, she was naked to the waist, but her briefs looked more like wrestling trunks.
>
> She lowered her crotch to my face, swiveled her hips, and dipped one of her breasts in Martin's beer. He screamed, "Now you've ruined my beer," and she bellowed back in a Ma Kettle voice, "Screw you, asshole," and offered the breast to Maddrix to lick off the foam. She continued to make her way around the bar, shaking her butt at this man, and bumping and grinding before that one. When she finished her routine we left the bar, laughing and joking about the experience on the way back to the post.

Bars and clubs were also typed by their clientele, which again implied territoriality. For example, "nice places" were usually avoided if the regular crowd was predominantly black or "lifer." Nothing in the taxonomy implied exclusive patronage by soldiers, for they frequented a number of different bars in the immediate vicinity of the post. They did have favorites but did not become territorial with respect to them in the sense that a given soldier or group of soldiers could always be found at a "home" bar. They could visit a "redneck" bar to laugh at the patrons, or a "dive" to make fun of the dancers; they could even stop by a "rough place" if they were with friends, if the place was within walking distance of the barracks, or if they were looking for a fight. On those rare occasions when the racial barrier to interpersonal relations was penetrated, a white might even drink at a black bar when accompanied by a black sponsor. A black could always drink with the whites, but few did.

It is clear, in sum, that drinking patterns outside the barracks are dictated by the structure and character of human relationships inside the barracks. In this regard it is essential to bear in mind that barracks relationships are rigidly timebound and ahistorical. They exist only in the present and the immediate past. For group relationships to endure in these confining time dimensions, it is essential to weave a web of commonality which provides a history and a sense of tradition for the group and which enables the members to distinguish themselves from all others in the Army. Drinking in different environments with different consequences can provide an experience that is clearly more significant than sharing a rerun on television.

DRINKING PATTERNS

Drinking outside the barracks fell into three patterns: recreational drinking, affirmational drinking, and ceremonial drinking.

Recreational Drinking

Recreational drinking was the most common pattern. It involved dyads, triads, and small groups who regularly hung around together. Often groups had a special haunt, one not too widely known or convenient to reach, and without a predominantly military clientele. Dotti's Tap was such a place for one group of soldiers.

Dotti's was a "nice place" that catered to working-class patrons in a town about five miles from the post. Located in the middle of the business district, the small sign outside escaped the attention of most persons driving by. The decor was that of a neighborhood tavern. The horseshoe bar was flanked by two pool tables, a bowling game, an air hockey game, and several pinball machines. The lighting was subdued, and the floor and toilets were clean. A trip to Dotti's was usually just a quiet night out with the boys. The observer noted:

On the bay Barker says "Anybody want to tip a few?" "Sure, why not, there's nothing else to do." I hesitate, and MacNamee says, "Come on with us. How are you going to find out what we do if you don't go where we go." Five of us pile in Johnson's car and drive to Dotti's Tap. . . . Gunderson and Roberts are already shooting pool when we arrive. We order drafts at the bar, and then drift toward the pool table. MacNamee challenges Cressey to an air hockey game. "Gee, I've never played before, but OK." He easily beats MacNamee two games in a row, and then challenges Barker. They put on a good show, loudly cheering their scores and hissing points scored against them. Watson plays the pinball machine as I drift back to the pool table. Gunderson is dominating the game with a barrage of banter, calling shots but sinking very few and urging Roberts to try the cue stick under his leg.

Barker and I bowl a couple of games, and then MacNamee and Cressey challenge us to a doubles match. The other patrons in the bar are mostly over 40, but pay little attention to the cheering and hissing that accompany our game. There is little talk among us not related to the games in progress. The guys also played the juke box that contained polkas, country-western, mod, jazz, and rock music. One woman with heavy makeup, teased hair, in a dirty pink knit pantsuit danced every polka with an older man. Between dances she hung on his neck, kissing him like a teenager with her first love, but the guys paid little attention to her. At 11:30 Johnson left, saying he had guard duty in the morning and needed some sleep. At 12:30 Gunderson said he was ready to go bar-hopping and suggested the Saddle Club, but Barker and Cressey wanted to return to post. Gunderson drove us to the barracks. No one was very drunk at the end of the evening.

Knowledge of where to go for recreational drinking was another commodity that could be used in the interpersonal market of the barracks.

Brownlee had invited me to go drinking and dancing with girls. He seems quite knowledgeable about the possibilities. "I'm really not sure where to take you. We could go to the Holiday Palace; it has lots of chicks and free beer, but it's a 45-minute drive. Then there's a Tip-Top that has OK chicks, but the drinks are expensive and you can't wear jeans. How about the Red Devil? It's only 10 minutes away, OK chicks, and a good band. We can stop by Walt's Lounge and load up on a few cheap beers to save money inside."

The distinguishing feature of recreational drinking is that it accompanies other activities; it is not the focal activity. The object is not to get drunk, but to enjoy the bar amusements, dancing, or food. Recreational drinking serves to affirm existing social relationships, but typically nothing "special" or "unusual" occurs during these sessions to add to extend the unique commonalities or traditions of the group.

Distinctive commonalities, however, can be arranged. By creating special occasions for drinking, individuals "in the know" can claim higher status by teaching less knowledgeable comrades while at the same time creating historical episodes that bind the clique closer together. In recreational drinking the focal activity is always something other than the consumption of alcohol. Groups of Fort Marshall soldiers who made special trips to the adult movie and bookstore sections of nearby cities created special occasions in which drinking was incidental. Such drinking was restricted to cliques, and the size of the clique was determined by the transportation available, generally no more than five in a single car. The observer recorded the following extended special-occasion episode:

Vine street is actually only a block long, but is tightly packed, mostly with bars. The flashing lights and neon signs seem stacked on one another, and look strange under the high-intensity street lights that practically create daylight conditions. Most of the places are dance bars where there is at least one nude female on a platform, dancing to a small band or a loud juke box. Each bar has a pitchman on the sidewalk, encouraging customers to enter. The pitchmen range from old men in tattered coats to a few young longhairs, but their line is always the same: "Evening gents, step right in; we've got some of the prettiest girls on the vine. Some of the tightest holes on the block, men, see for yourself." Other businesses include peep shows and pornographic shops, striptease joints, palm reading parlors, massage parlors, and even a topless shoeshine stand—$2 a shine.

At the last bar on the corner Gregory suggests we go in. The pitchman obligingly opens the door, and the scent of musk perfume and the sounds of loud rock music roll toward the sidewalk. There is a small partition inside the door so the dancers cannot be seen from the street, and with the help of the hostess we find our way to the bar. My eyes quickly adjust to the darkness, and I am staring at a topless dancer, wearing only a G-string, who is undulating to the music on the platform behind the bar. A hand runs around my neck, and a young girl in her early 20's softly asks me if I'd like some company. I look over and see three other girls have attached themselves to the others and are going through the same routines. The bartender comes along taking orders in rapid succession; I order a beer, and he pauses expectantly for me to buy the girl a drink. The others have all ordered drinks for their girls, as I get out $2 for my beer. The girl asks me my name, and I blurt it out before remembering Gregory's warning never to tell a whore your real name. She asks me my astrological sign; I ask her name; she asks me to buy her a drink. "Gee, I only brought $7, I really can't afford it." She coaxed for a while, then said to come back again as she slithered away. In the course of the next five minutes three other girls came over to me, urging me to buy them a drink. One girl even said, "Ya wanna fuck? They have some nice rooms in the back I'd like to show you."

As Darnell paid another $5 for a drink for his girl, her tongue disappeared in his ear. Gregory had been talking with his girl, and they got up from the bar and disappeared toward the rear of the building. Wolfson followed with his girl, and Darnell actively began kissing his at the bar. Most of the girls wore skimpy pullover tops and bikini bottoms. When Darnell and his girl retired to the sidelines, she unbuttoned her blouse, turned to me, and whispered, "See what you're missing?" Darnell ordered her another drink and was rewarded with more kissing and experienced hand work. I ordered another beer.

When they left the bar, the men had a new repertoire of conservational topics, and no one else in the company had shared this experience with them. The observer continued:

Immediately outside the door the conversation was animated. Darnell said, "I damned near shit in my pants when the bartender said $5 for the broad's drink." "Yeah, and all it is is ginger ale with a champagne label stuck on. My girl was pretty decent, though. She's doing the job to earn money and meet people. She said she was engaged, but is going to break it off. I even got her address and a date for Tuesday night. She promised it wouldn't be on a business basis, just a good time, so maybe I'll get a good-time free fuck." "How do you know that's the right address?" "I know the area. I used to date a girl who lived in that part of town." "Bullshit, I'll bet it's a pool hall." "Bullshit. I'll show you on Tuesday."

The remainder of the evening was spent in six or seven other places in the area. The criteria for staying or leaving a place were the age of the crowds and the appearance of the dancers. The conversation centered on the dancers' bodies and whether they were better or worse than those at their first stop. They also were amused by the other patrons:

In one bar we watched the female bartender and one of the hookers relieve a rather drunk man in his late 50's of his remaining money.

Gregory chuckled, "He said he wanted to swing, didn't he?" Suddenly a man appeared from the back room, followed by a young girl who was screaming, "If that motherfucker ever tries that again, I'll kill the cocksucker. If he even says that again, I'll kill the goddamned bastard." Gregory suggests we leave as Darnell starts for the door. Outside we laugh, "What a fucking hot bitch. She's a mean motha, isn't she?" It is now two in the morning, and the street is pretty much closed down as we head for the car.

Comparing their experiences during the evening permitted the men to test and affirm their status relations within the clique. The test was initiated by the junior member of the group, but was quickly reduced to a contest between the top two positions.

In the car Wolfson says, "I wouldn't mind coming back tomorrow night and fucking that little blond chick." Darnell agrees that he would like to come back. Gregory says, "For $40 a bottle, I'll just wait until Tuesday and get it for free." Gregory then laughs about Darnell spending $46 and Wolfson spending $50. Wolfson protests that he loaned $5 to me and $15 to Darnell. Gregory claims he spent only $23. Gregory then calls to a girl on the street, "Hey, Toni, you want a ride." Darnell begins taunting him to ask one for a blow job, so he rolls down the window and yells as we drive past another woman, "Hey, how about a blow job?" Everyone laughed as he slammed the car into fourth and sped away.

The contenders for top status then argue on how to get back to the post. The lower-positioned man asserts the driver has missed the turn; the driver does a U-turn, crosses a ramp, and finds himself going north on the southbound lanes of the freeway.

Everyone laughed at his predicament as he pulled to the side of the road and crept to a cross-over point. Gregory then vows we will go back his way. Later Wolfson asked him to stop the car so he could urinate. Gregory refused; Wolfson threatened to pull the emergency brake; Gregory said, "Go ahead, it's Wilson's car," Wolfson sat back in an angry huff, and Gregory then brought the car to a screeching halt.

Gregory was clearly in the top status position. The other two jockeyed a bit for the subordinate positions, and the observer affirmed the top position by allowing himself to be instructed in the ways of the world.

As we walk from the parking lot to the barracks, the talk is mostly about the girls and the shoeshine parlor. Wolfson says, "$40 a fuck is ridiculous; if it were $20 or $25 I could see it." Darnell and Wolfson laugh and joke about who spent the most money. I asked Gregory in his room what the bottle had to do with getting a girl. He said, "What you do is pay $40 for a fifth of something, then you go to a room and you can stay until you've finished the bottle. Hell, with 12 girls working one joint and each one only going to the back once a night, that's a hell of a lot of money."

The principal function of recreational drinking is to extend the web of commonality by means of distinctively shared experiences that serve to bind the group members to each other and give them a history. Such occasions not only provided a source of stories and conversation for internal consumption, but also elicited comment and discussion from those in the barracks who were not present. The morning after going to the city, the observer was asked by several different people about the evening and the activities of the group.

Affirmational Drinking

When the focal activity shifts to alcohol consumption itself, rather than drinking as an adjunct to some other activity, recreational drinking shades into affirmational drinking. At Fort Marshall, affirmational drinking was not usually planned in any formal sense, but just seemed to happen when a reasonably close-knit group ran out of things to talk about and was bored with routine activities. Affirmational drinking represented an attempt to infuse new energy into the social structure. Because the size of drinking groups off the post was determined by the size of the car available, most of the affirmational drinking was done in groups numbering less than six. The observer commented on the decision to go drinking:

When I entered the barracks, Gross and Cressey were with Murphy and Barker, watching television. I joined the group as Gross asked, "What're we doing tonight?" No one responds. "Hey, Barker, what do you say?" "We could go lift a few," making a drinking motion with his hand. Murphy is not yet 21 and says, "Where're you going?" "Don't worry, you'll get in. How about you?" "I guess so, it's my job." The whole exchange was pretty dispirited, and I felt I knew exactly what we were going to do before Gross asked. There was little enthusiasm for the excursion, so we watched the television to the end of the program.

The group stopped first at the apartment of some soldiers that Barker had met in basic training. Five men shared the apartment which was furnished with two broken couches, a mangy rug, a breakfast table, three straight chairs, and mattresses on the floor. Conversation immediately turned to the last party held in the apartment and snapshots were circulated. One picture showed the sweathog of one of the apartment mates. He proposed they get some beer and bring the sweathogs over, but the men from the barracks were not interested.

> Burris, one of the guys in the apartment, told a story of knocking Gross's sweathog to the floor after she refused to give him a blow job. Gross retorted that Burris had tried to kiss her on the mouth after she had previously sucked Gross off, and that his sweathog didn't understand men like that. Burris called Gross a liar, saying that he would never kiss a scum-bag on the mouth. He then suggested we round up a couple of hogs that night. Gross declines, saying we were going out for some "serious drinking," and invited them along.

Including the guys from the apartment would have necessitated another car, and since none was available, members of the group reaffirmed their identity with a few more stories of times past, and the barracks group headed for Dotti's Tap. All of the ingredients needed for a night of quiet recreational drinking seemed to be present, but the evening just didn't come off that way. The observer continued:

> Immediately after we ordered a round of beer, Cressey asked if anyone wanted to shoot pool. Murphy and I volunteered, while Barker and Gross remained at the bar. Cressey easily beat us both, and then Murphy and I played a loser's play-off. Conversation was restricted to the game in progress. Cressey said he grew up in neighborhood pool rooms in Boston, and Murphy said he did not play much until he came into the Army. We drank four rounds of beer while we shot pool, and another four at the bar after the game.

Gross appeared dissatisfied. He enjoyed high status in the group, but was in no mood for bar amusements. He wanted to move on to another bar.

> Gross suggested we walk to the hotel to see the 99-year-old topless dancer in tennis shoes. His description decided the issue . . . there were no seats at the hotel bar, so we stood in a tight group, sipping our beers. The older dancer was about 55 rather than 99, and wore white boots rather than tennis shoes. The other dancers were at least 40, and both had long since lost the battle of the bulge. The crowd was all white, all male, and pretty depressing; the patrons just drank or stared

at their glasses without conversation. We quickly finished our beers and left. On our way out, Gross called the older dancer a scum-bag, but she either did not hear him or chose to ignore the remark.

Conversation outside focused on the dancers, and Barker and Gross swore that the older dancer was wearing tennis shoes the last time they saw her. The group still sought a theme for the evening, having rejected rounding up sweathogs and bar amusements.

Gross suggested we go to the Saddle Club for another round, but Barker vetoed the idea, "I'm not going to that redneck hole. The women are all fat and the music is terrible." Maybe we should let Murphy off there so he can see his 300-pound sweathog." "Bullshit. I was drunk at the time; all I wanted was a blow job and when I got that I let her go. Let's go to the Starlight if you want to look at women."

The evening now had a theme: watching go-go dancers. The next stop was eight miles down the road. It was impossible for the group to carry on any conversation in the car because the music was too loud for anyone to be heard. At the Starlight the observer noted:

Gross ordered two pitchers of beer, and we sat around one table in the rear. The dancers here seem to be college age, and not bad looking. The crowd is mostly young and male and all white. In contrast to the hotel, the patrons actively look at the dancers. Cressey and I watched the show, but the others were more interested in their beer. Half way through the pitcher Cressey reached his limit and refused to drink more. Despite our teasing that he was a party pooper and a punk unable to hold his liquor, he adamantly refused to drink more beer. Gross repeatedly failed to get the waitress to talk to him, let alone give him a date. So he suggested we see some young dancers. I suggested the Red Robin that was about 20 miles away. Cressey protested that he had had enough and wanted to return to the barracks, but he was outvoted in the car. During the drive Murphy and I began singing above the tape music until I noticed Barker was beginning to weave on the road. I cautioned him to slow down, but he ignored me, and Gross said, "Aw, what the fuck." I remained quiet.

At the Red Robin the group ordered another pitcher of beer—their third following 10 bottles each. Gross suggested that they pick up some unattached females, but the others voted for some food. On the way to the car the disinhibiting effects of the beer began to take their toll.

Gross stopped to talk with two women and a man who were standing on the sidewalk. The rest of us walked on about a half a block when Gross began screaming that the women were sluts, whores, and scumbags, and the man was a cunt-lapping pimp. Murphy and Barker joined in screaming, "The whole fucking world's a scum-bag. Fuck all you motherfuckers," and other obscenities. People were out on the balconies of the nearby apartments when we drove off; the noise was that loud. As we drove off, Gross ordered Barker to slow down and drive near them. As we passed, Murphy and Gross spat on them from the window, and yelled obscenities again.

On the way to these bars it wasn't clear whether the driver was being reckless or his perception was awry; now there was no question. The observer noted:

Barker made a wrong turn that I pointed out. He immediately made a U-turn on one of the city's busiest streets. Cressey suggested we go to the Pizza Palace and everyone agreed. Unfortunately, we were heading in the wrong direction, so Barker pulled another U-turn. I then realized it was past 1:00, and the Palace would be closed. Another U-turn, and Barker raced up the street at 60 miles an hour. We were still close enough to the scene of obscenity screaming that I was positive we would be arrested. I don't remember much about the drive home except that I was scared all the way by Barker's driving.

Such serious drinking episodes were not the norm, but occurred with sufficient frequency that the observer was enjoined to spend more time recording what soldiers drank rather than keeping up with them. Heavy drinking was seldom reported unless a serious accident or an arrest ensued. Inability to function the next day was dismissed as resulting from " a little too much to drink last night." A night of serious drinking was typically followed by two or three nights of quiet television viewing in the barracks.

Depressed affirmational drinking always implied an intent to get very, very intoxicated. It was as though the group had become a closed system in entropy. No new events, episodes, or tales were available from the present and immediate past to generate and maintain conversation. Because the members had become bored with their relationships, it was necessary to seek out new places where old stories could be told again in the process of gathering new material that would sustain the bonds between group members.

The line between affirmational drinking and other forms of drinking is not sharp. Affirmational drinking may result at any time when relationships become dulled and require a provocative honing.

For example, the soldiers in the previous episode had planned for two weeks to attend the St. Patrick's Day festivities in New York City. They asked the observer to join them.

"Hey are you coming to New York with us?" "What's happening there?" "It's St. Paddy's day; there's a parade and everyone gets drunk and laid." "You got a place to stay?" "Sure, I rented a suite in a hotel downtown. We can leave on Friday after pay formation and have a three-day drunk. See, I've got two rooms; one bathroom we'll use, and we'll keep the beer and ice in the other bathtub. Last year I got laid, then I passed out in the hallway. My buddies stripped me to my drawers, carried me downstairs, and left me in a chair in the lobby." Everyone seemed quite excited about the prospects, and encouraged me to come along.

Three of the men stayed at the home of one whose parents lived in the suburbs, and took the train into the city. The day began as a special occasion with recreational drinking. The three, decked out in green hats and bow ties, consumed a case of beer on the train and while visiting the Empire State Building and the Statue of Liberty. The other two came on a different train, unbeknownst to the others, and spent the morning drinking Green Leprechauns concocted from gin and creme de menthe. Everyone missed the parade, but they did assemble at the hotel at one o'clock. Now they could begin to create a memorable special occasion of recreational drinking.

Gross had promised that the first thing he would do is throw the television out the window. When we enter he lifts the mirror from the wall, but unfortunately it was permanently affixed to the plaster, and leaves large holes in the wall. He mutters about having to be careful because the room is in his name, but then raises the mirror above his head as if to smash it on the floor. Unfortunately, Barker is standing behind him, and the mirror renders him practically unconscious. Gross then puts the mirror under one bed and begins turning flips on the other bed until two of the slats break. He quits on the pretext he will have to sleep on the bed tonight, and suggests we go out on the town. Unfortunately, it is raining steadily outside. We have three six-packs of beer in the room, and settle down watching the television. Two men immediately fall asleep on the beds.

The rain continued. Gross was determined that this would be a very special occasion, and he left the group, promising to return with five willing women. He returned, cursing and soaking wet. The men finished the beer while watching the "Wide World of Sports," and decided to eat at a very well-known Italian restaurant.

As we wait in line, Gross is cursing and becoming more obnoxious by the minute. "Fucking rain . . . hey, cunt, you're cold, but you're cunt . . . hey, lady, never take a cab in this town; those fucking Puerto Ricans are lousy. Take a horse carriage like that one over there. Horses give great fucks, and they love to be sucked off." Barker says, "Hey, calm down; this is a nice place and we're going to get thrown out." "OK, OK; hey, Murphy, watch this." Now he spits on the doorman, who is looking the other way. Barker says again, "This is a nice place. For my sake, cut it out." "Sure, OK." Gross then fakes a spit at Murphy. "You wouldn't dare." He does and Murphy retaliates. Barker and Reynolds are quite embarrassed and hope they will settle down once inside.

The purpose of special-occasion recreational drinking is to have something to remember and to talk about, and the organizers of the outing were determined to insure a vivid memory, despite the rain.

Inside the door a lady directs us to the hostess. Gross calls her a sweathog to her face, and before Barker can give the grandmotherly hostess his name, Gross interrupts, "Cunt, John Cunt." She directs us to the bar in obvious disgust. Gross is now swearing freely: "Look at all the cunt in here. You could fuck for a year and still have some left over. Wow, I'd like to get her wrapped around my face . . ." Then he resumes spitting: an elderly couple walk by—on the back of the man's suit; a young couple—on the girl's dress; then in Murphy's face, who just lets the gob roll down his sinuses, and hits Gross on his moustache where it lodges and sags toward his lips.

One way to affirm the integrity of the group is for the members to take care of one another. Gross was obviously out of control and required assistance. The observed continued:

Barker, Reymonds, and I have edged as far away from them as we can. Finally Gross says, "I'm not waiting anymore. I'm going back for some fucking whore durvs that are free." No one argues, but no one agrees to go with him, so he stays. As a foursome passes, he erupts again, "I'm getting out of this fucking place." One of the men turns around angrily and says, "Watch your mouth, buddy." Gross yells after him, "Hey, fuck you, mister. Get those sweathogs out of here." The man kept going, thank goodness, and Barker kept saying, "Calm down, Rod, cut it out; this is a nice place." Murphy finally agreed to leave with Gross, who called once more, "Barker, we're going." "Well, leave, damnit; we're staying here." After they left, to the visible relief of all, Barker said, "They're going to get thrown out of the hotel if they go for whore durvs; shit, I've been saying it for so long, I can't remember what it really is."

Murphy and Gross were asleep when the others returned to the hotel. The evening was spent dozing and watching television, not unlike evenings in the barracks. The special occasion was over. Group membership had been affirmed. The next morning, on the walk to the train station, Murphy attempted to resume the spitting behavior on the sidewalk, but was admonished by Gross to "cool it." The incident of the night before was not to be re-enacted, but to be retold time and again in the barracks as a reminder of the ability of the members to stick together through difficult circumstances. To the outsider, affirmational drinking may appear physically dangerous or socially embarrassing, but to the barracks dweller it is one of the primary means of regenerating the affective bonds between himself and his comrades.

Ceremonial Drinking

Ceremonial drinking at Fort Marshall involved more than a single clique, and going-away parties provided a prime occasion. Each soldier has an ETS date—that is, the day he is scheduled to leave the service. Soldiers at the post began describing themselves as "short" about a month from their departure, and marked off the days, hours, and minutes remaining on "short-timer" calendars. Not everyone merited an ETS party. Companies organized into a few large work groups, like platoons, tended not to have ETS parties for departing members. If any note was taken of a departure at all, it was among intimates in the manner of a birthday celebration. Companies that were organized into multiple, small work groups tended to have ETS parties involving many people from the company. Such occasions provided one of the few opportunities to affirm social bonds beyond the usually fragmented cliques. Whether an individual merited an ETS party depended upon his status in the barracks and the availability of sufficient people from his original cohort to organize the celebration.

ETS parties provided an opportunity to observe both the coalition of all of the work-group cliques into a momentary unity and the allocation of status within the entire barracks social structure. In the following description note should be taken of Lamsen, a low-status barracks dweller.

As we were leaving the barracks to buy beer for the party, Lamsen tagged along. Barker adamantly refused to take five people in his car, and suggested that Lamsen wait in the barracks since he had already eaten supper. Lamsen said, "Oh, I didn't know that you were coming back; I'll wait here for you," but he followed us to the car and watched us drive off.

The party was to begin at a small fishing pond near the post. The four ate at McDonald's, bought a case of beer, and drove to the pond.

On the way past the barracks Barker wondered if "the dirt bum" had found a ride to the party. I asked if he meant Murphy. "No, Murphy's just a slob. The real dirt bum is Lamsen. That guy never bathes. He gets up in the morning, combs his hair, and goes to work. He doesn't brush his teeth or bathe at night." I noted that I had not detected any particular odor about him, and Gross added, "Last week he stunk. He may have taken a bath over the weekend. Anyway, the guy really smells bad. Murphy is a slob; he wears grubby clothes and hates to shave, but he and his clothes are always clean. His area and locker are always a mess, but he's really not dirty."

The old-timers in the company had gathered at the pond when the group arrived. Four men brought their girlfriends, and the party totaled about 20. All of the beer was pooled with the men mingling, drinking, and talking. The observer commented:

During the night the groups are constantly changing, expanding, and contracting, with almost everybody interacting with everybody else at one time or another. Three of the guys with girls tended to isolate themselves from the rest of us, but the fourth readily joined in the milling and talking with apparent ease. Lamsen was definitely an outsider. He was not included in conversation, and was frequently left standing outside a group with someone's back turned toward him. I was also an outsider. No one seemed particularly interested in seeking my company; however, when I approached a group, a space was usually opened for me to join and be accepted.

Such large gatherings of several cliques with overlapping memberships had little in the way of shared tradition or history beyond their working relations and occasional off-duty contacts. They had no sagas of past carousing and debauchery to recount; thus the party was sustained by the beer, the storyteller, and music from a tape deck in one of the cars. Stories about the Army were always welcome:

The conversation was mostly exchanging funny stories. Gross related how he got into the Army: "After I missed nine months of reserve meetings, they got pissed. They decided to be nice and give me a second chance, though. I thought that was mighty nice of them, so I skipped the next four meetings. Then they said I was going back into the Army. I was at home one day when a registered letter came. The guy asked, "Does Rodney Gross live here?" I said I had never heard of the guy, so he took it back to the post office and mailed me a card telling me it was there. I knew what it was, so I ignored it. Thirty-nine days later I decided to pick it up before the FBI got it. The orders were for Fort Marshall, so here I came. A couple of weeks later an FBI man called up my old man. He said, "Do you know where your son is?" My old man said, "Sure, I know where my son is." That FBI agent must have gotten a hard-on a foot long; see, he thought he had me and would make his monthly quota. He asked, "Well, where is he?" My old man replied, "He's at Fort Marshall, and if you guys in the government would get your fuckin' heads straight, the kid wouldn't be in any trouble." Then he slammed down the telephone; we never heard any more about it, so here I am."

Being able to tell good stories was a priceless commodity in such social gatherings, and a really good yarn-spinner needed only the slightest opening to begin.

Frisco went around the car to urinate and someone called, "Don't piss on the car, Charlie." Everyone laughed, and Frisco launched into another story: "One time I was home, and I went out drinking with this guy I know. We were driving his big black Imperial—belonged to his old man really. Anyhow, we got out to piss on the way home after we were both shit-faced. I walked to the back of the car and faced the side of the road. He came up behind me. I'm standing there pissing away, and all of a sudden I feel something warm on my leg. I look around and this guy's pissing in my pocket. I told him, "Hey, man, you're pissing in my pocket." He said, "Oh," turned and finished pissing all over the back bumper of that Imperial."

Horseplay at such parties was inevitable after a few beers:

Murphy started it by throwing a lighted match at Edmonds. He retaliated with his own match, and soon everyone with matches or a lighter was chasing someone else, attempting to set him on fire. When everyone tired of that, we tried to throw beer bottles across the pond. Frisco succeeded, and everyone joined in. Lamsen succeeded, and everyone ceased the activity.

By 10:30, those with girls were ready to leave. It was very cold around the pond, so they returned to the barracks to continue drinking. They stopped for food on the way back and brought two cases of beer into the barracks. There others were incorporated into the festivities, as the first ritual was performed. The observer noted:

As we were eating, Frisco passed out beer to everyone. We were joined by Preston and Peterson (blacks), who accepted a beer and stood at the edge of the crowd in the Murphy-Barker area. Frisco decided we had to "shoot a beer" for Cressey, who was getting out of the Army. I allowed as how I had never shot a beer, and Williams gave me an unopened beer can with a half inch hole punched in the side near our mouths, and pulled the tab. As each of us finished, we threw our can on the floor in the middle of the circle. Frisco finished first, then Cressey, then the rest, then me. I was kidded about being last, but Williams defended me: "He's never done it before . . . you have to know the trick." Later Barker explained that you have to open your throat and let the beer pour down as fast as it comes out of the can. "If you try to swallow, you lose it and it runs all over you."

These drinking rituals were neither inevitable nor invariable at ETS parties; rather they were invented at the moment and performed as if they had long-standing traditional significance:

Murphy then proposed a "beer-for-Cressey" ceremony. He opened a bottle of beer and proceeded to each person, urging him to have a drink of Cressey's beer. He carried the beer bottle in both hands at his stomach, and lifted it to each of us in turn with great formality and solemnity.

A considerable number of soldiers had recently arrived in the barracks. The old order was clearly passing, but some way was needed to communicate to everyone how the barracks was organized and who determined the policies. It was also necessary to initiate the newcomers into the ways of the village:

After everyone in the circle has taken a sip, Murphy decides that every-one on the bay should wake up and participate. The new black accepts with no argument. The new guy in my area accepts, and gets up to join us. The three new guys next to Murphy and Barker accept. Next is Simpson, and I expect some trouble. Simpson awakes, is told to sip from Cressey's beer, looks at the crowd, and takes the beer. He also gets up. The new guy in Peterson's area takes a sip and gets up. The last man on the bay is a new man on the far end. He refuses to drink and is booed roundly. Murphy persists in pushing and poking the guy and telling him to drink. He refuses and rolls to face the wall. We leave the area and return to the other end of the bay; whereupon Murphy decides he isn't finished yet. We return to the new man, and after much pushing and yelling he finally sips the beer, pleading that he didn't understand what Murphy wanted to do at first.

The barracks residents were now united, and the new men were ready to learn why "this is the most fucked-up company in the whole Army." A new out-group had to be defined.

Murphy, Roberts, and Frisco troop to the other end of the building, determined that the other platoon share the ceremonial beer. They return shortly, bragging that only one man refused, but they would get him yet. The ceremony is then forgotten. No one presents the empty bottle to Cressey; it is thrown out the window with all the other bottles.

Having had the outsiders defined for them, the new men were now ready to learn the rites of the in-group.

Cressey, "the torch," then made his final showing. He got out his lighter fluid and sprayed it on his wall locker. Frisco set it on fire as he continued spraying circles and zig-zags on the floor. We all cheered as he put away his fluid for the last time, but there was no formal passing of the torch to the new generation.

The next "lesson" involved dealing with the low-status people. One target was the individual whose highly polished floor was burned some weeks earlier.

Murphy instructs Simpson to shoot a beer. We all crowd around him and he is successful at shooting, but not at making friends. Roberts then decides to throw Simpson's television set out the window. It is an old cabinet model that will not fit through the window, and the pane breaks as Roberts tries. Simpson just stands back, looks relieved, and mutters that it didn't work that well anyway. The television is left leaning between the window and the desk. Next Rembolt is told to shoot a beer. He swallowed about half way through, and Gross jerked the can from his hand, finished it, and threw it disdainfully on the floor. Rembolt smiled in embarrassment and left the party.

From the day they arrived, the newcomers heard stories of the kind of barracks they joined. The oral history reached back little more than a year and recounted exploits of the "real crazies" who weren't afraid of anything or anybody. The newcomers had been told that the barracks had settled down a lot since the "crazies" left, but that some of the tradition was carried on by those who knew them. Now the drunken revelers re-enacted some of those scenes from yesteryear.

For some unknown reason Cressey pours a beer over Frisco's bed-pillow, sheets, blankets, and mattress. Frisco laughs, walks to the hall-way, and returns with a fire extinguisher which he empties on Cressey's bed. Gross comes in with a 24 oz. glass of urine, and tries to get people to try his "beer." Everyone recognizes it for what it is, and

Roberts takes it toward the latrine. Instead of dumping it there, he proceeds to the other platoon area, and returns, bragging that he poured it "in that fucking faggot Bezoni's bed and somebody else." Ten minutes later Gross comes screaming down the hall. "Roberts, your mother sucks cunt. You cocksucker, you poured piss all over my bed." Roberts denies it, and the incident is quickly forgotten.

As if on cue, a staff sergeant who lived in one of the private rooms was awakened by the melee, came to the bay, and demanded quiet. The observer noted:

Very bald Sergeant Blumer came into the bay, and in a disgusted tone demanded that we hold down the noise so others could sleep. Frisco yelled out, "Fuck you, shine. If you can't take it, move out with the rest of the goddamned lifers." Blumer left in angry, disgusted resignation only to return in a few minutes and demand that the party stop at once and the mess be cleaned up. Preston said, "Cool it, Sergeant Blumer, we'll clean it up like we always do, and it would be just so much easier if you would just go back to your room and don't hassle us." Blumer stalked out again, shaking his head in disgust. Murphy and Barker then began beating on the metal wall lockers, and Cressey disassembled his bunk.

At 1:00 they sent out for more beer, but the party was over. The observer concluded:

While Frisco was gone we began cleaning up the bay. Murphy and Gross threw beer bottles out the window; Barker and I used the trash can. When we collapsed in bed the bay was as usual except for the broken window, the burned floor, the disassembled bed, and the debris outside. When Frisco returned with the beer, he awakened Murphy with great effort and urged him to come to the window. "Hey, Murph, you know there is 62 beer bottles out there?" "Yeah, I know," and Murphy slumped back in his bed. Frisco and Gross drank another beer in silence, then went to bed.

DRINKING FUNCTIONS AND RULES

Whether the drinking is recreational, affirmational, or ceremonial, one of its primary functions is to provide the participants with a tradition, a history of common experience that gives a sense of depth to their relationships. At Fort Marshall, drinking together was as important for the dyads as for larger groups, as evidenced by the frequent recounting of experiences shared by "drinking buddies."

Darnell and Gregory apparently went to the city and picked up a whore. Gregory serviced her first, then during Darnell's turn, Gregory removed their money from her purse. They have told this story several times with obvious relish at each recounting.

Drinking also provided one of the few opportunities in the Army to express dependence and nurturance. The classic example was putting a buddy to bed after a drinking bout:

Bousman has a severe hangover, and is lying on his bunk, moaning. "I don't even remember going to bed." Walter says, "That's because I carried you to bed." "Watch how you say that." "Well I did; I carried you over my shoulder up three flights of stairs and then dumped you in your bed." "No shit. Simpson says you threw me against the wall." "Aw, fuck Simpson, you never touched the wall." "I felt like I did more than touch the wall." "You didn't even get into the second fifth; here, take a little rum to help your head." He pours a coffee cup of rum and coke that is about 90% rum.

Drinking episodes also provided small groups or cliques with a shared history. At an ETS party the observer noted:

The guys recount once more the Varsity Grill story. They were drinking in the college town when some other patron made an offensive remark. A magnificent fight broke out that resulted in "tearing the place apart and putting one of the college boys in the hospital." They have never returned, but the story is recounted whenever two or three of the members that were present get together.

The classic story of group bonding, frequently celebrated in movies and novels, is going to town in a body to avenge an insult to one of the members. Garrison Army life is not very much like the movies, but the psychological consequences to the group are the same.

About 1:30 Miller and Dobson wake up Murphy. Miller reports that he was hit with a pool cue in the Screaming Eagle by a civilian named Chuck, and that Reynolds was also beaten up by Chuck and his friends. Dobson wants to return to get even, but no one expresses much interest. "It's too late now; we'll go this weekend; I'm too tired."

Two days later the avengers' ceremony was enacted. The observer noted:

Seven men were sitting in Murphy's area when I entered the barracks. Barker asked if I want to go fighting with them, and explained they were going to the Screaming Eagle to help out Miller. I asked where Reynolds was, since he was also beaten up, and Miller contemptuously said, "Aw, he doesn't believe in this sort of thing." Lamsen came in, but declined to accompany us. He was razzed, but otherwise left alone. Dobson returned with two recruits from the other platoon, and proclaimed we had waited long enough. He kept repeating, "Willie is the best guy I know. We can't turn our backs on him when he needs friends." On the way over, Dobson kept giving Miller a pep talk of do's and don't's: "Be sure to keep him in the building. You'll go in first with us right behind. Wait until we all get there, then we'll surround him and hold off his friends. Don't let him get the first punch, and don't fight him if he has a pool cue. Don't worry about the cops; there's only one phone, and we'll cover that." At the bar Miller entered first, but Chuck was not there. Everyone looked disappointed, but relieved, and quickly ordered beer and turned to the pool tables and pinball machines.

A final example of the contribution of drinking episodes to group solidarity occurred after an ETS party where the floor was burned, a window broken, and the newcomers roused from their sleep to drink the ceremonial beer. The commander levied restrictions on the barracks and extra duty on ten of the major instigators. Someone had informed, and both the newcomers and old-timers were incensed.

Bousman said, "I don't go for tearing up the barracks like they did, but punishing just a few isn't right. Hell, we were all involved in it." Barnes added, "I'd like to know the son-of-a-bitch that squealed; us privates have to stick together." Murphy, the company legal clerk who received punishment, commented to the newcomer, "Don't sweat it. I just filed the papers in my desk; the punishment will never appear on the records. If the CO asks, I'll just say I forgot to forward them, but he'll never know."

The norms or behavioral rules for drinking were simple. The first was a prescript to share alcohol in the barracks with buddies. The sharing affirmed status relations and defined levels of interpersonal intimacy. The observer noted:

Lohman called across the bay to Waller, "You want to go for a beer?" "You buying?" "Sure I'll buy you one." Marconi is walking by and says, "How about me?" "What about you? I didn't take you to raise; if I buy a beer for you, I'll have every leech in the barracks begging me. "Lohman's tone is almost hostile, and the atmosphere is tense as he and Waller leave the barracks. Marconi just stands in the hall and watches them leave.

The second rule was that the individual should not get sick. Individuals who broke this rule tended to be excluded from barracks drinking groups.

Lamsen was associated with the Gross-Murphy-Barker clique initially, but he has gotten sick and vomited several times, and has not been invited to drink with them since that time. On a couple of occasions I have heard him bragging about his drinking capacity and the great times he has had, but no one seems much interested. Today Barker got up late and was going off post to eat. Lamsen asked him why he didn't get up and eat in the mess hall. Barker responded with contempt, "I didn't know you were a lifer. You like Army food, don't you, lifer? When do you re-up, lifer?" Lamsen protested he was not a lifer, but quickly retreated to his area away from Barker's taunts.

The third rule was derivative of the general barracks norm against informing to the leaders. Individuals who informed about rowdy parties and disturbances were shunned, verbally attacked, or physically assaulted.

Among first-tour soldiers there were a few individuals who showed signs of problem drinking or alcoholism. It appeared as if they could adapt to the structure and operations of barracks living, since they conformed to the major norms, but they happened to like alcohol better than social company. They described themselves as loners, but it was difficult to know whether their isolation antedated or followed their drinking. The observer noted:

Raymond is known as the company alcoholic. He is 24 years old and has been in the Army six years. He claims that he did not drink heavily until Vietnam, although his father is an alcoholic and has been drinking beer as long as he can remember. In Germany he had trouble waking up in the morning, and went AWOL a couple times, but says he has had no serious problems until he came here. He says he never drives when he drinks, but walks or hitch-hikes to the bars near post to prevent accidents. He describes himself as a loner who enjoys beer and bar hopping. He says he drinks $368 worth of beer each month because he enjoys it, but must substitute for others' guard duties to finance his recreation. In this company he has been reduced in rank twice with a promotion in between and currently holds the rank of private. He says, "I enjoy drinking because I like beer. When I drink, I don't want to play pool or listen to anybody's problems. If they want to be friendly and just shoot the shit, fine, but I don't need anybody crying in my beer. I know my limits, and when I reach that point I stop drinking."

The alcoholics were the exception, however, and drinking, whether formally sanctioned or "on our own time," served principally to bring people closer together by providing additional common experiences and by defining and affirming status differences among them.

SUMMARY

This chapter has described alcohol consumption by barracks-dwelling soldiers. Three basic occasions for drinking were discussed: sanctioned drinking, unsanctioned drinking, and drinking external to the formal organization. The first two occasions typically occurred on post, while the latter was more characteristically outside the barracks and away from the post.

Off-post, soldiers frequented four kinds of bars and clubs: "redneck places," "nice places," "tough places," and "dives." The kind of setting selected depending on the activities sought for a particular evening and on the kinds of people that made up particular cliques.

Drinking outside the barracks was of three types: recreational drinking, affirmational drinking, and ceremonial drinking. The first two types were generally within single cliques, while ceremonial drinking involved different cliques. The categories were not sharp or mutually exclusive, since the function of all drinking was to set group boundaries and to affirm group membership. Recreational drinking was mostly adjunctive to other activities, such as bar games and amusements. It provided content for social interaction and frequently resulted in episodes producing a unique history of shared experience for the group members. In affirmational drinking the focus was more on alcohol consumption per se. If the mood was depressed, very heavy drinking resulted in distinctive episodes—even a very severe hangover would do—that rejuvenated the group by providing commonality. When several cliques came together, affirmational drinking shaded into ceremonial drinking, which could involve all of the barracks residents who affirmed their common relationship in "the craziest company in the Army."

Alcohol in the barracks demarcated groups and cliques by binding the members together through shared experiences. This was as true for formally sanctioned drinking as for unsanctioned occasions.

To participate required an absolute minimum of social skill, the willingness to share resources, and the ability to drink without getting sick. As on other occasions, drinking scenes were marked by claims to status, especially in ceremonial drinking. Although the young, first-tour soldiers drank heavily, evidence of problem drinking or alcoholism was rare.

In conclusion, drinking patterns among enlisted men were entirely consonant with the social structure of the barracks already described, and appeared to be integral to maintaining that structure by drawing members of the cliques closer together through their shared experiences while intoxicated.

5

SMOKING WITH THE BOYS

Unlike alcohol, there is no sanction for drug use in the Army except when prescribed by a physician. The unprescribed use of amphetamines, barbiturates, opiates, and hallucinogens is illegal, and that is all there is to it from the view of the formal organization. On their own time, however, soldiers used all of these substances regularly. The purpose of this chapter is to describe the range of experience soldiers had with illicit drugs before they entered the Army, to argue that drug use is entirely consonant with the social structure of the barracks and with life in the Army as described thus far, to demonstrate that drug use is patterned similarly to alcohol use, and to consider the complementary functions of drug and alcohol use in maintaining the social order. Finally, it is argued that drugs and alcohol are not interchangeable since they contribute differently to the generic conditions of social structure.

DRUG USE AS NORMATIVE

To understand drug use in the Army requires an appreciation that such use is *normal* in the context of the barracks. Drug use is no longer the province of an isolated, deviant fringe, but is so thoroughly embedded into barracks activities that at Fort Marshall it was almost as difficult to imagine an evening when someone was not using marijuana as it was to imagine one when someone was not drinking beer.

Given the normative character of drug use, it was not difficult to elicit information if minimal assurances were given concerning confidentiality. However, interviewing about drug use was com-

plicated by the inclination of soldiers, when questioned either individually or in groups, to turn the conversation quickly to
dissatisfaction with life in the Army. The following group interview
was typical:

Interviewer: "Tell me about drug use in the Army."

Pvt. A: "Well, sir, there's a lotta dope used in our unit, no deny-
             ing that. It's mostly grass with a few pills now and then if
             we can get hold of any."

Interviewer: "Any chemicals like acid?"

Pvt. A: "Sure, sometimes [group laughter]. Let's see, there's blot-
             ter acid, and microdot, and mescaline, and [more laugh-
             ter]; but sir, when you're in a unit as screwed up as ours,
             drugs is the only way to make it. ("Yeah, man, dig it,"
             from the group) Like, take for instance our platoon
             sergeant. Last week he got a hair up his ass and ordered a
             full field inspection at six o'clock at night. Man, I just
             couldn't believe it; six o'clock is on my time, and he comes
             up with his off-the-wall mickey mouse inspection. It takes
             three hours to prepare for one."

Pvt. B: "And then he didn't even look at the displays! Just came
             in the barracks and poked his head in one or two rooms. I
             didn't even prepare for it. Fuck him, I just split."

Pvt. C: "Yeah, and remember the time he promised me a pass for
             the weekend, and I was all packed when I saw on the
             board I was up for guard duty that weekend. I was mad. I
             went to him and said . . ."

Pvt. D: "Yeah, and remember when we had Sergeant Kearney?
             Now there was a stupid fucker. . . ."

In like manner the interviewees discussed the sergeants they had
known, the lack of meaningful work, the quality of food at the dining
hall, the lack of privacy in the barracks, the poor equipment, haircuts
and shoe shines, and so forth. Soldiers were not opposed to talking
about their drug use, but without guidance from the interviewer,
they preferred to talk about their life in the Army. Drug use was
simply not a central concern for these men. It was like interviewing
about oral hygiene: after the respondents acknowledged that they
brushed their teeth, they had little else to say on the subject.

PRE-ARMY DRUG USE

Most of the interviewees at Fort Marshall were in junior and senior high school during the nationwide proliferation of drug use that peaked in the late 1960s. Virtually every one of them had either been exposed to or had used drugs before coming into the Army.

Every Army company had an extensive reservoir made up of the pre-induction drug experiences of its members. The most common experiences were with marijuana, chemical hallucinogens, amphetamines, and barbiturates. Moreover, every company was likely to have at least one member who had used cocaine and heroin and who knew how to use a hypodermic syringe. A soldier who had not used a particular substance had no difficulty in finding an experienced teacher among his comrades.

It is now widely believed that drug use declines sharply when individuals enter the Army and undergo the isolation and stress of basic training. Use often increases during Advanced Individual Training, which is less stressful and provides more leisure time. After assignment to a permanent duty station, use typically returns to or exceeds pre-Army levels. The following sections examine more closely the patterns of drug use among soldiers at their permanent duty stations.

DRUG USE AND BARRACKS SOCIAL STRUCTURE

Chapter 3 demonstrated how the barracks social structure at Fort Marshall consisted of a segmented series of groups with overlapping memberships (dyads, triads, and cliques) that could momentarily unite in the common defense by means of a superordinate series of social categories. These categories, discussed previously, included "privates vs. lifers" and "old-timers vs. newbies." Drug use was the basis for still another category, "cool vs. straight." Here, too, membership usually was determined during the first week of acquaintance and incorporation into the existing social structure.

As was noted earlier, the first issue to be settled in the barracks was whether the newcomer was a "regular guy" who would abide by the barracks norms regarding theft, military standards, anti-army sentiments, and squealing. Because drug use was so very prevalent in the barracks, a second determination was necessary, and almost as important as being a "regular guy": whether the newcomer was "cool." That is, did he use drugs or at least tolerate those who did? "Being cool" was simply a derivative of the "regular guy," an acknowledgment that everyone should be allowed to "do his own thing."

Although it was not unknown for Army law enforcement agencies to place undercover agents in the barracks in the guise of privates, the determination of whether a new man was "cool" did not require elaborate questioning or prolonged observation. First, marijuana use in the Army was sufficiently high that the odds were overwhelming that a given individual was "cool." Second, Army drug users were not fools. They knew the rules of admissible evidence and did not worry about hearsay or circumstantial evidence. Unless they were apprehended selling or possessing illicit drugs under rather strictly defined search and seizure procedures, there was little danger of legal entanglement. Third, given the character of the social world, it is very difficult to be a good spy, particularly for a person under 25. A good spy is not obvious in any way, doesn't ask too many questions, and never asks socially inappropriate ones such as, "Where and from whom do you buy your drugs?" He has mastered the language of those being infiltrated. He has a plausible military history, and can talk knowledgeably about where he says he has been. He readily joins into the ongoing activities of the group. As if these requirements were not difficult enough to meet, he must also avoid provocation or entrapment if his testimony is to be accepted in a military court of law. Many soldiers, with certain justification, regarded the use of drugs in a cobehaving group as the ultimate test of whether or not a man was "cool."

Again, the appearance of a new man in the barracks was not greeted with much overt suspicion—that was an everyday occurrence. Drugs provided yet another avenue of commonality on which to build social relations; the newcomer was usually as eager to demonstrate acceptance of drugs as the residents were of ascertaining his drug preference. Critical bits of information were passed so nonchalantly that the actors themselves were seldom aware of the process. The first level of knowledge was verbal. The observer noted:

> I explained my work and asked the new man where he was from. "Okinawa; I was there for 13 months." "I hear there's a lot of drug use there." "Yeah, you can get anything you want. We were pretty isolated up on the mountain, and we used to smoke a lot of dope."

Clothing, hair styles, jewelry, music, and art provided additional cues. Signs of a traditional "head" (drug user) included parting the hair in the middle of the head, wearing a beaded necklace or bracelet, wearing wire-rimmed spectacles, listening to hard rock music, wearing tie-dyed or embroidered clothing, and displaying dayglo posters with black lights. A soldier who used drugs or tolerated their use did not necessarily display any or all of these signs, but if he did, the most plausible inference was that he was "cool."

> Marco had his hair parted in the middle last night, and was working on his jeans. He had split the side seams and sewn in towels to create flared legs, and was busily sewing on patches. He chuckled as he showed me the patch on his rear pocket, "Kiss my Patch," and the "One Way" patch with an arrow to his crotch. He was also wearing a "Mr. Natural" T-shirt.

If any doubt remained after talking with and observing the new man, the ultimate test was to ask him to smoke.

> Parrish was the meanest man in the company and feared by most everyone. He was getting short, with less than two months remaining in service. He was said to have an "attitude problem" in that he refused to salute officers and was always two minutes late for everything. Tonight he lit a "J," ambled over to the new man, struck up a conversation, and passed the cigarette to him. He said when he returned to his area, "He's cool; no sweat."

Being judged "cool" implied either drug use or approval of those who used. It was not absolutely necessary to use. Nonusers with high status among users had used in the past, but for various reasons chose not to use at present. For example, there was the case of the soldier who was said to have "fried his brain" during high school. Another example was the soldier who reported, "I don't criticize drug users; after all, I get drunk a lot, and what's the difference? I also burn incense in my room because I like the smell." The observer was also judged "cool" in that he was assumed to approve of use, but was prevented from using because of his job.

The category "drug user" was a functional social superordinate to the cliques. It was impossible for every user to observe every other user in the act of using a drug. Thus the practice developed of having a known member vouch for the "coolness" of a stranger. Vouching worked well in face-to-face encounters, but was useless when a soldier was transferred to another unit. Other mechanisms were required to proclaim membership as a drug user and to learn which barracks mates were also sympathetic. Such initial exchanges were extremely important since they defined the potentials for social affiilation in the new environment. Therefore, signs and symbols evolved which denoted drug use and thus encouraged further self-disclosure. One of the more subtle signals was the handshake. Drug users tended to grasp each other's thumbs when they shook hands in ways that were borrowed from blacks. The thumb handshake was not invariably a signal of drug use, but provided a cue. Other cues were embedded in the language of users. Dubbing a car "the roach coach," or speaking of "getting blown away" or "wrecked" or "getting off" or "getting high," had specific meanings for the drug users. Again, use of these constructions was not invariably associated with use, but added evidence for a plausible inference. The linguistic constructions could be used in any verbal statement, whether or not it was related to drug use, and the signal still functioned to define the speaker as a user. For example, "burned out" with drug-using circles meant having used too much, too long, or too frequently, to the point that the user was exhausted and incapable of functioning.

> Craft was spraying his tent with insect repellent. A bug crawled across the ground, and he sprayed it. As the bug lay on its back struggling, Craft said, "What's the matter, little bug? You all burned out?"

There were other ways to proclaim membership without incurring risk. The soldier in the field with a packet of cigarette papers in the band of his helmet was issuing an invitation to other users to open lines of communication. Similarly, wearing a religious symbol on a chain around the neck had a meaning for those familiar with it, as did wearing a cocaine spoon or a roach clip. Clothing styles also functioned as signals of inclusion and invitation. The observer noted:

> The six guys from the cooks' room, where I have often smelled mari-juana burning, are seated together. They look the part of heads. Their hair exceeds regulation length and is parted in the middle. Two wear wire-rimmed glasses with tinted lenses. One has on a T-shirt with a picture of a marijuana plant and the slogan, "The flowers of all the tomorrows are the seeds of today." They all wear faded blue jeans with embroidered flowers or patches that read, "Keep on Truckin'."

Everyone who proclaimed membership in the drug-using group through language, clothing, personal appearance, or possessions did, at least, use marijuana. The converse was not true, however, for many drug users were reluctant to identify themselves publicly. Yet all users knew the signals and could identify persons most likely to be users without extensive face-to-face interaction with them.

To maintain a group boundary requires that the out-group be as carefully specified as the in-group. Among drug users there were two out-groups. The first consisted of the sergeants and officers, who were an out-group for all lower-ranking enlisted soldiers. The boundary here was maintained by means of "getting-over" stunts.

> The platoon sergeant was furious with Roberts and Sexton this morning. They had taken some old fatigues, stuffed them with newspapers in effigy of an old sergeant, and had hung the effigy by the neck in their area. The sign said, "Lifers, Beware!"

For drug-using groups, "getting over on the sergeant" typically involved demonstrating his ignorance of drugs and drug use.

> Bunsen again told the story of the platoon sergeant complimenting him on the "tomato" plant he was growing on his window sill, and praising him for taking pride in his room. "It was a marijuana plant, but the stupid fucker never knew."

The second out-group for drug users consisted of the otherwise regular guys in the barracks who were not "cool": those who did not approve of drug use and made no secret of their disapproval. These men were found in elite units, and they objected to drug use because it was incompatible with their images of themselves and the unit. One way to define them as outsiders was to taunt them about their inability to detect drug intoxication. But more importantly, they defined themselves as outsiders by their moral judgments. The observer noted:

> Warner and I began talking about drug use in the platoon. "I can understand why the guys smoke, but I can't see it for myself. Basically, they're insecure, immature, and unable to face their problems. They are seeking an escape and find it in drugs and alcohol." "Is that the only reason they use?" "No, part of it is lack of imagination. You can only watch so much television, play so much basketball, and things like that. It's not like leaving the Army behind you at the end of the day and going home to a wife and family. When you have to face the barracks every night, you tend to go up the wall, so they smoke to get away. The barracks is home for me, so I take pride in my room, and spend a lot of time fixing it up and keeping it neat."

Besides viewing themselves as superior to the users, the men who were "uncool" posed other threats. The observer continued:

> I asked Warner about use in the barracks. "I told them that's one thing I'm firmly against, and I'd turn their asses in if I ever saw or caught anyone using. They can do it on their own time, but not when everyone might get in trouble."

When they threatened to turn others in for drug use, nonusers were really maintaining the boundary between themselves and the users, for they subscribed to the barracks norm of not informing, and were simply warning the users of the conditions under which the norm could be broken fairly.

> "The problem in the barracks is that the men just don't trust one another. The privates have to stick together. Take the drinking party on duty the other night when Donnally turned in that list of names. That's not right. The first sergeant asked me who smokes in the platoon, but I don't go for squealing." As a matter of fact, Warner did find three men smoking in Patton's room, but just told them to get it out of the barracks, and they complied.

Although the nonusers provided a convenient out-group for the users, they had much in common with them:

> Warner continued, "One night Randolph came in high on speed and was so paranoid, he didn't think he could pull his guard shift. Wilson took his place and covered for him. I respect him because he at least had enough sense to realize he was unfit for duty. The same thing happened to me, only I was so drunk they had to carry me to my room. Turpin covered for me that night. Maybe we're all a little bit insecure."

The boundary between drug users and nonusers in the barracks was not so impermeable that the nonusers were oblivious to what the users were doing. After all, they spent a good deal of time working, drinking, and talking together. The observer noted:

> McDonald was telling me about drugs in the platoon. "Only about six of us in the barracks don't do drugs, and I'll tell you who . . . I've never tried them myself, and am totally against it, but it's up to the individual. The only time I get concerned is when it interferes with duty like when they are speeding or on acid. One time, Turpin and I had to get up early, and there were about five other guys already up—people who usually don't get up early at all. At formation I realized that just

about everyone was up, and I knew they were all speeding. I found out
that someone had brought in 100 tabs of speed. The whole platoon was
speeding for two days, and they didn't think anyone knew about it."

Another way of marking the boundary between users and
nonusers was through verbal banter or put-downs that usually resulted from a nonuser's assertion of moral superiority.

McDonald started his drug harangue to the amusement of everyone.
"Now, what a man does on his own time and in the confines of his own
home is his own business. I personally don't condone illegal acts like
drugs anywhere or anytime, particularly in an elite unit like this. Don't
ask me specifics, that's just the way I feel. I was brought up to respect
the law, and I'm pretty inflexible about that point. Maybe I am a redneck, but I've got *balls*. It always takes a man with balls to speak out for
what's right, and to keep police departments free from bribery and
corruption. Even though I may get my own ass whipped, it's because of
people like me that you can be assured of a safe sleep tonight." As he
walked to the door, someone said, "Don't wrinkle your cape when you
go to sleep." "Fuck you."

The drug of choice for the nonusers was alcohol, and occasionally the boundary between the in-group and out-group was marked
by verbal or even physical assault. Such incidents were sufficient to
maintain the in-group belief about the proclivity of drinkers for vio-
lence. There was always the potential for the kind of "heads versus
juicers" conflict that caused divisiveness within the American units in
Vietnam:

Bunsen has been temporarily relieved of duty, and spends his days
lying around the barracks. McDonald comes into my room, complaining of being tired and overworked, and Bunsen says, "I know
what you mean, sleeping all day with the weekends off is tough on me,
too." McDonald interrupts, "I'm going to beat your fucking ass, Bunsen, before I leave here; step outside and I'll beat the shit out of you
with one hand tied behind me. You fuckers on drugs never do any
work, and are a disgrace to the corps." he then turns on Marcusi: "The
same goes for you, Dago. I'll put your fucking head through this wall."
As McDonald returns to calling Bunsen "fatso" and "tubby," Marcusi
shrugs and says, "How did I get into this mess? I'm just an innocent
bystander." He then puts his arm around McDonald's shoulder and
says, "Come on, let's go watch 'Police Story.'" "Don't touch me, you
wop. I'll beat your ass, too." Marcusi steps back, smiles, pinches
McDonald's cheek, and leaves the room. McDonald glowers and then
explodes, "That did it," and follows Marcusi out. There are curses in

the hall; when I look out, they are eye-to-eye with clenched fists. I call to McDonald to come get his alarm clock because I was going to sleep. He tells me he had about six beers that evening, and apologizes to Bunsen and Marcusi the next day for being drunk.

As discussed previously, much of the verbal banter and social interaction in the barracks involved claims and assertions of status or position within the group, made with the medium of goods and services available for social exchange. The rule did not change with drug use. Blatant proclamation of affiliation with drug users by word, dress, or deed was an assertion of status in the drug-using community. Not only did those who talked or groomed themselves in distinctive ways proclaim identity with drug users, but they also won approval from others in personifying the barracks norms of pushing military standards to the limit and demonstrating contempt for the Army. A leader who criticized drug-related dress, demeanor, or deportment was therefore likely to evoke "private versus lifers" alliances that would result in sympathy, support, and status for the "persecuted" drug user.

The very symbols of drug use could also provide more direct benefits, such as a pleasing ambience for interaction.

Quincey stops in Marcusi's room. "Man, this is really some room; there's another like it down the hall, but this is something else." Marcusi motions for him to slip off the light as he plugs in the black light affixed to the ceiling. The whole room is immediately transformed into another world as Quincey gazes in amazement. Four geometric posters almost seem to move in the illumination. A picture of a rising sun also glows in the darkness. On another wall is a poster of a long-hair in yogi position, smoking dope, with the caption "Dope will get you through times of no money better than money will get you through times with no dope." Quincey moves cautiously around the room, chuckling at the sign on the desk, "Off limits to E5 and Above," and recites the poem on another poster by Craig Lawrence Green. A glowing mobile depicts the hat, moustache, and shoes of Charlie Chaplin that hangs from fish netting tacked in folds holding soda caps. Several dayglo stickers are affixed to the locker, and the window shade and walls are speckled with dayglo paint. From under the bunk Marcusi takes his prize possession, the skull of a cow painted in six different colors. He also shows them a pair of cork-sole clogs he has painted in a similar fashion. Quincey is fascinated with the room, so Marcusi puts the skull on the pillow and gently moves the mattress, giving the illusion that the skull is moving by itself. "Freaky, man, far out," says Quincey as he leaves the room.

Most barracks "heads" had to rely on the personal supplies of drug-using buddies. Drugs came into a unit in dribs and drabs, depending upon who was last home and successful in "scoring," so the drug users were not assured of a constant supply. Finding drugs for sale in the Army was mostly a matter of asking other drug users. The observer noted:

> Cresswell and I were sitting on the barracks steps, and he was muttering, "Damn, I could use some dope right now . . . aw, fuck, I wish I knew who had some dope to sell . . . shit, I don't have any money anyhow. . . ." Godfrey came by from the motor pool, and Cresswell casually asked, "You got any dope to sell?" "Nope. Just sold my last half ounce." "You got anything else?" "Nothing for sale. Did you check with Adams?" "Yeah, but he doesn't have any to sell."

If a user smoked marijuana in the presence of another user, he was obligated to share, but not to sell. Nevertheless a drug user had the right to approach any other drug user regarding a purchase, even if they were only casual acquaintances.

> Spitz told me he had gone to Darnell's apartment to buy some marijuana, but Darnell was not there. On the way out, he saw two men from another company to whom Darnell had once introduced him. "I kinda poked my head in the door, said, "I didn't know you two guys lived here," and saw they had some dope. "I said, 'You got any for sale?' They said, 'No, nothing but our personal stash; come on in and have a bowl with us.' I ended up smoking the whole afternoon with them."

Local contacts for buying drugs were comparatively rare for soldiers, and were based on past associations in the Army either during basic training, Advanced Individual Training, or service at the current post.

> Bunsen told me there are 200 hits of speed around the company. They were obtained from a guy who used to be in the company, but has been discharged and is now living in a town about 20 miles from the post.

When local contacts were used, the transaction usually occurred off the post. The observer noted:

> As I drove up to the barracks, Frisco called out, "Can you give me a ride to the quick-stop grocery store on 245? I've got to make a phone call." "Why not call from here?" "No, I have to call a guy in Lockwood to see

if he has any dope; I don't want to call from an Army phone." As we drove off post, Frisco explained, "This guy was supposed to get me a pound. I have to call him to see if he has it. If he does, he'll bring it out to me and give me a ride back." "Do you always work out of the quick-stop?" "No, I just don't like to call from post." Outside the phone booth, I listened to the call. "Hey, man, this is Frisco . . . OK . . . yeah, that's cool . . . we're at the quick-stop just before post on 245 . . . about 15 minutes? We'll go across the highway to the 500 Club for a beer . . . OK, see you, man."

Contacts with civilian dealers were mostly a matter of chance. Even in a large city, soldiers had little luck, because they lacked familiarity and connections.

Peters, Gino, Grady, and Loveless were laughing and joking in the barracks. They had just returned from the city, where they had gone to do some "dealing." They were talking to some "cats" when a cop walked up. They all ran in different directions, eventually regrouped, and drove back to post.

Most buying took place in hometowns where contacts were known and trusted. The buyer was usually interested only in his drug of choice, typically marijuana, so someone in the market for a hallucinogen or pills had to contact a soldier who regularly used those substances. Learning who had what for sale was no problem; it was a staple of conversation among users.

At about 11:00, the people started coming back from the weekend. Darnell, Bunsen and Wolfson came into Patton's room to catch up on the gossip. Wolfson said he couldn't find any grass at home; Patton said he saw Godfrey with a whole bag of rolled "J's" over the weekend, and that Walters had some grass he was trying to sell. Bunsen mentioned that he had a chance to buy some LSD for $3 a tab. "I tried one, and it was good, but that is too much money for any LSD." The others agreed. Darnell mentioned he had some good chocolate mescaline a few weeks back, and wondered whether there would be any more around.

As drug consumers, soldiers were not very sophisticated as to what exactly they were using. The important thing was the psychological effect of the substance. The observer noted:

There seems to be a lot of THC around lately. Loveless and Kenny were discussing it, and I asked what the initials stood for. "Tetrahydrochloride [sic]; it's supposed to be in grass, but not in the tranquilizer PCP. It makes you feel mellow. The stuff that's going around now is not really THC, but just some chemical on a tab." Kenny disagreed and argued it was THC, and sold me an orange tab for $2 to have analyzed. I then asked Grady about the chemistry of THC. "I don't know; I just take 'em. It's not as harsh as PCP." He used his hands to describe PCP by pounding his fist into his hand, while for THC he slowly drew his hands open. "I could take THC all my life and be happy."

Neither were users very much concerned about weights and measures. Marijuana was sold in kilos, pounds, lids, and ounces without reference to a scale. The quantity was determined visually, and so long as both parties were satisfied, there was no reason to be more exact.

Bunsen explained he had bought the hash from Peters. "I actually got more than a gram. See, hash comes in a stick about six inches long, and Peters didn't know how to cut it. So I broke it into four pieces that we agreed were about half a gram each. I took the three biggest pieces for $7 a piece. I could have got a whole ounce for $100, but didn't have the money. Let's see, there are 32 grams to the ounce, right?" I asked why Peters didn't cut the hash. "He doesn't deal much with hash, so he doesn't know that much about it. Christ, he only really deals in dope; just about all the chemicals he gets from me."

Selling drugs was the complement to buying them and occurred in the same casual fashion. The observer noted a typical transaction:

Frazier comes into the area, looking for a ride to the snack shop for a late-night free meal. He watches television a while and says, "Hey, Murph, you got any weed you want to sell?" "No, but I can get you some," "Like a nickel." "Sure, it's Jamaican; I plan to get a lid for myself. You can try it to see if you want any. I'm buying this weekend, and you can pay me on Monday. I'll be taking orders till I leave on Friday."

The observer drove Frazier to the snack shop, and then Frazier proposed that they look up a buddy of his from Korea who was assigned to the nearby medical unit.

Frazier wasn't sure where his friend lived, so we entered one barracks and were told by three different people they had never heard of his friend. He walked to the next building, smelled some marijuana at one door, knocked, and said, "Is Boren in there? This is Frazier." We entered the room where three men were drinking beer, smoking joints, and watching television. No introductions were made, and shortly the heavy blond said, "Any of you want to buy pills?" "What do you have?" "Phenobarb; three for a dollar." "No, man, it's too near pay-day."

Selling drugs in the Army was more a friendly gesture that maintained personal status among drug users than a business proposition. Clearly there was money to be made in dealing drugs (one soldier reported buying a pound of marijuana for $80 and selling it in ounces for $200), but most soldiers found the risks in transporting and storing large quantities not worth the effort.

> Bunsen said that at home he buys a pound or two in Ann Arbor, and then sells it to his friends. "But I just don't want to take the risk of carrying that much in my car across the state lines."

Another soldier reported a similar story that revealed he was hardly a big-time operator:

> "One time I flew back here with five ounces in my AWOL bag. At the airport it was the only bag on the luggage turntable, just going round and round. I thought it would be a perfect set-up for the narcs who were just waiting to see who was going to pick up that bag. Finally, I picked it up and started down the hall. Here came a cop with a dog. I ripped the tag off with one hand, set the bag near a post, and just kept walking. The dog came within eight inches of it and kept on walking. I circled back and picked it up, but I was scared shitless."

In fact, one of the major concerns for a soldier selling marijuana was to avoid having to store large quantities. The observer noted:

> O'Neill told me he almost got into a fight today with Darnell. "You see, I sold him an ounce of grass yesterday, a big ounce at that, but he didn't have any money; said he'd pay today. Today he says he still doesn't have the money and wants to give it back to me. Now I might have been wrong, but I tried to make him take it and pay for it. He pushed me, and I was ready to hit him when Gregory stepped in. I hate to have the stuff lying around here. I'd really like to sell it, but there's so much of it around this week."

People who sold drugs on post seldom considered themselves "dealers" or "pushers." They saw themselves as entrepreneurs with a reputation to protect. Their sales activities secured favored status within drug-using groups, in addition to providing money. Mary Jane was such a person, a civilian who had begun dealing while engaged to a drug-using soldier, and who retained her contacts by hanging around Boomtown:

> "I deal mostly in grass now, half pounds and pounds. No more of this ounce shit for me, I'm too well-known. Besides, it's a hell of a lot of work selling ounces; frankly, it's exhausting because you have to do lots of running around and really work at it full time. In dealing pounds, I don't even have to leave home, and I still make as much money as before."

To stay in business, it was necessary to carry only quality merchandise.

> "I like cocaine, too; it moves fast. I don't mess with any shit [heroin]. That's how my ex-fiance and I got such a good business going. We tried most everything, and wouldn't sell it if we didn't like it."

Like any business, there were fair and unfair marketing practices. Mary Jane continued:

> "I do it mostly for the money—hell, I made $1,100 in one month last summer—and because it is fun. But I don't believe in price gouging; I can't see it. Last fall I bought 200 hits of speed for $160. I sold them to Ron Barquist over in the signal company for $180; that's about a 15% mark-up that is about standard profit. It's fair, I figure, 'cause I go to some trouble to get it, and I have to live, too, y'know. Well, he was selling them $1.80 a hit, 100% profit! Now that's a real rip-off, and I really got mad and let him know about it. I told him that if I ever sold to him again it would cost him $330 just to teach him a lesson. Ripping people off like that gives all of us a bad name."

And so it went from day to day as barracks mates gossiped about prices, supplies, getting ripped off, and "scoring big." The "brand names" were continually changing, along with debates on the merits of Jamaican, Lebanese, Colombian, and Panamanian grass, the scarcity of "Buddha" or of "elephant weed," the contrasts between THC and PCP, and the effects of "Orange Sunshine," "Strawberry Acid," "Purple Haze," "Window Pane," "chocolate mescaline," "cosmos," and "microdots." It mattered not a whit that only one man in the group may have tried the substance; the effects were private experiences that could not be challenged, and besides, "Drugs work differently in different people." For the barracks dweller it was not drug consumption that was so important, but the talk that preceded and surrounded consumption. One of the most critical and valued commodities was something new and different to talk about. In some circles talk may be cheap, but in the barracks it had to be manufactured if social groups were to remain alive. Recounting drinking episodes was one way of generating talk; buying and selling drugs was another.

Such talk produced a sense of belonging to a group that was more extensive and more stable than the cliques of coworkers, a group more enduring than drinking buddies who repeatedly indulged to generate memorable episodes which maintained their boundaries, a group marked by commonalities that went beyond the present moment, and a group that permitted the individual to rise above the cliques, to maintain multiple clique membership, to change cliques when transfers eliminated the existing ones, and to enter existing cliques even though a stranger. The talk surrounding drug use provided a "we" in the barracks. Whenever a newcomer was told of the kind of people he had joined, the only stories available to link everyone together were from the drug users. The observer recalled:

> In the mess hall, Cressey told me about the history of the barracks. "We are the crazies. Not the real crazies, they're all gone, but I knew some guys who used to run with them. Hell, everyone was high before they brushed their teeth in the morning; guys used to fire up [inject needles] right in the barracks. They didn't give a shit what they did or who knew about it; they just didn't care. One guy was a narc. They hung him by his heels out the third story window and threatened to drop him. He still didn't get the message, so they strapped him in his bunk while he was sleeping, then poured lighter fluid around the bed and lit it. He didn't get hurt, but it sure scared the shit out of him. Funniest thing, he transferred out of the company the next day."

A similar story was recounted in another barracks:

> Bunsen chuckled and said, "I know why you're studying us; we are the 'head' platoon. Just be careful that you don't have any accidents like poor Wilkins. He started running off his mouth about turning a list of names into the orderly room. Gregory arrested him and brought him before the court where Darnell was the judge. Wolfson was the prosecuting attorney, and Loveless tried to defend him, but Wilkins wouldn't say anything. He got sentenced to the shower, but on the way, the lights went out and he must have stumbled into a couple of door jambs on his way. I think the cold shower was good for his bruises, but he got transferred out of the unit anyway."

In part these stories of the history of the group derived from the illegal status of drugs, but in another sense they were simply reflections of the general barracks "rule" against informing about barracks activities to anyone in formal authority. Thus, whenever there was reason to invoke the rule, "Privates stick together," the drug users provided the foci around which all privates, users and nonusers, were mobilized. An individual could be harassed for informing, but he was in no real danger unless a number of cliques could be united into a single group to enforce the norms. Drug use, with the stories that surrounded it, was one of the few ways to unite the barracks.

OCCASIONS FOR DRUG USE

Drug Use During Duty Hours

Both marijuana and beer were used during duty hours, but marijuana was more convenient. It left no telltale odor on the breath, and there were no containers to dispose of. Guard duty, of course, provided the best opportunity to use with almost no risk of detection.

> Barner came into the barracks between guard shifts, looking a little glassy-eyed. He joined two other guards who were drinking beer, and later explained to me, "We usually just drink between shifts, but on guard everybody smokes. The lifers get a little uptight if they see you walking with a rifle in one hand and a beer in the other, but no one notices if you're smoking a cigarette."

Any isolated duty like walking patrols, barracks orderly, or MP patrols after midnight provided a suitable occasion to smoke a "J." For such tasks, remaining awake was the only requirement.

The noon hour was considered a good time to smoke. Work groups that were located at a distance from the dining hall often took a circuitous route in the "roach coach," and one such group dubbed itself "The let's-get-fucked-up-for-lunch-bunch." The observer noted:

> Five of us leave the motor pool in Randolph's car. As we drive off post, Miller said, "Roll up the windows so we can get it nice and smoky in here." The joint comes to Randolph and then to me. "You don't smoke?" "Not while I'm working." "You'll get high with the windows up; blow some smoke this way, Miller. . . ." "Did you hear about the 42 tons of grass they burned in Virginia?" "You shoulda been in Germany; I was the biggest cutter there. I could cut a gram of speed in five

minutes. . . ." "Where we gonna eat, Consolidated or the hospital?"
"Hospital has better food." "Let's eat at Consolidated so I can get some
more dope." "OK, you convinced me."

After lunch, two of the group went for more marijuana while the
other three waited in the car, sleeping and listening to the radio.

Miller and Rogers return to the car, and Miller gives Randolph a metal
cigarette case, explaining that he and Rogers have to go to the orderly
room. We drive to the motor pool, but the gates are locked. "What time
is it?" "Five to one; we might as well go to the car and smoke a joint."
"Good idea." The joint is passed until it burns down. "You got a clip?"
"No, but drop the roach in the cigarette lighter." They pass the lighter
back and forth, inhaling the smoke until there is nothing but the paper
burning. "Hey, man, you want some speed?" "I got six hits." "I could
sure use some to get through the day." Randolph takes six small white
pills from a baggie in his pocket and gives three to Carson, who swallows them immediately. Randolph swallows two, snorts some powder
from the third, and then swallows it.

It was not necessary to be in an automobile, for the barracks
served equally well during the post-luncheon nap. The observer continued:

Zambioski and I entered the barracks about noon. He called to a black
near the orderly room. "Hey, Woods, you fucking nigger, what are you
doing loitering in the hall? You got any smoke?" His tone was obviously joking. Woods looked apprehensively toward the first sergeant's
door and said he didn't have any. Upstairs, Zambioski awakened Rutta
with the same approach. Rutta said, "What about the narc?" "It's okay,
he's cool." With that, Rutta withdrew a hand-rolled cigarette from his
pocket, and they sat on the bed, smoking and talking about how little
time they had left in the service.

In the field, the observer watched a card game near a small
campfire:

"Where'd Mendez go?" "Probably taking a piss." "Don't play that one,
I'm getting all the fucking diamonds again. . . ." About 15 minutes
later, Mendez, Barry, and Walters returned from the camp perimeter.
Judging from their meandering walk, sly smiles, and occasional giggling, I inferred they had been smoking. Dobson said, "Where'd you
guys go?" "Oh, just went for a walk [knowing smile] about 50 yards
that-a-way." "Thanks a helluva lot; you take off and don't tell me."
"You were playing cards and we didn't want to bother you." "Fuck it,

let's go back out, c'mon." Walters had gone directly to his tent, and Mendez said, "We just came back, maybe a little later." I said something about how I could tell they had really enjoyed their walk. Barry smiled, but Mendez looked at me apprehensively until Dobson cut in, "Don't sweat him, Mendez, he's cool." Mendez immediately relaxed and began talking about the experience, drug effects, and his feelings about use.

On duty, alcohol and drugs were used in moderation, which not only reduced the chances of detection, but enabled the individual to function reasonably well in the improbable circumstance that he had to exercise some degree of judgment or take on a difficult task. Occasionally, events would conspire against even the best-laid plans:

> Bunsen admitted to me that he was tripping on acid when he wrecked the jeep. "Yeah, I took some 'nice' before I went on duty and was tripping my fucking brains out. I wasn't even supposed to be driving, but the sergeant changed plans and I had to take Mercer to his area and then drive to my own. He drove to his post; I could barely see. All the car lights had trails that were beautiful. When I took the wheel, I really got into the needles on the dashboard and BANG, there's this dumb broad stopped at a stop sign. Somehow I pulled myself together. They couldn't prove I was drunk—no smell or anything like that—so all they did was suspend me from duty pending an Article 15 [nonjudicial punishment] for dereliction of duty."

Accidents were rare, however, for as with alcohol, drugs were mainly used after duty hours. Because of their illegal status, drugs were used and shared in private, secluded places where the possibility of surveillance was minimal. Quite naturally the barracks became a favored, if not ideal, place to indulge in drugs.

Drug Use in the Barracks

Once a few of the influential residents had vouched for him, the observer was able to blend into the barracks drug scene without becoming a disruptive influence. After his first night, he commented:

> At about 11:30, the only people awake in the barracks were several blacks clustered in the Prescott-Peterson area. Gross began talking with Prescott in a relaxed, familiar manner: "Hey, man, what's happ'nin?" I followed him, hoping to observe the interracial interaction, and watched them intently before looking around the group. I looked down as Prescott looked up from his bunk, and I suddenly realized he was

rolling a joint. He immediately threw the unrolled paper on the blanket next to the baggie of marijuana, laughed, and exclaimed in mock astonishment, "Where'd that come from? I've never seen that before. Who put that shit on my bunk?" I laughed along with the others and said in mock seriousness, "Don't try to deny it; I saw that fall out of your pocket." Prescott protested again until I said (this time in earnest), "Hey, man, just roll your joint and cut the shit." He shrugged amid the laughter and returned to his rolling. After he rolled two joints, he lit one and encouraged us to stay and smoke. Gross said, "No, you guys go on. I'm about to turn in." I agreed, as we left the area after Prescott had taken the first hit, and Peterson had lit a stick of incense.

Smoking marijuana in the barracks was hardly secret knowledge because almost everyone who spent appreciable free time there was a "regular guy" who was "cool."

After the touch football game we returned to the bay. Murphy took his TV from his locker, turned to "Get Smart," and casually withdrew a "J" from his pocket and began smoking. He offered it to Gross and me, but we refused, Gross because of his New Year's resolution to quit, and me because of my job. Murphy continued to smoke openly and in a very relaxed manner, using a matchbook (since he could not find his roach clip) to handle the butt. Barker came from the shower and got a quart of beer from the refrigerator. He took a long swallow, passed it to Gross, who took a swig, and then passed it to me.

The use of drugs in the barracks was scarcely more circumspect. After his third night, the observer noted:

When I entered the barracks, Gunderson and Rogers were lying on their bunks, listening to Franklin's tape recorder. Four men in the Murphy-Barker area were drinking beer and discussing their 40-to-0 football loss earlier in the evening. After several beers, Gross told me that Gunderson and Rogers were on cocaine, and I paid closer attention to that area. Most of the evening they just lay quietly on their bunks, listening to "The Grateful Dead." Occasionally they got up to imitate the guitar or drum player.

Barracks partitioned into individual rooms offered even more privacy for using drugs, but the distinctive odor of burning marijuana was a very public statement of what was taking place behind closed doors. Nevertheless, the occupant of an individual room did have greater flexibility in determining what others could know about his drug use in the barracks. The observer continued:

I wandered down to Patton's room because I heard a TV on at that end of the hall. When I knocked on the door, he yelled. "Who is it?" stirred around, and eventually opened the door. I saw some wooden matches on his bed, and he said, "As you can see, I am a natural arsonist. You can't get these big wooden matches just anywhere; you have to order them from a professional supply house." I noticed bits of marijuana on his bed under some match books, and suspected he had been rolling "J's." Loveless and Nelson then came into the room, and Loveless pulled a "J" from his pocket. He and Nelson began playing around with it, and Loveless finally lit it. Patton, looking very surprised, said, "Hey, man, you're crazy. Get that stuff out of my room." Loveless held the smoke in his lungs, then rushed for the outside door, where he exhaled. He and Nelson finished the "J" on the fire balcony.

In some prestige units, such as the Military Police, Military Intelligence, and the President's Honor Guard, there are professional norms against using drugs, and there are definite pressures to inform on those who do. These arise from an interest in preserving the unit's image. In such units, drug consumption in full view of the "uncool" was somewhat risky, so the users left the barracks, consumed the drug, and then rejoined the barracks group. The observer noted:

Gino came into my room, obviously stoned and not worrying about it. He said, "I was up on the hill behind the barracks—near the chapel, you know, but it was like Grand Central Station. I was sitting up in the woods, smoking, when three people walked by and damn near tripped over me. Then I watched two medics walk by on the road, and finally a car turned around and shined its lights right on me. That was too much, so I went to another section of the woods that Grady had shown me one time. Finally, I got to smoke my 'J' in peace. It was really nice— peaceful and quiet, you know."

Detecting drug intoxication depended largely on the circumstances and the experience of the observer. When there was no reason to conceal it, the intoxicated state was obvious.

Egan came into the room. His walk was slow, his eyes dilated and glassy, and he smiled constantly. Gino asked if he was with the guys on the hill. Walters and Grady also came back looking dazed, but ever-smiling.

Under other circumstances, however, detection was virtually impossible. A good example was the case of two soldiers who stepped outside the barracks to take a hallucinogen; they returned to gossip in the presence of a companion opposed to drug use.

> McDonald had told me several days ago that he could easily spot any-one on drugs. As we were talking, Gino and Grady returned from dropping some acid outside the barracks. The conversation centered on McDonald's recent leave, the upcoming inspection, the rumored transfer of the unit to another post, and the possibility of the first sergeant being promoted to sergeant major. Gino then mocked McDonald: "You smart motherfucker. Here we sit gossiping, while Grady and I are tripping our brains out. Inspector McDonald, the super undercover narc." McDonald didn't condemn them directly, but launched into his usual tirade: "Anyone on drugs deserves whatever they get, be it prison or an overdose. It's all their own business, but I have no sympathy for them at all. If I ever caught anyone using on duty, I would put them on sick call or turn them in." "Bullshit. I was speeding on duty with you night before last, and you didn't notice a thing."

A minor variation on stepping out of the barracks was using while driving, colloquially known as "going trucking."

> Bunsen said, "The food was so bad in the mess hall tonight it looks like we'll have to make an early food run. You wanna go trucking?" On the drive to the store, Bunsen and two others circulated a pipe with a block of hashish in it. Cramer was drinking bourbon and seven, and offered to share it with me. After buying orange juice, cupcakes, and apple turnovers, they relit the pipe. "I wonder what the MPs are doing on the strip tonight?" "Probably got a call to pick up a guy out of uniform. Hey, man, pull into Frank's so we can get some wine." As Grady went to get two bottles of Wild Mountain, Bunsen relit the hash cube, quite unmindful of the two county police cars in the lot next to us. In the parking lot, Grady asked, "Anyone want another hit?" but no one accepted because it was very difficult to keep the hash cube burning evenly.

Storage of drugs in the barracks presented a minor problem: pills and powder were easily concealed, but marijuana was bulky and required a little ingenuity. The most cautious users stored their drugs in abandoned buildings, broom closets, and heating ducts. Bolder users kept marijuana in their cars or in their bedposts. The rule here was to maintain the supply in a "public place" that could not be traced to the individual user. Only the most cautious went to such bother, however. The vast majority kept marijuana in their wall lockers among their personal possessions.

> The group started talking about storing marijuana. "I always use a bedpost. If anyone finds it, I just say that it belonged to the guy who had the bed before me." "Shit, I always keep mine in the bottom of the tennis ball can with two balls on top of it." "What a pain. I keep mine in the pocket of my uniform in my locker. On inspections, they just want to know if I have the uniform displayed. They never pull a complete shakedown unless they're out to get you."

Thus drugs were used openly and regularly in the barracks and the immediate vicinity in ways that are essentially equivalent to the use of beer and liquor.

PATTERNS OF DRUG USE

Like drinking, the use of drugs assumed recreational, affirmational, and ceremonial patterns.

Recreational Use

The previous chapter described recreational use of beer that was so thoroughly integrated with other activities that the participants hardly considered it "drinking." The same was true for marijuana and certain other illicit drugs. As a case in point, four Fort Marshall soldiers went to a "redneck" bar one Saturday night to shoot pool and laugh at the other patrons. They smoked marijuana on the way to the bar, and drank beer inside. They then went to the German-American Club to drink beer and dance polkas. On the way they smoked more marijuana. At midnight the group decided to go to the hotel dive to watch the stripper. On the way they smoked marijuana, and drank beer while watching the show. On the way back to the barracks, they smoked more marijuana.

On other occasions, however, the activities that accompanied drug use were not equivalent to those associated with beer drinking. Drug use was seldom associated with competitive activities, such as barroom games. Instead, drug users tended to seek altered perceptual awareness or heightened sensory input. The user might indeed play a pinball machine, but his attention was focused more on the sounds and flashing lights than on the total score. Thus, with recreational drug use, a seemingly innocuous experience could be transformed into a "big night out."

> Gino said that he and Grady had just returned from a large toy store. "We dropped some acid after supper, and were really fucked up. The toy store was absolutely freaky with all of the colors on the boxes mixing and trailing. Gino really got into the stuffed animals. He just stood there staring and stroking, staring and stroking."

The observer recorded a similar description, somewhat analogous to bar-hopping:

> "The four of us dropped some acid and drove to the shopping mall . . . we just walked around looking at the stores, fountains, and the people. . . . Stevens and I started following some chicks, and ended up walking down the service road behind the mall. I don't know what happened to the chicks . . . then I went to the car, sat on the fender, and really got into the traffic and the people. . . . Back in the mall, Stevens and I met these two chicks again and said, 'Have you seen two other guys tripping their brains out around here?' They said, 'Sure, over there/ and there they were, staring at the fountain. . . . Then we drove to a carnival and walked around, watching the light trails and the people on the rides . . . wow, man, what a trip . . . all the headlights on the highway were trailing. . . . We ended up in the woods near the barracks, talking about what it means to be a soldier and what we planned to do when we got out. . . ."

Another recreational use of drugs was sampling the new substances continually coming on the market.

> Bunsen said, "I'm into 'nice' right now. It's a combination of speed and acid and THC. You take it and your body goes into a roller coaster ride with alternate highs, lows, and great rushes in between."

> The conversation turned to smack, and I asked Grady whether he had used. "No, er, ah, well yeah, I've tried it twice, but will never do it again. It was too good." He told me he actually didn't know he was taking heroin. He and Masters met a friend of Masters at the shopping center. The friend had some 'cosmos' to sell, so they decided to check it out. He wanted to sell them a large bag for $75, but Grady said he only wanted to try $10 worth. By his hand gesture, the packet must have been about the size of a match box. "I opened the packet, divided it in half, and then sniffed my half through a straw. It felt like liquid dripping down the back of my nose, down my throat, and then this tremen-

dous rushing feeling. I didn't know what 'cosmos' was, but Masters later found out that while it was white like heroin, it actually was a combination of lots of leftovers after cutting and packaging heroin, coke, crystal, and other dust."

The chief difference between recreational drinking and recreational drug use was the lack of drama associated with the latter. Drug use focused on the private perceptual experience of users engaged in sedentary or mundane activities. Yet there was a social component, as shown in the account, given above, of an evening that concluded with a discussion of serious concerns.

Special occasions for recreational drug use offered different kinds of heightened sensory experience. Soldiers reported going to the "adult entertainment" district of a nearby city while under the effects of amphetamine. Their reports, however, focused on the flashing lights and the pulsating music rather than on the girls, the pitchmen, and the topless shoeshine parlor. Yet the special occasion was in some sense a group experience in that three men went to the area together. Similarly, dyads reported hallucinogenic interludes that consisted of walking through the woods singly and then coming together to talk or share in the contemplation of a leaf or a sunset. The experience was at once social and profoundly individual. Inasmuch as nothing much happens *to the group* while using drugs, users had few memories of the group experience except from their own personal sensations. This did not mean, however, that the social dynamics that marked other social groups were suspended when drugs were introduced.

The social aspects were vividly illustrated in the most frequent special occasion for drug use—the "party." The ingredients for a party included drugs, music, subdued lighting, congenial company, and possibly a strobe light or a black light with psychedelic art or colors. A party was not planned; it just came about when the critical ingredients were present. At a party nothing very memorable happened, certainly nothing as dramatic as ripping a mirror from the wall or throwing a television from the window. Yet the conformity pressures and other group dynamics appeared equal to those observed in drinking groups. The observer described the setting:

Gino asked me for a ride to his apartment, and Bunsen decided to come along. He lives about a mile from post, and mentioned that the lieutenant and several state policemen also live in the same apartment complex. He lives in a three bedroom garden apartment with two other men in the company, and they have had no trouble paying $315 a month rent and meeting other expenses. The place is furnished, but is maintained in typical bachelor fashion with magazines strewn about and dishes piled high in the kitchen sink.

In return for the ride, Gino invited them to stay awhile, and played the role of congenial host:

Gino put on a Paul McCartney album, sat on the sofa and casually opened the drawer in the end table where he kept a baggie of dope, probably ¾ of an ounce or so. He then took the water bong from the coffee table, and casually stuffed it with a little grass. After lighting it, and taking a deep hit, he passed the bong to Bunsen, who refilled it and took a hit. I declined to smoke. "You mean even if we were in my hometown you wouldn't smoke?" "How about a big party after I get out of the Army?" "We'll get you high yet."

A party wasn't planned, but those who wanted to "party" knew where to go. Three other men from the company came through the patio door and sat on the couch and floor. The presence of the observer was noted, then ignored:

Mercer said, "You taking mental notes tonight? You really must have a lot of stuff on us . . . it's confidential, though, right? Well, I just want you to know I haven't had any grass for at least the last two days." [laughter] "I thought you quit." "I slowed down for a while because I was drinking a lot, too, and it was making me sick." Collins had a bong now, packed it, lit it, and passed it to Preston. "Preston, I don't believe you. You said you weren't gonna smoke any more, and now look at you." "Hey, man, cut me a break. Can I help it if I'm sitting right beside Gino? Shit, I gotta be sociable, don't I?" The bong was then passed among the five smokers, making the circuit three or four times.

The conversation centered on the "great party" the night before with "at least 50 people" circulating through the apartment. The stream of conversation was free-associational and stimulated by ongoing events. One man reading *Jonathan Livingston Seagull* was kidded about speed reading; the night before he read 26 pages in an hour and a half while stoned. From there they went to *Trout Fishing in America* and *The Charles Manson Story*, which some of them had recently completed. The evening was punctuated by new arrivals and early departures. Offering the bong signified inclusion in the group in the same way that offering a beer did.

There was a knock on the door, and a Puerto Rican entered. "Hey, man, is Dave in?" "Nope. I think he's out with his girlfriend." "Oh. I got some heavy things to think about," and he sat on the edge of the group near me, but no one offered him the bong. Another knock on the patio door, and another person entered. "Hi, George; what's happenin'?" "I got pissed at the old lady for spending a lot of money today and had to get out of the house." He sat down on the floor, set his motorcycle helmet beside him, and took the bong from Collins. After 15 minutes the Puerto Rican left silently without exchanging a word with anyone.

Two girls came into the apartment and were introduced as Sue and Jean. One way of affirming inclusion was to define exclusion.

The girl named Sue sat down on the floor by me and began talking freely while furiously chewing her gum. Soon she drew a water bong from her tote bag and said, "Wanna try my new bong?" Just my luck, she offered it to me first and I had to explain that I wasn't smoking that night. She then filled it with Gino's grass, lit it, and passed it among the group. Shortly thereafter she got up and moved to the couch. I got the distinct feeling I had become the group deviate for the evening.

Horseplay was not restricted to beer parties, as the observer noted:

Collins was constantly teased about his reading, and he finally set the book aside and playfully threw a pack of matches at Mercer. Immediately the air was filled with matches, paper wads, and empty cigarette packs with every man for himself. Collins hid behind a "Battle Cry" game board while Mercer attacked him with paper wads and playful jabs in his ribs. They laughed constantly, but Gino stopped the fracas because ashtrays were being overturned and were messing up the apartment.

Collins told a story about bear hunting with Mercer, and they suddenly began a "mind game" reminiscent of the hypnotism routine described previously during a barracks beer party.

Collins and Mercer began staring at each other. Collins constantly waved to Mercer across the room, having fun, and making him wave back. Mercer would try to resist, but he would inevitably give in and they would break out laughing. Bunsen then got in on it and started waving to Mercer. Collins said to me, "We always kid each other about something."

Next it was time for party stunts:

Mercer picked up a broomstick and held it under his nose, pretending
he was chinning himself. First there was laughter, then cheers and
encouragement as he pretended to struggle over the stick. Gino came
from the kitchen and lifted him over the stick by his ears to the rousing
cheers of the spectators. Next Mercer decided to break an imaginary
egg over Collins' head. He crawled a few feet across the rug and sat
facing Collins, who was also on the floor. He then cracked the imaginary egg over Collin's head and imitated the flow over his hair with his
fingertips while vividly describing what was happening. Everyone else
got into the act by commenting, "Yuck, what a mess . . . it sure is runny
. . . oh, look at it drip off his ear." By the time Mercer cracked the third
imaginary egg, Collins was no longer laughing, and almost seemed
concerned about the mess on his head.

"Parties" also provided an opportunity to instruct novice drug
users.

Jean talked to Gino on the couch. Gino stated with a certain pride that
he and several others had done acid a few times. He explained some of
the effects like "tracings and framings" and noted how an experienced
person ought to be present with people when they drop acid for the
first time to "talk them down" in case they start to lose touch with
reality.

Pressure on the observer to smoke continued throughout the evening:

Once I noticed Gino staring at me with an irritated look in his eyes.
"You know, you really piss me off just sitting there watching us getting
blown away while you're straight." The room was quickly silent in view
of the possible confrontations, and Collins said, "Hey, he's had some
hits, man; he's as fucked up as the rest of us." "Oh, yeah?" Gino said,
and that was that. Actually, I had *not* taken any hits, and whether or
not Collins thought I had, or was just covering for me, I'm not sure. At
one point, Mercer took the bong, chuckled, and said, "I'm loading this
one for you and you're gonna smoke it." He offered it to me; I refused,
and Bunsen covered, "Look, he's not gonna smoke; if he won't smoke
with me, he won't smoke with you, so don't hassle him 'cause he's not
gonna smoke." I suggested again that we have a party after I left the
Army.

Conformity pressure on the observer to smoke was most likely
due to the special circumstances of the party rather than apprehen-

sion about the observer's reliability and trustworthiness. He had witnessed many of these same people smoking under different circumstances, and little pressure had been exerted on him to join them. The pressure was a special case of the barracks norm prohibiting members from setting themselves apart as morally superior. In the barracks all were equal save for the "finks, snitches, nurds, gung-ho lifers, snobs, and queers" who were excluded from daily participation in the informal activities. In support of this interpretation was the case of the man who persisted in reading during the party, and was subjected to pressures more intense than those put on the observer.

> Whenever Collins picked up his book, Mercer and Preston began taunting him and throwing paper wads. Collins finally threw a wadded paper bag in momentary anger and ran out the patio door. He was gone at least 45 minutes. Sue said to Gino, "Why do they always pick on him?" "Aw, they're just teasing and having fun."

After more stories, a mock joust between two men armed with a broomstick and a belt, and a nonjoking exchange of insults, the party broke up about midnight.

Special-occasion recreational drug use, like its alcohol counterpart, served to bring the barracks residents together, expand the web of common experiences among them, and provide an opportunity to assert and resolve status claims. The principal difference was that special-occasion drug use resulted in few new stories for the social memory bank—stories like spitting on passersby in a restaurant, bilking a whore, or tricking someone into throwing a boot through a window. The content of the social memory was no more specific than "we did a lot of partying together," and individual memory was mostly a blur of private perceptual experience attributed to drug effects. The observer noted a conversation with one of the roommates of the apartment:

> "Man, we partied every night for three months in the apartment. Three straight months every night; marijuana, hash, speed, acid—you name it, we did it. I can't remember half the people who used to come by— the guys in the company mostly—but at the end I was so wasted I couldn't tell when I was fucked up and when I was straight. I remember one time really getting into my painting at my easel while stoned and another just staring at the aquarium, but mostly it was just smoking and rapping."

Affirmational Use

There was no direct drug-using analog to depressed affirmational drinking. Such drinking occurred when group relations became dulled, and it was necessary to provoke a memorable incident, even if it was no more than trying to remember how they got back to the barracks. Most drugs taken by soldiers did not have such powerful intoxicating effects, at least in the course of a single evening, and apparently permitted more conscious control of behavior than occurred with hearty indulgence in alcohol. In addition, drug use at a party, for example, set the stage for more intense interpersonal interaction, for there was little external distraction by way of dancers, games, or fights. Because intense interaction was rendered impossible by a group entropy, drug-using soldiers in such circumstances were more likely to engage in serious drinking than in more drug use.

Going-away parties provided occasions for affirmational drinking or drug use. Drinking a final beer with good old what's-his-name was equivalent to sharing a final "joint." Soldiers made frequent references to changes of personality and behavior while smoking marijuana; they claimed that smokers were more subdued, relaxed, and congenial. The observational evidence did not support this claim. The evidence suggests that the setting and social context were as important in determining behavior as the pharmacological effects of the drugs being used. In the following description of an ETS party where marijuana was the main diversion, the personalities and activities remained quite recognizable from previous episodes. Invitations to the party were extended in the usual spur-of-the-moment fashion, as the observer noted:

> When I entered the barracks there was and informal wrestling match going on in the Murphy-Barker area. I watched with the others, and Eagleton said, "Going to the party with us?" "Where?" "At Marty's place; he's getting out on Friday." "Marty won't mind if I come?" "No, man, come on; we're really going to get blown away tonight." He took a couple of ounces of marijuana from his coat pocket to show me.

The barracks contingent drove to the apartment that Marty shared with his girlfriend. There were about a dozen people already there when they arrived; four were with girls. No introductions were made. All of the chairs were taken, so after an awkward period of standing and milling, people began sitting on the floor. The conversation then became more animated.

Groups were formed briefly and divided again all night. The only patterns were the couples who tended to remain seated. The tape deck was on continuously. Marijuana was used by everyone except me. The larger group usually broke into smaller groups for smoking that was very heavy at first, and then only occasionally for the rest of the evening. The group on the couch used a small water pipe, and the others were either smoking plain joints or were using holders made from polished stones with holes drilled through them. The stones were good for giving shotguns, and Kenny offered everyone a shotgun at least once. The joints were passed among three or four people, and very seldom did they jump between groups. Everyone was also drinking beer except the three with wine. Miller and MacNamee each brought a lid of grass, and were responsible for rolling the joints.

A popular conversational topic was women:

"Is Green porking that bitch beside him?" "Yeah, he says he's going to take her with him when he leaves." "No! He'd take that?" Gross then began recounting sweathog stories of blow jobs, anal intercourse, armpit intercourse, and spitting in his personal sweathog's face. Later in the evening, he left to bring her to the party, but she was not home, and he returned alone.

Stories of Vietnam were also popular:

Marty came over to our group and started telling Vietnam stories. He knew some guys who blew up the first sergeant's hootch because he was down on the drug users. "Most people just snorted heroin, but a few used needles. Vials cost $3 and $6 and some guys used 20 a day." "Wouldn't that mess them up pretty bad?" Eagleton pulled a picture from his wallet. "Here's what it does to you." The snapshot showed him as a virtual skeleton beside his Vietnamese bride. I asked about withdrawal. "I was Medevaced for hepatitis, malaria and shrapnel wounds. I was in the hospital for 60 days, and I kicked at the same time."

The multiple smoking groups coalesced into a single body twice during the evening. The first time was to hear once more the "Varsity Grill" story, with a new element added. On this telling, a member of the group who had already left the Army was said to have provoked the fight by "mouthing off," but had been first to head for the door, leaving the others to finish the brawl. Everyone enjoyed the story, and the talk turned to the oldest man in the unit and those who were next to get out of the Army.

The second display of unity was during a fire ritual.

Marty's girl had pretty much ignored the party by sitting on the floor, sewing cuffs on a pair of trousers. She brought in some of Marty's fatigues and started to throw them away. Gross asked for them and then began tearing them to shreds. Murphy joined in the tearing, and then Gross piled them in the middle of the floor and lit them with Murphy's lighter. Marty laughed, but his girl seemed angry. Gross stamped out the flames, and she took the smoldering clothes outside.

Several men went into the bedroom to lift weights, later returning to the group to flex their muscles and tell how much they had lifted. From time to time the group in the bedroom would begin shadow boxing or playfully slapping each other. The observer noted:

When I walked into the bedroom, MacNamee instructed Miller to squat and hyperventilate. He then gave him a shotgun. Miller stood uneasily and fell across the bed in a mock faint. The bed collapsed. Marty passed it off, "That always happens. It has a bad leg." He fixed the bed quickly, and was then coerced into squatting for shotgun. After inhaling, he exclaimed, "Wow, what a rush." Murphy was next, and then Kenny.

The party began breaking up about 11:15, with the couples leaving first, followed shortly thereafter by the barracks group. Their silence during the ride back was broken once inside the barracks.

Gross started a high-pitched scream that was picked up by Murphy and Roberts. All the lights were turned on in the bay, and Murphy was singing loudly. Then everyone turned in quietly and went to sleep to the music of Roberts' radio.

A reasonable conclusion from this extended example is that soldiers who have spent an evening smoking marijuana behave about the same as if they had been drinking beer. The stories, personalities, and activities are unaltered in structure, but are moderated by variables such as the physical setting and the persons present. Both marijuana use and alcohol consumption were found to be effective means of affirming group membership.

Ceremonial Use

The final pattern, ceremonial drug use, is structurally identical to ceremonial drinking. At the ETS party that started near a fishing pond off post, the observer noted:

Most of the interaction took place between two cars parked parallel to each other about a car length apart. All of the beer was pooled in the trunk of one car; on the seat of the other car were two baggies of grass and papers. Frisco was rolling the joints and starting them on their rounds among the men who were drinking beer, laughing and talking. There was no pressure at all on me to smoke, although I was offered several "J's."

The ritual of "shooting a beer" had a striking analog in the practice of "shotgunning" with a marijuana cigarette.

Frisco was clearly the man with the dope. He not only rolled the joints, but ate the roaches and introduced shotgunning. A shotgun is administered by holding a "J" firmly between one's lips. The receiver stands close to the "J," exhales deeply, then inhales. As he inhales, the administrator blows through the "J." The dope burns much faster than on a normal drag, and a larger amount of smoke results. The receiver draws the smoke through his nose or mouth, and a good receiver wastes very little smoke. Hyperventilation is natural when drawing in the smoke from the air. Frisco seemed to enjoy shotgunning everyone, and regularly made the rounds.

When the group returned to the barracks and forced everyone to sip the ceremonial beer, another packet of marijuana appeared.

Sometime during the beer-sipping ritual a large bag of grass appeared. It must have contained at least five ounces and apparently belonged to Eggers, who started rolling joints and encouraging Frisco to do the same.

The newcomers were not slow to perceive the meaning—dope was acceptable in the barracks:

I went to my area where the new guy was sitting alone, drinking a beer. We started talking first about work, then his assignment in Korea, and then about his home near the post. He looked the part of the "head" with long hair parted in the center, a bushy moustache, wire-rimmed glasses, and "far-out" language. As we talked, he pulled a lid of grass from his locker and lit up a small ceramic pipe. I refused a hit and explained why. He accepted the explanation and continued to smoke, finally sharing with another new guy.

Other occasions for the ceremonial use of drugs included the initiation of the inexperienced into the use of new substances. Already cited episodes indicated the need for an experienced user to "guide" a novice through his first acid trip to prevent panic or "freaking out." Soldiers reported taking precautions regarding time, place, and setting before initiating a friend in the use of LSD. The need for such measures seemed to diminish with experience and increased sophistication. Nevertheless, a soldier's first trip on acid retained an element of ceremony as the more experienced users demonstrated what he could do with his mind while intoxicated.

Gino says that Wolfson is tripping tonight for the first time on strawberry acid. Shortly thereafter, Wolfson comes into the room, sweating, jittery, and rubbing his hands up and down his arms. "Man, it's cold in here. Motherfuck, never again; no grass, no speed, no acid, no nothin.'" Gino chuckles, "He's really gone," and runs his hand slowly in front of Wolfson's face. Wolfson recoils and says, "Hey, man, don't fuck with me."

Gino explains that this is Wolfson's first time and he is really having trouble distinguishing reality from unreality. Wolfson sits on my desk, rubbing his arms and face, then he breaks into a fixed smile, then chuckles nervously. Gino says the guys were really giving him a hard time downstairs.

Wolfson says, "Yeah, man. They had me dying, dead in a coffin I was, then they buried me—Christ, is this stuff bad—never again." Gino tells him he is a huge turtle, and Wolfson chuckles, "Yeah, and they had me believing I was a turtle, too." Gino then goes to the desk and wiggles his fingers while telling Wolfson a spider is approaching. Wolfson tenses, curls up at the back of the desk, pleads, "Hey, don't fuck around," and slams Gino's hand with my clipboard. Gino continues, "They're crawling all over the room. There's a big one right behind you," and notes in an aside how paranoid Wolfson is. Wolfson shakes his head nervously in denial, looks over his shoulder, and then begins killing the "spiders" with the clipboard. He then gets up, mumbling, "Motherfuck!" and walks unsteadily from the room. Gino says, "He's obviously hallucinating and not controlling himself very well."

Obvious in this example is the grand time that the more experienced users were having in teaching Wolfson about the potentials of strawberry acid. The ceremony provided an occasion for them to affirm their status as experienced users, as did the patronizing asides to the observer.

The parallels between drug use, particularly marijuana smoking, and alcohol use are too close to be coincidental. Both alcohol and drugs were used on duty at the same times and places, and under very similar circumstances. Both were used in the barracks in much the same ways. With the exception of depressed affirmational drinking, both were patterned into recreational, affirmational, and ceremonial uses. Both were used in ways that served to weave increasingly fine the net of interpersonal similarity and commonality. Both provided opportunities to assert, establish, and maintain status within groups and cliques. Drugs and alcohol were complementary means to the same end: preserving the social order in the barracks. These functions, however, were seldom discussed by the users themselves.

What do drugs do for the maintenance of barracks social structure that alcohol doesn't? There are essentially two fundamental problems of social organization faced by barracks soldiers. The first is how to keep social relationships vital and alive in circumstances in which there is neither an expectation of future interaction nor a storehouse of past affiliation. The second is how to create and maintain group identification and group boundaries under unstable conditions: how to create a sense of "we" and define a contrastive "they," given the constant personnel turnover in an Army unit.

Alcohol use contributes in a major way to the solution of the first problem, while drug use contributes heavily to the solution of the second. Alcohol and illicit drugs each make a *unique* contribution to the social structuring of barracks living; as a result their use cannot be taken as interchangeable.

Alcohol is particularly helpful in generating distinctive, memorable episodes involving brawls, "broads," and bad news so that the participants can recall and recount evidence for the meaningfulness of their relationship and what they have been through together. Drug use is far less effective in this respect; it is personal and private.

Illicit drug use creates two large, superordinate oppositional categories: user and nonuser, or "we" and "they." These explicitly defined categories cut across cliques, build stable perimeters despite unstable personnel, and engender a sense of group identity.

Drug users at Fort Marshall were united in their individual histories of defiance of a general societal norm; moreover, they were united in the risks of sanction, in a belief in the acceptability of their actions, and in language and dress. There is nothing quite like opposition—or better yet, persecution—to create and maintain categorical boundaries. Alcohol users enjoyed no such commonality.

SUMMARY

The observations recounted in this chapter suggest several conclusions. Experience with or exposure to mind-altering substances invariably precedes entry into the Army. Illicit drug use in the Army is regarded as normal rather than deviant by both using and nonusing barracks residents. It is therefore not surprising to find drug use entirely consonant with the social structure of the barracks. For example, drug use defines the social categories "cool" and "straight," which cut across dyads, triads, and cliques. Membership in the "cool" category offers opportunities for status claims, provides for the exchange of goods and services, and enables the exercise of social power to a greater extent than is accorded to nonmembership.

Like alcohol, illicit drugs were used both during duty hours and after duty. Use was unscheduled and opportunistic, depending upon what was available and at what price. When drugs were not obtainable, alcohol was substituted. Like alcohol, illicit drugs fell into recreational, affirmational, and ceremonial patterns of use.

The use of drugs and alcohol had discernibly different effects on barracks social structure. Drugs were less effective than alcohol in defining cliques and small groups, but more effective in defining social categories that did not rely on face-to-face interaction. Alcohol bonded small, face-to-face groups, while drugs bonded larger social categories that cut across small groups and cliques. However, the contents of the social interaction, exchange of goods and services, exercise of status claims, and bids for social power were clearly present in both drug and alcohol use patterns.

6

THE
LEADERS

This chapter describes the reactions of company leaders, in particular the response of the sergeants and officers of Fort Marshall, to the use of drugs and alcohol. It is important to recognize that the leaders knew that drugs were used in the company area, that alcohol was often used in destructive ways, and that some response was required. The essential questions revolve around how much the leaders knew and how they responded to such knowledge.

WHAT WAS KNOWN

There were three principal ways in which leaders learned of drug and alcohol use: casual observations, inspections, and talking to those who were caught. Drug users talked freely to those with whom they had daily contact so that any first-line supervisor might make reasonable inferences regarding who used drugs. The observer noted:

> Rogers did not make the morning formation. Reynolds told Sergeant Badder that he knew where Rogers lived off post, and Badder suggested he drive out to pick him up. Rogers got in the car, explained how his car wouldn't start that morning, and said, "Hey, I've just got to get some dope. I'll have to see if Marconi has any." "Miller's got a bunch; he's supposed to come down to see us this morning." "Oh, great! Where'd he get it?" Sergeant Badder doesn't comment on the conversation; he drives to the barracks.

Alcohol use on duty was also not unknown.

> The lieutenant came into the office as we were eating our sandwiches and drinking beer. The guys put their beer in the desk drawer; Wilson

went to the refrigerator and began stuffing beer cans in his pockets. The lieutenant catches him in the act and sees a six-pack remaining in the freezer. "What's going on here?" "Just prepared for the afternoon; that is, after work, sir." [general laughter] The lieutenant seems angry: "Well, don't drink that shit in the office." "Oh, no, sir; that would never happen." "I know it has happened; you guys are gonna get me in heavy shit here one day; just cool it, dammit."

A company commander commented that he had often smelled burning incense and marijuana when staff duty officer at night, "But it's damned difficult to catch them at it." Judging from the following group interview, it was not all that difficult:

Interviewer: Do the sergeants and officers know?

Pvt. A: Sure, they know. Like, take Sergeant Brooks, he's cool. We were smoking outside the kitchen, and he just says, "I wish you guys wouldn't smoke that shit around here."

Pvt. B: Or what about that time in the field when the lieutenant caught us smoking around the fire. Just told us to knock it off and not use it anymore on maneuvers.

Pvt. C: Remember when Darcey was talking to the lieutenant, and that pint of Southern Comfort fell out of his pocket? Lieutenant just looked down, says, "Somebody must have dropped this," and put it in his own pocket. I thought Darcey would cry seein' that bottle in the lieutenant's pocket.

Pvt.B: That's nothing. The CO found a pint of vodka in my desk in the barracks. The orderly told me about it. He just took it with him out of the room; never did say nothin' to me about it. Shit, they don't care.

Inspections provided another opportunity to know that drugs were used. Periodic searches of vehicles for misappropriated government property frequently revealed stashes of marijuana. A commander reported, "I sometimes find a bag of stuff in the broom closet; I've even found it in the heating ducts, but there's no telling who it belongs to." The observer noted:

There was a shakedown inspection earlier this week. The only result was a pipe found in the cooks' room and two small stashes in Kenny's area. Kenny told me months ago that he never keeps his stash in the barracks. It was found in a desk leg, and he has denied any knowledge of it. He doubts any charges will be filed.

Finally there were enough who got caught in possession of marijuana to provide incontrovertible evidence that it was being used. Most of the apprehensions occurred as a result of user stupidity, bad luck, or both.

Just before the holiday the commander inspected the privately owned vehicles. He checked the lights, windshield wipers, and tire treads and reminded the owners of safety hazards he discovered. He also checked the trunks for the presence of a spare tire and any unauthorized Army equipment. As he finished the inspection, another car came into the lot driven by a man who had had a medical appointment that morning. He apparently thought the inspection was for drugs, for he attempted to pass a bright yellow envelope to a buddy in another car. A quick-thinking sergeant inquired into the contents of the envelope and discovered a half dozen marijuana cigarettes. The captain inspected the car carefully and found several other brightly colored envelopes with similar contents.

On another occasion a man reported to the orderly room, wearing a field jacket bearing the name tag of a man who had reported it missing. The first sergeant instigated a search of the man's car for other missing equipment, and turned up a tranquilizer pill and a plastic oxygen mask to which a pipe had been cemented so as to provide simultaneous inhalation through the mouth and nose. On still another occasion the observer noted:

Walker told me about his drug bust: "So the MPs pulled me over after I went through the stop sign, and asked to see my driver's license. I always keep it in my glove compartment, and I left the door open. This one MP looks in and sees my bag of dope. I had to get out of the car, submit to a search, and go into the station for questioning. They don't have anything on me, however, 'cause they didn't have probable cause to search the car."

Sometimes an investigation could not be avoided.

Rankin said, "So I decide to quit dating this broad, and the next thing I know she has filed a statement with the CO that I've been smoking in the barracks. He relieved me of duty for two weeks pending the investigation. They hauled me in for questioning about four times; took me to this room where two cops battered me with questions. I was really shaken, man; one time I almost cried. I finally told them I had smoked once in high school. My lawyer says my rights were violated, and they can't get anything on me, but that bitch really did a job on me, I'll tell you."

Thus from casual observation, formal inspections, apprehensions and investigations, the leaders knew that drugs were used in the company. By the mid 1970s, it was acceptable to admit this knowledge, in contrast to a few years earlier when it was customary for leaders to issue a general denial. One new commander, for example, remarked to an observer, "Did you know there are drugs in the company? We found two joints on the inspection this morning. I'm not ashamed to admit it." The typical response of commanders and first sergeants was, "Yes, we have our share of drug users, but we know pretty much who they are." Those named as drug users were those who openly proclaimed membership in the drug-using barracks groups or those who had been investigated or prosecuted for use. When actual observations of barracks life were compared to the lists of users provided by the leaders, less than one fifth of the users were identified. Aside from the occasional broken window or the empty beer bottles on the ground outside the barracks, the leaders certainly did not know much about routine nightlife in the barracks, and had little appreciation of the role of drugs and alcohol in the day-to-day existence of their charges. They agreed, however, that drug use was undesirable and ought to be eradicated.

IMPEDIMENTS TO KNOWLEDGE

Why did the leaders not know more about what went on in the barracks? Why were their attempts at intervention sporadic and unsuccessful? The reasons resonated with the confusion, despondency, and despair that marked barracks life in the mid seventies.

First, with respect to knowing what was going on in the barracks, the real question was whether the leaders really wanted to know. Over the years, organizational theory and managerial guidelines from industrial models had been imported and adapted in wholesale fashion. The Army, particularly in garrison, came to be viewed as an industrial complex with inputs, throughputs, and outputs of goods and services. True to this model, first-line supervisors confined their attention to task performance. When performance fell, the job of the supervisor was to refer the individual to experts for help, not to attempt to intervene himself. Thus, many sergeants reported, "As long as they do their jobs, it's none of my business what they do on their own time." Commanders similarly responded, "I told them in formation I would not tolerate drugs in the barracks, but what they did outside the barracks was no concern of mine."

Using the performance criterion alone, there was little reason to know more about the individuals because most drug users do their jobs very well. Indeed, the less said the better, as in the case of a company armorer. The armorer, or keeper of the arms room, has one of the most responsible positions in the lower enlisted ranks, because one missing weapon can cost the commander his job. In one company the armorer wore longish hair parted in the middle, wire-rimmed glasses with tinted lenses, and love beads. He told his company commander he was a Buddhist monk, used drugs regularly, and wanted to return to Thailand to be closer to good supplies of drugs. The commander was reluctant to see him transferred because on a recent inspection the arms room had been one of only two duty sections that passed with distinction; all other sections had failed miserably.

Being too particular about drug and alcohol use also created interpersonal unpleasantries for a sergeant or officer who had to assign someone else to the duty. If the task was not too demanding, it was easier to simply ignore the soldier's condition.

Sawyer and Ludlow finished their "J" as we pulled into the parking lot. Sawyer was bitching about having to go on duty at midnight. After Sawyer went into the barracks to polish his boots, Sergeant Bloom asked us whether he was in any condition to pull his guard shift. Ludlow said, "We've been drinking most of the afternoon and evening, but he should make it all right." "Well, if he can stand up for 10 minutes at guard mount, I guess he can make it through till morning." Bloom was sergeant of the guard, and seemed willing to cover for Sawyer if he had any trouble.

In the main, the cadre equated ineffective performance with drug use, and when first sergeants railed against long hair, sloppy dress, and poor military courtesy, they usually characterized the offenders as "the drug users." Exposing the essential falsehood of the equation could be shattering to Army leaders.

The commander talked about Tryon who was under investigation for selling drugs. "I just can't believe it. He was one of my outstanding troops. I appointed him to the color guard for parades; even got him out of duty to practice on the pistol team; recommended he be given advanced, specialized training in the most elite unit in the corps; and now this." He repeatedly shook his head while muttering, "I can't believe it . . . if I can make this kind of a mistake, what does that say for my judgment? . . . it's not true, but it's all there in the report."

Even when the cadre deemed it necessary to know more about drug use, the powerful norms in the barracks against informing made access to the information difficult. The prisoner's dilemma interrogation was tried, as the observer noted:

> Gino told me how the first sergeant had called him into his office and explained that he knew Gino had bought dope from men in the company and wanted their names. Gino denied buying anything from anyone. The next day Mercer was called in. The first sergeant said that Gino had squealed on him, so he might as well spill the beans on the rest of the users. "When Mercer told us about it, people really got uptight thinking he had really squealed. I almost jumped him myself till I found out the first sergeant was trying to set him up."

Commanders also established networks of informants in the barracks who told what was going on in exchange for a few kind words or sympathetic attention to their problems. Few men were willing to play this role, especially when anyone could find out from the clerks who had seen the commander or first sergeant. In addition, many sergeants supported the norm against informing. A first sergeant commented, "If I find out about something on my own, then I'll take action, but I don't want no goddamned snitches coming whining to me with every little thing that happens when I'm not looking." At the time of the kangaroo court episode reported previously, the sergeant was said to have known about it, but made sure that neither he nor the junior sergeants were in the area at the time.

Problems in the upward flow of information were common in two divergent views of the nature and purpose of the barracks. One view was outlined by a colonel:

> "The barracks are actually only a half-way house to and from the civilian community. They're a kind of transient hotel for new men until they find an apartment, a lady, or both, and a place for the old timers to go when their wives throw them out of the house. The notion of a platoon working and living together is gone; we've abandoned the barracks to the hoods and thugs."

Given this vision of the barracks as a transient hotel, there was little reason to exert more effort than routine cleaning and monitoring for damage, because, by implication, the kind of people who lived there merited nothing else. The barracks, in this view, were analogous to a slum where the only possible response was more law enforcement. The colonel continued:

> "Take the shooting in the barracks last month. They say it was drug-related, but it wasn't. One guy comes into the other's room, spills soda on the floor, the other tells him to clean it up, he tells him to shove it, and the other pulls out a pistol and shoots him. What that's really about is how much the lines of communication have broken down. Several men saw that gun in the barracks two weeks before the shooting, but no one said a word. A few years ago, a man couldn't have kept more than a pen knife without the sergeant knowing about it. I told the post commander I could stop the nonsense in the barracks; just order the sergeants to live there. "No, no," he says, "they might not like that and resign; we wouldn't want that." Of course he's right, but I could stop that crap in a minute if my hands weren't tied."

The contrasting and more prevalent view of the barracks was as the home of the single enlisted. The Army listened carefully to soldiers' demands for more privacy and launched major construction efforts to remodel barracks into individual rooms. Soldiers were encouraged to hang curtains, pictures, and other decorations to personalize their habitat. The problem with this vision was that closed doors made casual surveillance virtually impossible. In an open bay a sergeant or officer could stop by, watch television, and converse informally. With private rooms the sergeant or officer needed the pretext of official business in order to knock or enter with a pass key. Even official business could be awkward when both parties considered their room "home." The observer noted:

> Another duty of the staff duty officer is to insure that the fire lights are on in each building. We walked down the halls of the various barracks quickly because most of the doors were closed. One door was open, however, and two men were watching television in their underwear. The captain poked his head in the door to say good evening, and the men came to attention beside their bed. He told them to "carry on, as you were," but they simply relaxed to an "at ease" position with hands behind their backs. His attempts at small talk—the heat of the evening and the television program—were met with formal "yes, sirs," and both he and the men seemed uncomfortable during the interchange. He was not invited into the room to join them watching television, and under the circumstances he could hardly invite himself. He later explained, "I don't like to go into the barracks too often; after all, it is their home and I try not to intrude or harass them."

Another reason for the cadre's lack of complete information about barracks life, including drugs and alcohol, was an acute awareness of being out of touch with the men. Social boundaries are both inclusive and exclusive, and the usual tensions between privates and their sergeants became transformed during the Vietnam war into a struggle between "heads" and "juicer-lifers." Many of the older sergeants were just as sensitive to the sneering epithet "lifer" as were the privates in the barracks. One way of avoiding the taunts and jibes was to avoid the barracks whenever possible. This avoidance was then rationalized by asserting that modern generation of soldiers was not only different from, but actually inferior to their predecessors. Some sergeants complained that privates were too well educated, while others contended that with the end of the draft the privates were nothing but "dummies" and "street bums." In either case they were said to have no pride, no incentive, no ambition, and "no talent for anything but lying around smoking dope." For their part, the noncommissioned officers maintained that present-day enlisted men were a different breed: "When I was coming up and we were told to do something, we did it without question. Now you have to explain why, wheedle, cajole, and beg them to do it."

Racial differences aggravated the already strained lines of communication. Not long ago the elaborate greeting among blacks, called "the dap," angered many whites as they waited in line behind two brothers blocking a passageway for several minutes while saying good morning. Sergeants were so sensitive to charges of race prejudice that one black first sergeant felt compelled to announce in formation, "There, I've assigned a white and a black to this detail, so I don't want to hear any crap about discrimination." The blacks immediately began hounding him about being a "Tom Sergeant," and argued that he should have selected the men for their ability rather than their race, while the whites groaned about having to do "nigger work." Across the "generation gap" the senior black sergeants saw the young blacks as threats to all they had achieved, and the senior white sergeants perceived the young blacks as a threat to their traditional authority. A reenlistment sergeant commented, "You know why all the niggers, I mean blacks, are enlisting in the Army? To steal. They're all going into the medics for drugs or into supply."

Finally there were drugs. The senior sergeants watched their men become addicted to heroin in Vietnam. They returned home to find their teenage children smoking marijuana. They saw their troops continuing to use, and they did not understand. If only they would settle down and act reasonably and responsibly, a sergeant remarked,

"Like last Friday I went to the club, drank 10 or 12 beers and seven double shots of whiskey. I just drank beer on Saturday and sobered up Sunday so I'd be ready for work Monday, but these kids. . . ." Drugs also perplexed many of the younger officers, and one company commander puzzled:

> "I don't feel I can really counsel the drug-using troops. What do I say when they say I can't understand because I've never used? Some reports say marijuana is harmful; others say it's not. Who am I to say they shouldn't use?"

Thus the cadre mused on about drugs, discipline, and morale with a sharply inadequate knowledge of what actually went on in the barracks. A clearer vision of reality was obscured by the belief that the first-line supervisor was to judge only performance, by contrasting views of the function of the barracks, by endorsement of the norm against informing, and by the usual problems implicit in comprehending the younger generation. To this list must be added the most paralyzing reason of all. To know more carried the implication of doing more, and the leaders had no idea of what exactly they would do with more accurate information.

Many placed the inability to act at the feet of inexperienced sergeants and officers. One major said:

> "In every war the Army rapes itself. It takes its most promising senior NCOs, makes them warrant officers, and then boots their ass out of service when the war is over. During a buildup promotions come fast and easy, so we are left with old sergeants ready for retirement, the incompetents who couldn't make warrant, and inexperienced kids. It takes about 10 years for the U.S. Army to recover from a war."

The life of a first-line supervisor in the Army is not an easy one; it is filled with interpersonal unpleasantries that require considerable training and experience in personnel management. Attempting to intervene can be embarrassing, as in the episode in the barracks when the sergeant attempted to break up a raucous party and was hooted from the area. Intervention can also be provocative:

> A heated argument was going on in the orderly room. As we entered the private leaped to his feet, opened his shirt, and shouted at the sergeant, "I'll kill you, you old son of a bitch. Get up from that desk, motherfucker, and I'll beat the piss out of you." The sergeant calmly soothed, "Now, Kincaide, you're going to get yourself in a peck of

trouble running your mouth like that; I'm just going to make one little call to the MPs to see if they have a place where you can cool off." The argument continued in the presence of two senior sergeants who made no move to interfere.

Finally, attempting intervention can be dangerous:

At the firing range Parrish was his usual sullen, insubordinate self. While his squad knelt and fired, he stood glaring up and down the firing line with his rifle at the ready. When the squad ceased firing, he glanced over his shoulder as the sergeants and men began edging for cover amid whispers that Parrish was crazy. The ensuing silence was broken by Sergeant Snell's quiet but firm, "Soldier, you haven't fired your weapon yet." Parrish turned toward Snell, moved to lower his rifle, and then turned back toward the range. He knelt and emptied his clip on automatic firing.

Given the interpersonal embarrassment, provocation, and danger of first-line supervision, it is not unreasonable to believe that the barracks tales had some basis in fact when residents reported, "We tore up the place for the hell of it, and the sergeants got scared and ran away."

If the sergeants proved ineffectual, the officers were often tempted to fill the breech. One company commander growled, "Yes, I get here at 5:30 for wake-up. Some of my sergeants don't believe you can get a man out of bed without court martialing him." As the commander went from bunk to bunk, gently shaking the sleeping bodies, the sergeant growled to the observer, "See what I mean? No respect for the NCO; he doesn't even think I can do my job; imagine the company commander getting the troops up."

Coupled with the belief that the NCO corps was inexperienced was the belief that the best way to train NCOs was formal schooling in classroom settings. The Army runs a virtual university of courses in leadership principles, human relations, equipment maintenance, and office organization. Promotion points are weighted in favor of such training, and the ambitious sergeant acquires all the formal instruction he can. One problem with this scheme is that the sergeants felt it favored the least competent. Whenever there was an opening in one of the schools, the officers were thought most likely to appoint the sergeant they could best do without; hence the most competent sergeants stayed behind and managed the company while the least competent were sent to school and promoted. There seemed no system of reward for looking after the troops.

Secondly, the supreme faith that schooling equaled training served to absolve the unit from responsibility for poor performance, and displaced it to outside "experts." A battalion commander commented:

> I know we have a big problem with leadership among our junior sergeants. They were promoted too fast, and don't know the first thing about leadership. They hang with the younger troops who are their buddies, and then find it difficult to give them orders. I've set up a leadership class for them taught by a psychologist from mental hygiene.

The course failed dismally because, in the words of the instructor, "They just wanted to talk about their problems in the unit, not the general principles of leadership, organizational dynamics, and personnel management." On another occasion the observer reported:

> The company commander returned from an inspection of the barracks. He was most upset with a sergeant's behavior that he diagnosed as inability to divide the labor and provide follow-up supervision. "I just don't understand it. He's had years of experience and plenty of schooling." I inquired what would be done. "I'll counsel him, and if things don't improve, I'll have to take disciplinary action." I asked if the counseling would include pointing out the problems of dividing the work and providing supervision. He looked incredulous and said, "Christ, no. That's just common sense."

One man's "common sense" may be a profound insight to another, yet the notion that training is best left to the experts in schools often prevented sharing of insights. Reliance on the experts created conditions for the diffusion of responsibility to the point that deficiencies in soldiers were seen as inherent. The observer noted:

> Sergeant Green commented on the poor quality of individuals now in the Army. "Take the promotion board I was on last week. A man from this company comes in with his brass on wrong and needing a haircut. I could have died of embarrassment. He didn't know how to approach the board, and when I gave him the give-a-way question, 'What do you use to clean your weapon in the desert,' the fucker said, 'Oil.' Shit, oil will collect dust so fast the weapon will jam in a minute." I asked what the sergeant major's reaction had been. "He just shook his head afterwards and said, 'See what we've got to work with.'" I asked whether the platoon sergeant and first sergeant didn't have some responsibility for the performance. "You're damned right. The sergeant

major should have kicked ass clear down to the squad leader, but the young troops they just don't care any more."

The third problem in equating classroom instruction with training was the chasm between what is written in notebooks and what is enacted in the unit. A first sergeant, unmindful of the irony as he watched his sergeant rush to the automobiles after work, commented, "The job of the NCO begins at when duty ends." Sergeants "knew" that the best rewards for enlisted men were praise and time off, yet it became too embarrassing to ask for the most recent use of these rewards. The more dedicated sergeants could easily recite the 11 principles of military leadership; they noted the second principle, "know your men," by carefully compiling personnel data cards on each of their charges, yet they could not say why they collected the information or what they might use it for. The dictum "know your men" usually was reduced to a *pro forma* interview with the company commander and a similar interview with the work supervisor.

The private has been briefly coached by the first sergeant, just to be sure he hasn't forgotten the correct procedure and the CO has reviewed the man's personnel file. He knocks twice on the office door and stands at ease until he is bid to come in. He then marches to the front of the CO's desk, comes to attention, salutes, and says, "Private Charles Wilson, reporting to duty as ordered, sir."

The CO returns the salute while seated, and says, "At ease." Wilson moves his right foot 18 inches from his left and folds his hands behind his back. The CO then stands, smiles, and extends his hand. "Sit down, Wilson, sit down; welcome to Delta Company." Wilson takes the chair indicated, but sits erectly, almost at attention; "Thank you, sir." "Where's home, Wilson?" "Vermont, sir." "Vermont, yes, pretty country up there, but lots of snow. Do you ski?" "No, sir." The CO continues to ask idle, free-associative kinds of questions designed to put the private at ease. When the responses exceed two words, the CO shifts to the second order of business.

"How long have you been in the Army, Wilson?" "Eighteen months, sir. I took basic training at Fort Dix, AIT at Fort Knox, and then went to Okinawa with the 35th Engineers." "What's your MOS?" "Seventy-one B twenty, sir; motor mechanic." "Well, we can sure use a good mechanic. You'll be working for Sergeant Slocum at the motor pool; he's a damned fine man who knows his job and runs a tight ship." "Yes, sir."

"By the way, why are you only a private, E-2, with 18 months of service?" "I got busted from E-4 for fighting in Okinawa, sir." "Well, you start out with a clean slate in this company. Do your job and behave like a soldier and we'll see what we can do to get your stripes back. We've got a really fine unit here; we take care of the equipment and take pride in the company." "Yes, sir." "You will want to stop by the barber shop today; that haircut might be all right in Okinawa, but it definitely won't do in Delta Company." "Yes, sir."

"I'm sure you're going to like it here. If you have any problems at all just see Sergeant Slocum at the motor pool or the first sergeant. My door is always open on Tuesdays and Thursdays from 4:30 to 6:00, stop in any time if I can help you out in any way." "Yes, sir."

Wilson comes to attention again; they exchange salutes; he executes an about-face pivot, and marches from the room.

The notion that anything worth knowing about an individual is contained in his official records was not confined to the lower enlistees, but pervaded the entire rank structure. A senior sergeant complained to the observer:

"I'll tell you why I'm getting out. It used to be the Army was a friendly place. A private first reported to the battalion sergeant major who escorted him to the first sergeant of his company. He'd always say, "Top, got a real fine troop here for your unit, and I want you to treat him right." He'd say that even if the man was the worst dog to come through that year, but the man felt he was wanted. Then he'd talk to the first sergeant, the old man, and then his platoon sergeant. The senior NCOs always had a chat with the battalion commander. Hell, when I came to this unit nobody said nothin' but "Sign in." After three months I still hadn't seen the battalion commander, so I raised a little smoke over at EEO. I finally got to see him, but what a farce. I report in my fatigues with my nametag reading "Hooker," which it is. The colonel puts on his big phony smile, slaps me on the back, and says, "Sergeant Warren, welcome to the battalion. I been hearing some good things about your work over at the mess hall; we need good cooks." I damned near laughed in his face I was so disgusted."

It is not so much that the senior officers and NCOs did not know how to deal with their men; they could all recount leadership strategies that worked in the past, and while they faulted the younger officers and men for inexperience, they also recognized that the Army had changed. The organization seemed to have become even more impersonal with the advent of computers and centralized services. Everyone, from the private to the general, felt estranged and helpless in view of the social constraints against individual action. The organizational factors that constrained even the more experienced leaders must now be examined.

Once upon a time life in the Army was simpler—not necessarily better—but simpler. Each company maintained its own dining facilities with its own cooks, menus, and maintenance. Each battalion or regiment had a surgeon for the treatment of minor ailments. Each company provided finance clerks to the paymaster's office that were felt to be responsive to the company, because the clerks lived in the barracks. Save for the running battles with the bureaucracy in Washington, commanders had considerable discretion over the time and activities of the unit, and the proverbial "GI ingenuity" was both celebrated and encouraged. In that world it was possible to take Wednesday afternoon for the company baseball game, to hold the evening meal until the game was over, and to sit down together, eat, and replay the game. Many sergeants lived in the barracks with their men, and order was maintained by having the unruly dig and fill holes or, as a last resort, spend time in the guardhouse. The degree of truth in this idyllic image of the Army of the past is irrelevant, because it is to such a world that the officers and sergeants contrasted their current situation. In many ways the cadre saw themselves as overwhelmed and powerless against a bureaucracy that had extended its tentacles even to the company level.

As an example, one company commander told about his difficulties in improving the quality of food served to his men:

> "I know the food is greasy, sloppily prepared, and unvaried. What can I do? I contribute four cooks to the consolidated mess, but not the chief cook. I took it up with the major in charge, but he says nothing can be done until the mess steward rotates out. In another couple months, maybe things will improve."

Another commander complained that one of his men had been told to wait two weeks for a hospital appointment to check a condition that was interfering with his work:

> "I went over to the hospital, but the civilian at the appointment desk as much as told me to go to hell. I was so mad I was ready to go to the I.G. [Inspector General], but the colonel finally got him an appointment by calling the commander of the hospital; they're both on the old man's staff."

Even colonels are not always successful. One battalion commander was enraged to find, upon returning from the field, that there was no hot water in the home of one of his sergeants:

"So I called the facilities engineers, but they said they would have to pay overtime for one of their civilian plumbers to come out on the weekend; couldn't it wait until Monday. Monday, hell, he was tired and dirty from a week in the field, and that's his reward. I told them I had trained plumbers in the unit who would correct the problem. He said that was against regulations. I pleaded with him to open the warehouse so we could get the necessary parts, but he stubbornly held to his position."

In a similar episode there had been no heat or hot water in the barracks for three days in January. The first sergeant lamely apologized to the formation:

"I know you haven't had any heat or hot water up in the billets. I have spoken to the company commander, and he is taking it up with the colonel. Be patient; the lieutenant and I are doing everything we can to remedy the situation, and we'll take it to the post commander if we have to."

In another case, a private was threatened with eviction from his apartment because his family allotment had not been paid, and he did not have the money for the rent. Two calls to the Central Finance Center in Indiana pinpointed the problem. The man had changed his residence without informing the finance office. The first month his check had been forwarded, but the second month it had been returned. Regulations prohibited soldiers from receiving money allotted to the family, and the finance personnel insisted that a new check be written from Indiana for the soldier's wife. He argued that he would be evicted before the check arrived. A determination from the finance officer was necessary, but his pinochle game could not be interrupted until after lunch. Amid conflicting claims of whether the soldier could be paid his due, he received the money after four hours of negotiation. His first sergeant commented:

"I don't blame the younger men for getting out. People like me have too much time in and are stuck. In the old Army, the finance clerks lived in the barracks. They either worked overtime to take care of the men in the company, or they became accident-prone in the shower. Those clerks over at finance don't care about us; they're just putting in their time. I keep a duplicate set of records in my possession at all times. Why when I went to Korea last time they had my records so screwed up I wasn't paid for six months. It's all so impersonal now; pay, promotions, assignments are all done by computer in Washington. There's no way the individual soldier can have much say at all. Look at Sergeant Andrews, with his asthma condition he should be in Arizona; he put in for it, but look where he was assigned—in this swamp; the computer just matches MOS with openings; there's no concern for the individual. If I were younger, I'd get the hell out, too."

Nothing rankled the leaders more than the changes in the legal system. For any violation of the Uniform Code of Military Justice, soldiers are advised of their right to counsel and a hearing before a military judge. Cases would be thrown out of court or delayed for months when the paperwork was not in proper form, down to the last comma. The authority to confine a soldier to the stockade has been sharply curtailed, and all instances must be approved by an officer in the Judge Advocate General Corps. Pretrial confinement was carefully monitored, and harsh prison conditions have disappeared. Restrictions on confinement authority, in the words of one captain, "took the sword away from the company commander." Another captain commented to a legal officer:

"You people don't seem to realize how important, swift, sure punishment is in the control of an Army unit. I always felt that strapping on my .45 and marching a troublemaker to the stockade had a powerful influence on the rest of the men." The JAG officer conceded the point, but noted the law was not written to reinforce the authority of the command, but to protect the rights of the individual soldier.

In addition to changes in confinement authority, the rules of evidence have changed. To the eternal consternation of the officers and NCOs, a private's word was as good as theirs in the absence of witnesses. A private explained his brush with the company commander:

"So there I was sitting on my bunk, smoking a "J," when Chilly Willy comes up behind me. 'Egan, are you smoking marijuana?' I dropped it on the floor and says, 'No sir, not me; I don't know where that came from.' He storms out and comes back with a sergeant as a witness, but they didn't find anything in their search."

Searches also required "probable cause," thus the accidental discovery of drugs was not usually grounds for prosecution. A commander reported:

"That was JAG on the phone; they want to drop the marijuana charge. The man was suspected of stealing from the barracks. The sergeants took him to his room to change clothes, and a "J" falls out of his shirt. They search the room and find more dope, but now the lawyer says he will have trouble proving it was a legal search. Damn it all, anyway!"

The only alternative to prosecution, from the viewpoint of the commander, was harassment. A command-directed urine analysis provided one avenue of action:

"A private had just returned from two days AWOL. The captain had just called JAG, and had learned that the absence was not sufficient ground to initiate revocation of suspended sentence proceedings against the man who had recently been punished. The captain said, "Now what am I going to do with that fucker in my billets? First sergeant, send him over to the drug center for a piss test. If he's positive, maybe we can get rid of him through the treatment program." A few minutes later the first sergeant reported back, and the captain exploded, "He refuses to take the piss test, does he? Well send Sergeant Wahl over there with him, and they can just stay there until he pisses in the bottle."

Drug and alcohol treatment programs were viewed with cynical distrust by leaders who equated use with poor performance, since the users they most commonly saw were also below standard in their military appearance and performance. A veteran first sergeant commented:

"The drug treatment programs are a farce; just a way to get out of duty. In Vietnam the drug counselors were the biggest pushers in the company. If three months of my counseling doesn't straighten the man out, there's no hope, and he should be kicked out of the Army."

The treatment centers provided a convenient place to dump undesirables, as in the case of the man who processed into the unit, admitted a past problem with alcohol, got very very drunk the first night, and defecated in the shower. He was immediately sent to the alcohol rehabilitation facility. Others who had drinking problems were left alone so long as they could perform their duties.

One of the major problems with the rehabilitation facilities was the perception that they were unsympathetic to the problems of the commanders. The following telephone conversation is illustrative:

The captain was speaking to Mr. Evans of the Alcohol Rehabilitation Center. "I'm sorry, I don't know where Cosway is. I send men over there time after time; I get no word of where they are or what they are doing; I get no word on their progress; no recommendations; no nothing from you folks until they go AWOL. Then you call me and expect me to do something about it. Damn it, you lost him; you find him."

In another case, a lieutenant and a civilian counselor tried to get one of their clients reinstated in the unit. The commander and first sergeant flatly refused, and recommended that the man get a "fresh start" in a new unit. The civilian had the temerity to suggest that the first sergeant was biased. Later the first sergeant exploded to the observer:

"The civilian was just pissed off because I wouldn't send over Akerman's clothes. Well, that's not my job. I had Akerman in Korea. He can't be trusted; he has a pending Article 15 for leaving without being relieved; he has too much rank to pull details; he cannot lead; he cannot have access to weapons. I'm biased, am I? The little fucker was on drugs the day he processed into this company."

With respect to drugs, thoughtful commanders also have to deal with personal self-doubt about punishing marijuana use, even when they have a good case. One such commander confessed:

"I honestly don't know what I should do about drug use. Some authorities say marijuana smoking is dangerous; others say it is not. Texas used to have the stiffest marijuana laws in the country, but they recently softened them. In some places, possession is just like a parking violation. I'm willing to enforce the law, but I wish I had some clear idea of appropriate punishment to fit the crime. I'd send them all to prison, but I'd also look like a damned fool when trained judges are letting kids off with a $5 fine."

A very senior colonel took a similar position:

"If we just didn't have to enforce the law. No one really believes drugs affect readiness, but we're bound to uphold the constitution. I had a driver one time—damned fine soldier, too—but he was using drugs. I told him to stop; he said he wouldn't give them up. I had no choice but to get rid of him. What a waste."

In summary, the officers and sergeants closest to the troops did not know what to do to improve life in the Army. They groused about the Army bureaucracy, the impersonal organizational climate, the changes in the legal system, and saw themselves in a hopeless morass of paperwork and regulations that made most of their efforts ineffectual. They acknowledged that the junior NCOs were inexperienced and that the schools were failing to train leaders equal to the task, but they had no remedy. The senior leaders were either cynically or philosophically resigned to a social system that they neither comprehended nor controlled. A colonel suggested that the observer read General Bruce Clark's handbook, *Guides for the Company Commander:*

> "Clark has some good ideas, but he's a little too gung-ho. He thinks an officer should eat, sleep, breathe, live and die Army 25 hours a day. You just can't expect that kind of devotion and commitment in the garrison Army. He ignores the demands of wives and families and second jobs; he lives in a world where everyone lived on the same post and were social friends as well as work associates. Those days are gone, and we must muddle through."

The fact that of 180 NCOs in one battalion studied, 30 attended a free beer call after work, that only three of these were junior sergeants, and that mandatory attendance was required at an NCO social in another battalion further attested to the change in social order noted by the colonel.

A battalion commander felt it was his responsibility to teach his company commanders to wage bureaucratic warfare "with determination and a firm resolve." He was completely unwilling to recognize that such campaigns are waged in the trenches where the civilian bureaucrats and the regulations always outlast a military leader on a three-year tour.

Another colonel viewed drug use as simply an extension of the patterns observed in the larger society:

> "You know, I think that marijuana is becoming fairly widespread. It's just like an officer going down to the club for a few drinks; the younger kids are now using or at least experimenting with it. It's just like in the civilian society; the Army's just following the same patterns. . . . It used to be that people really thought marijuana was hazardous to your health, but attitudes are changing; it's been shown that it's almost harmless when compared to alcohol. . . . Marijuana is just like alcohol during prohibition; I think it will be legalized in another five years."

A collage of confusion, alienation, and perceived helplessness in a world of eroding values and social restraints marked the beliefs and attitudes of leaders at Fort Marshall. They were fundamentally unconcerned about alcohol misuse, or drug use, or even the men in the barracks. Their basic concerns were promotions, maintaining authority, and avoiding the suspicion of incompetence. For each officer and NCO these issues posed significant psychological questions: Where do I fit in this organization called the Army? Am I really important? If I am, what is the evidence that tells me so? The plaintive cry of the men in the barracks expressed in one group interview—"Nobody gives a shit about us"—was echoed by the leaders as they struggled to maintain a stable place in the amorphous social order.

In view of this depressing and seemingly hopeless organizational climate, it was perhaps not surprising that the leaders saw that the solution to what ails the Army is beyond individual effort, lies outside the company, and is even out of reach of the battalion. Soldiers of all ranks agreed that the solution to all their problems and quandaries lay in meaningful work, or in Army jargon, "a mission for which we were trained." A senior commander summed up this sentiment well:

> "The traditional and only effective solution to the Army's problems— alcohol, drugs, race, whatever—is work. Work the men 18 hours a day for 10 days, give them three days to get drunk, and then work them again. I have fully trained electricians, plumbers, and masons who cannot work because of lack of appropriations, and because of inevitable opposition by civilian contractors and labor unions. I have truck drivers who are limited in how far they can transport what kinds of cargo because of prohibitive regulations supported by the trucking lobby. I have fully trained medics who could man public health clinics, if we had the money and support from the medical establishment. Instead, I have these men pulling routine maintenance and post beautification details. It's no wonder we have problems that appear insolvable. We can't even train like we should with the fuel shortages and budget constraints imposed on us."

The privates concurred that they had little work to do that was either interesting or in line with their training. They agreed that they were more satisfied with their lot in the Army on those brief occasions when they had work to do for which they were trained. However, they were far less sanguine about the role of a mission in solving the social ills of the organization. A private during a temporary duty assignment commented, "Sure we're happier when we're working, but that doesn't change drug use. The only thing a mission does is keep the cadre occupied so they have less time to hassle us." Observation confirmed the private's conclusion. Moving a company away from post on a temporary assignment and providing mission relevant work did improve job satisfaction for both the privates and the leaders, but aside from the temporary disruption of distribution patterns, drug and alcohol use did not change. In view of the patterns of use that bind people together into cohesive social units, it is not surprising that work and mission are fundamentally unrelated to drug and alcohol use.

The discussion thus far has focused on what the leaders know of life in the barracks, the limitations on their knowledge, their attempts to intervene, and the reasons they use to explain their failure to be more successful. The evidence presented leads to the inescapable conclusion that, with respect to drug and alcohol use in the barracks, the two traditional panaceas or solutions to human relations problems in the military—leadership and a mission—are fundamentally irrelevant. Irrelevant, that is, under the assumptions and social structural constraints described. If drug and alcohol use is viewed as a "social problem" in the contemporary Army, then it is imperative to inquire how patterns of use might be altered by granting other assumptions and different structural constraints. Such an inquiry is possible by leaving aside for the moment the typical Army leader's response and concentrating on the behavior of a "deviant" leader—an exception to the general rule—a man who implicitly understood social structure and small group dynamics sufficiently well to know where his men were coming from.

THE EXCEPTION: SERGEANT WILEY FOX

Wiley Fox was hardly the Hollywood ideal of a lean, mean Army sergeant. He was of medium build, bespectacled, with gray, receding hair and an ample girth that testified to the rich food and European beer he loved so well. On leave in his small southern hometown, he would have easily passed for a middle-aged shopkeeper. Dressed in his black suit, white shirt and tie, Wiley looked like a parish pastor. Puttering in his yard, wearing bermuda shorts and a sports shirt, he resembled a recently retired courthouse clerk whose only passion was photographing roses. In Army fatigues he looked a bit like the good soldier Schweik who would have marched more smartly if the quartermaster had only issued him boots a size larger. In his dress uniform he suggested a mild-mannered Omar Bradley who looked after his men with fatherly concern. Wiley's career specialty was military intelligence, and his unassuming manners probably contributed to his effectiveness, for few would suspect such an innocuous fellow until it was too late.

Yet Wiley Fox was a warrior who was prepared to be absolutely ruthless in carrying out the professional duties that he described simply enough—"killing people." He had been severely wounded in Vietnam, but immediately returned to the war zone upon his recovery. He exulted in war not because of the killing and carnage, but for the intellectual and emotional thrill of pitting himself against an equally cunning adversary. Listening to his war stories was like listening to the tales of a big game hunter, even down to "the one that got away." The observer noted:

> Sergeant Fox told me about a woman who controlled the black market in one of the port cities in Vietnam. "She was one of the real society matrons of the city, but we knew she was getting her cut from every crate that came off the pier. I watched her for weeks; knew where she went, when, and with whom; but she was clever and well guarded. God, I wish I could have shot that bitch."

Wiley loved the Army and his country with a passionate, old-fashioned patriotism that sounded strange amid the cynicism of his contemporaries. He became unabashedly misty-eyed when he talked of flag and country, and the sincerity and rhetorical style of his speech transformed the trite, jingoistic cliches of politicians into profound, inspirational truths. He transferred into the unit from Korea, where he suffered a series of mild heart attacks, but his determination to "go down fighting" was such that he managed to re-enlist for another six years without having a medical examination.

Intellectually, Wiley was clever, but not particularly subtle. He believed the war in Vietnam had been lost "because the politicians forced us to fight it with one hand tied behind our back," that drug use among American soldiers was "a carefully planned communist trick to undermine morale," and that drug use in garrison was the work of "pushers" who embodied all of the evil, sinister intentions portrayed in the media stereotypes. Politically, he was a conservative who supported expanded defense spending and opposed social spending that went "mostly to welfare chislers and those too lazy to work."

When Wiley came into the unit, he worked as the company operations sergeant, but quickly grew bored with the paperwork. He desperately wanted to have a platoon of his own, but none was available. After considerable wheedling, he convinced the company commander and first sergeant to give him a platoon. He was ecstatic at the prospects, but confided to the observer:

"All they give me is 34 men. That's not many, but it's a start. Damn, if I only had 60 men I could set this battalion on its ass."

Casual inspection revealed that the platoon looked no different than countless others. The uniforms ranged from neat to disheveled, and haircuts from evenly trimmed to ragged. The physical appearance of the bay was undistinguished in muted institutional greens and grays with a tile floor that was usually scuffed. The men spent their days as did most others in the unit, doing chores in the motor pool, cutting grass, shoveling snow, going to the field for training, and occasionally getting a job for which they had been trained.

To the observer familiar with other barracks, however, there were striking differences. The bay was partitioned into cubicles by wall lockers like other bays, but here each area housed four to six men instead of the usual two or three. Bunk beds were the rule, and there seemed to be more wall lockers than residents. A quarter of the bay was a lounge area with a carpet, easy chairs, and a few magazines. The barracks orderly had a desk just inside the door, and Wiley kept his desk near the lounge area rather than in the platoon sergeant's office.

More remarkable still was the ambience, the feeling tone of the barracks. Soldiers were usually hanging around the bay at all hours of the day, engaged in relaxed conversation that often included racially mixed groups. Radios, played at low volume, punctuated the laughter at traded stories. Owing to the unusual amount of traffic during the work day, the orderly often swept the center aisle three or four times, but invariably with a smile. Even more unusual was the fact that when soldiers entered the bay, they reported to their sergeants that the assigned task had been accomplished and that they were ready for the next.

Wiley orchestrated all of the platoon movements from his desk in the bay. He was always soft-spoken with a mild southern drawl, and referred to the men by their first names or their last prefaced by "mister." The observer noted:

Sergeant Fox greeted each man as he made his way through the bay on his morning tour. "Morning Robert, how are you today? Have a good leave? . . . Barry, got some work for you today; hurry up with your breakfast . . . Kenny, you had an appointment with the JAG; was that today or tomorrow? . . . Mister Dexter, top o' the morning; you were late coming off leave, but don't worry about it; I covered for you . . . William, did you call your folks? . . ."

From his desk he needed only to mutter to himself, "Now where is so-and-so," and someone would go scurrying off to summon the man requested. It was not that he could not assume "command presence," but that he usually chose not to.

> At the end of the picnic only a half dozen or so men remained to kill the keg. Sergeant Fox suggested they police up the area, and I reached under the table to retrieve a cigarette package. Fox snapped out in a tone that permitted little argument: "Captain, leave that goddamned paper where it lies." "Sergeant Fox, how do you know I wasn't responsible for putting it there?" "Leave it lie! In my Army, officers don't pull police call."

In addition to his gentle speech he had the habit of touching the men when he addressed them individually. In this way their attention was riveted on him as he spoke.

> One man requested that he be allowed to go get snow tires for his car. Sergeant Fox granted the request, but grasped the soldier gently on his upper arm and counseled, "Now, whatever you do, drive carefully. In this snow drive very slowly, and if some damned fool follows you too closely, just pull off the road and let him by. You read me? OK, son, see you when you get back."

Later in the morning a similar touch accompanied a routine inquiry:

> As we approached the truck a black private was brushing snow from the hood. Sergeant Fox laid his hand on the private's arm and asked, "You get it started all right? Good, I'm counting on you to have it ready to go at any time. How are your ears? Don't let them get too cold; if they get too cold, you be sure and go inside." Listening to the sergeant, I got the impression this was the most important man in the entire battalion, and judging from the private's expressions as he listened, he had the same impression.

Like his gentle speech, his gentle touch could be modified to suit the occasion.

> Sergeant Fox talked about handling each man as an individual. "Now you take Noble, he must have had a rough time growing up, and I'll bet his father beat him plenty. You can't talk to him like the other men; you first have to get his attention and make him afraid." "How do you make him afraid?" "I slammed him up against the wall and tapped him in the

stomach a few times; that's all it took; now he listens when I talk to him."

Although he never would have used the term, Wiley understood the meaning, function, and importance of group boundaries. The observer recounted:

I asked him how the bay came to be laid out as it was with a lounge and all. "Well, the first problem I faced with the platoon was getting the men to pull together. I sat them down and said that now that I was their platoon sergeant, I would have to have a place to sleep in the bay, and since I had the most rank, I would take that quarter where the lounge is now. If they're gonna pull together they have to have some opposition, and at the time I figured it might as well be me. Well, they drew themselves a little closer in the circle, looked at each other, and then began arguing that just because I was the platoon sergeant didn't give me any right to hog a quarter of the bay.

"I gradually allowed as how maybe I had been a little greedy, but then asked them what they had in mind for the married men. After all, it's a platoon bay, and the married men should start keeping their field equipment in the same place as everybody else. After some more discussion someone got the idea of getting more lockers for the married men that could also be used to partition the bay more effectively. Since all the sergeants also had to have bunks on the bay, they finally invented the idea of squads, so the cubicles you see are squad areas. The married guys traded their bunks that they never use for the lounge area that everybody can use. Then we set to work painting the whole bay, replacing the broken windows, and furnishing the lounge."

Given the nucleus of an in-group, the structure grew by continual infusions of distinctive activities. There was always something going on in the platoon, ranging from sitting in the lounge being quizzed for the promotion board, to planning a 50-mile hike for reconnaissance of the river, to building washstands and showers for the next field exercise, to showing up the other platoons by shoveling all the walks before the others were up and dressed. The objectives of these activities were to fill time, allow each individual to contribute his skills, and most important, to provide a means for the men to know each other.

Sergeant Fox talked about keeping up morale during inclement weather. "You gotta do something with them or they start bickering and squabbling among each other. When we were on that temporary duty assignment it rained one afternoon, and they immediately commenced to grumbling. I loaded them on the truck and drove to the local historical society museum. You should have heard them moaning on the way: "This won't be any fun. Who wants to go to a boring old museum." When they came out they were singing a different tune: "Gosh, I didn't know this area went back to the Revolution. Did you see that old cannon? Yeah, and can you imagine farming with them wooden tools?" They grumbled, but they talked about that museum all through supper that night."

The out-groups were usually the other platoons in the company, and could be defined as an amorphous, sinister "they." An armed robbery in a neighboring company provided such an occasion. As Wiley told the story:

"That desk at the door is for the barracks orderly and a CQ in the evening. It's extra duty, but the men don't object. After the robbery I told them that nothing like that would ever happen in our platoon. If anyone comes in here with a gun, someone just distracts him while others get behind him, jump him, and stomp him into the ground." He then added with a chuckle, "I think the round-the-clock barracks guard was their idea."

The platoon was also remarkable for the absence of the usual grumbling about having no real mission. For Wiley, the mission was "whatever the company commander orders us to do," and he had the ability to endow the most mundane tasks with the drama of combat.

The platoon was on snow alert, and the men were lounging around the barracks, but with an air of excitement and impending drama. Sergeant Fox talked about the need for coffee and soup for the men who may be shoveling sand from the trucks. The married men volunteered thermos bottles, and someone suggested sandwiches from the mess hall. One man drifts into the discussion group, and Fox counsels, "Now, Roy, you get back to bed. You worked hard last night, and we have to be rested; snow and cold will beat you every time if you're not rested." "But Sergeant Fox . . ." "But nothing; you get some sleep. Now third squad; you all checked your equipment? Everybody got gloves, scarfs, and hats? I don't want anyone going out unless all his equipment is in order."

If the task at hand could not be accomplished with a combat motif, other strategies were employed:

"Whenever possible, I always say, have some fun. When I was operations sergeant, I got a piddling little two-man detail to pick up some trash in a long ravine. Well, I went to the stable and got a horse so one man could ride and carry the sacks while the other filled them. Hell, I had men volunteering for that detail." "How about mowing grass?" "Grass details are the most fun of all. I organized drag races with the riding mowers. Even persuaded the MPs to ticket a man for going three miles an hour in a two-mile zone. Company commander then called him out in front of the formation, read the citation, and told him not to get caught next time. Everybody laughed, and the man felt right good for being recognized as a fast worker."

In another sense, however, Wiley Fox defined his mission more broadly and more aggressively than simply waiting for an order from the commander:

"Most of these younger sergeants have spent their careers in Vietnam or in getting ready to go to the war zone. They don't realize that in garrison there really isn't very much for a soldier to do. Garrison is mostly just sitting around maintaining equipment that is seldom used. The most important job of a platoon sergeant is to aggressively seek out work. If I can find only two hours of work a week in line with a man's interests, I have a better soldier. You always have to study the individual, and then play to his strong side. I remember one unit in Germany I had a man who was interested in photography. They were planning a new darkroom at the hobby shop, so I got him a job every afternoon designing and installing the darkroom. Another man was mechanically inclined, so we would scour the city on garbage hauling days for discarded bicycles. He fixed them up and we would lend them to anybody in the unit who wanted to borrow them. We got so many that we damned near had a platoon on bicycles. Then there was the Puerto Rican who didn't speak English very well. I didn't know what to do with him; all he ever showed much interest in was music. Then I hit on the idea of training him to modify American electrical appliances to work on the European circuits and vice-versa. It wasn't long until he was one of the happiest people in the unit. The Army doesn't like to admit it, but most of our "work" can be done in three or four hours a day."

Wiley approved of drinking, but strongly disapproved of drug use. Every two weeks or so, the sergeants in the platoon chipped in to buy a keg of beer that usually lasted for two days before it was gone. Whatever the issue, he was ready to bet anyone a case of beer because "The important thing is that the men talk to each other. Makes no difference who buys the beer; just so we have a reason to get together." When asked how many men used drugs when he formed

the platoon, his answer was equally quick—"Five." He believed he
had eradicated drug use:

> "First I got some films from the education center; you know, showing
> what happens to people on drugs. Then I took all five of them to the
> emergency room in a city hospital, and we watched the addicts come in
> all drugged up with scars running all over their arms. I also arranged
> for a marijuana sniffing dog to come through the barracks, and I let
> everyone know that I won't tolerate that stuff in my platoon. I tell
> them, "Go ahead and use whatever you want, but I'm going to catch
> you; it's only a matter of time, and when I do, you'll know you've been
> had. They quit using quite directly, and I haven't had any problem with
> drugs in the platoon at all."

A more likely explanation for Wiley's success is that he sup-
planted the role of drugs in the barracks with his own strategies for
bringing men together, giving them things to talk about and issues on
which to take a stand. In addition, his relationship with each man in
the platoon was so personalized and so intense that to be caught in
disapproved activities would have betrayed a trust that each man was
committed to maintain. The personalized concern began at the first
meeting, with Wiley interviewing the new man about his hometown,
family, friends, interests, girlfriends, and talents. The observer recalled:

> I asked him why he collected so much personal information. "I need it
> to be effective. Take Richards over there; he comes from a large family,
> his father ran off, and he has to send most of his pay home. Now when
> something goes wrong with the family, he'll go AWOL if he has to help
> them out. He likes mechanics, so I got him a part-time job at a filling
> station; he sends his pay home, but makes enough at the station to get
> along here in the barracks. Donohue just broke up with his girl—
> happens every two weeks—so he'll probably need a little extra time off
> this weekend. Keefer lives in California; he needs a little help getting an
> Air Force hop if he is to get home."

Each introductory interview was followed up with a letter to the
man's family, expressing the sergeant's delight in having the son in
his platoon, advising them to be sure to contact the Red Cross if their
boy was needed at home in an emergency, and requesting that they
write or call him with any questions or concerns. Furthermore, although the company policy forbade accepting collect phone calls,
Wiley left standing orders that all such calls from members of his

platoon were to be transferred to his home phone and that he would accept the charges.

Because everyone had his phone number, Wiley was available at all hours of the day or night. He describes a particularly trying night:

"Sorry, I'm a little bushed this morning; been up since 2:30. Got a call from the city jail; four of my men were locked up. The desk sergeant apologized for waking me, but said one man insisted that I be called. I says, "That's exactly right; he did just what I told him to do; I'll be right down." Two of them were jailed for fighting, and I got them out directly. The other two were caught stealing tires off an auto transport in the railroad yard. That's tampering with interstate commerce, so they'll be seeing a federal judge, and I couldn't do much for them. The police were most cooperative. The arresting officer took me over to the hotel. What a dive; I've never been in such a filthy, stinking place. I said this wasn't right, and he agreed, but said there wasn't much they could do. I suggested he contact the military police and have the place put off limits to soldiers, and he thought that was a good idea." "Why bother? All four of those men are duds who have been giving you grief for weeks." "They're still my men, and I'm their platoon sergeant. If I don't help them, who will?"

Not only did the men have his telephone number, but they were also encouraged to visit him and his wife at their apartment. Thus Wiley Fox was never off duty. Whether through phone calls from the barracks orderly or visits to his home, he was always apprised of what was happening in the platoon, and was likely to appear on the bay at anytime. He was in constant motion, picking up rumors, praising, counseling, joking, and planning out loud the activities for the next day.

Wiley did not last very long as a platoon sergeant—about six months at most. The unit was in the field for the annual winter exercise. He had prepped his men for weeks on ambush tactics, security precautions, and grading procedures, yet he did not feel that the unit was truly ready. He laid out the strategy in his pep talk as the platoon huddled around him in the barracks:

"We're not ready; we're going to make a lot of mistakes, but we can't slip too often. The only way to win this one is to run the judges ragged. We'll keep them up and running for the first 36 hours, then we can take a few mistakes. Keep your eyes on the lieutenant who will be following me; the minute he looks sleepy make sure he takes a tour of the entire perimeter; we've got to run him into the ground."

The first day of the exercise dawned clear, but with light snow. The sergeant had worked all night preparing for loading the equipment. In the field, the snow melted and turned into sticky mud. By ten in the morning the tents were in place, the foxholes dug, and Wiley had completed his first tour of the area. He stopped at a jeep to talk with one of the squad leaders, complained that he feared his angina "hissies" were acting up again, and then slumped to the ground. The squad leader knelt in the mud and slipped the nitroglycerin tablet under the sergeant's tongue as he had been instructed. The field ambulance would not start. Slowly the nitro took effect, and Wiley was helped to a jeep for the ride back to the hospital.

When he returned to duty, his request to return to the platoon was denied, and he went back to a desk job in the intelligence office. The platoon quickly reverted to the typical patterns of behavior described for other units. Wiley could not comprehend why his platoon fell apart:

> "It's not supposed to work that way. In the Army, no man is indispensable. I set it up; I showed them how to work it; but when I left they forgot everything. Why? It's supposed to just keep going with new men and different faces. The parts are interchangeable in the Army, yet the platoon fell apart when I left. Why? No single individual can be that important. Why, Doc, why?"

From the observer's viewpoint, why the platoon fell apart after Sergeant Fox left is the wrong question. For the very reasons elaborated throughout this book, the platoon did not "fall apart," but simply returned to its natural state. The more interesting and important question is how Fox succeeded in the face of the many obstacles and social changes characterizing the modern garrison Army.

One element of the sergeant's unusual success was his personal trademark: an olive-drab pickaxe handle that he carried as a walking stick. He could be quite persuasive when he quietly laid it on the desk in the Finance Office while discussing one of his charge's problems. At the time of the study, "The Godfather" had just been released to area theatres and Wiley moved merrily from place to place, joking about making offers that could not be refused. Even in jest, the simple presence of the axe handle made him quite intimidating:

> "So we get this mission to form up like a bucket brigade and pass bales of shingles up to the roof of this warehouse. In the summer that's damned hot work. I says to the men, 'Why are we standing here in the

sun when we have a machine to do this work? Let's get that fork lift over yonder and use it to get this job done.' The men said, 'We already thought of that, but the man in the warehouse said we couldn't have it.' 'Well, then, take it! We got a job to do,' I says. Then I went to see the warehouse foreman with my walking stick. 'Don't you ever deny the use of your equipment to my men,' I said. 'They got a job to do and you aren't using the fork lift right now, anyway.' He just looked at the axe handle and said, 'Gee, I'm sorry, Sergeant Fox, I didn't realize it was you. You can be sure it won't happen again.' I thanked him for his kind attention and understanding."

During the study, we never saw Wiley use his axe handle except as a symbol, but he told of using it once in another way:

"One time in Germany, I was eating in the mess hall when a racial fracas broke out. Oh, Lawdy, they were throwing dishes, busting chairs and carrying on something terrible. I just continued eating. Two blacks came over to my table and one of them started running his mouth: 'Hey, old man, you better move out of here, we gonna tear this place apart.' I told 'em it made me no never mind, we were going to have to put the place back together again the next day anyhow, and I saw no reason to leave before I finished my dessert. The mouthy one started poking and provoking me, so I reached down for my axe handle and laid his head open. I told the quiet one to get his buddy out of there before he got hurt. Then I finished my coffee and dessert."

Like the sex stories soldiers tell each other in the barracks, it does not really matter whether this actually happened. When Wiley told the story with the handle lying on his lap, you believed him.

Another element in this leader's success was an ability to create indebtedness to himself. One strategy involved a private construction company he managed on the side. Wiley specialized in remodeling taverns in record time. His men could lay a floor, hang a ceiling, affix paneling, or replace the plumbing, all between business hours. The owners paid handsomely for this service, but they lost no revenues because of it. Wiley paid good wages, and he especially liked workers who were also soldiers, badly in debt, and in a position to do him favors. On one occasion he hired his first sergeant "just to watch the bar so the men don't drink too much while they're working—you'll get the usual wage and all you want to drink."

Those who couldn't be bought might become obligated in other ways. When a new colonel came to the battalion, Wiley saw to it that all the appliances worked, that new rugs and drapes were installed, and that the quarters were spotless. In the refrigerator he left a quart of whiskey and a can of beer—"An old Army custom," he mused, "that the colonel would understand and appreciate." Finally, Wiley pushed the Army system to the legal limit—and sometimes beyond. There was practically nothing he wouldn't do for his men.

> "I'm a little depressed today, you'll excuse me. The colonel is mad at me. We just had a little talk. I don't know what he is so upset about. That whole pile of plywood had been setting in that field rotting for months—no plastic cover or anything on it. My men needed plywood to accomplish their mission. Well, damn, you can't win them all. But I don't understand it, the wood was going to waste, anyway."

Such devotion did not make him the easiest person to work with—unless you were willing to abide by "Wiley's Law." Whenever anyone asked him for anything or whenever he made a request, the wording almost always began, "Wiley's Law says . . ." meaning "Let's do it my way." Those who followed the law got along well with him, but he could be an undeniable rascal with those who did not. This may have accounted for his surprisingly low rank of sergeant first class after more than thirty years of service. Who knows how many times he might have achieved and lost rank for doing what he thought best for his men, but insisting that it be done by "Wiley's Law." There is little question that he paid a considerable price somewhere along the line for his unorthodox ways.

I asked Wiley to reflect on the changes during his thirty years of service:

> "When I came in, the men felt close together. You could leave your billfold on your bunk for a week and it'd still be there when you came back. There was only one car in the outfit, so we all had to chip in for gas, but of course only a certain percentage could be on pass at one time. We used to play baseball and cards and do marching drills just to pass the time. Maybe that's part of what's wrong today: we've lost the ability to entertain ourselves."

Had the men changed?

> "Yes, when I came in, a lot of guys had trouble writing their names, and a high school education was really unusual in some outfits. Now the guys are better educated, but dumber, if you know what I mean. They have high school diplomas but can't read a lick. No, it's not the men who have changed, it's the way they are led."

How have the leaders changed?

"They don't care anymore. We're not putting the Army first anymore; there's too much moonlighting, and the Army comes second. There's no sense of community like when all the sergeants got to know each other and spend time together. We've got to get back to professionalism at every level. You can't run an Army where the first four ranks are all recruits. We need professional privates who can drive any rig in the lot and handle any weapon in the arms room. They could teach the younger guys more than the sergeants. But the Army doesn't see it that way; it's either up in rank or out of service. They think that every NCO should be bucking for sergeant major of the Army; hell, there's but one of them. Everybody is evaluated on education and test scores that can be read by the computer. Qualitative management they call it; brought to you by the same goddamned dummies who got us into Vietnam."

The colonel saw the situation differently: "Show me a private with fifteen years experience and I'll show you a private with one year of experience repeated fifteen times." The colonel thought that the basic leadership problems rested with the junior sergeants who insisted on being pals with the boys in the barracks instead of exerting their authority. The colonel thought that men like Wiley Fox "were all right for babysitting and housekeeping, but I wouldn't want to take them into combat—you know, of course, his test scores aren't really that good." The colonel thought that the Army was just like the civilian world, and that the "drug problem" would iron itself out in a few years—"just like the racial tensions we experienced a couple of years ago." The colonel thought that the Army could be conceptualized within an industrial model, and that what was really needed was management experts trained to master a bureaucracy. The colonel looked to a bright future; Wiley Fox could only see the past.

Faced with such opposition, why do sergeants like Wiley Fox persist? Why do they insist on being rebels who are repeatedly washed out of the mainstream and into the eddies? When confronted with these questions, Wiley could only respond with the cliches that he had always regarded as eternal truths, or perhaps the truths that others had always regarded as cliches:

"I am a soldier and an American. I am proud of both. Whenever I go to Washington, D.C. I always go to the Tomb of the Unknown Soldier and think of the words, "The soldier is the most despised creature on this earth until there is war, then he is hero to all." Why do I bother with this platoon? I really don't know. Maybe it's that I've seen too much killing in the last thirty years. These men are soldiers. They only exist for one reason—to die. The only challenge in being a soldier is in staying alive. To do that in combat you have to know and be able to count on your buddies. You can endure anything so long as you know your buddies are in the next foxhole. Why do I bother? It's my job. You never know; the time might come when I, too, must count on them to follow that final order, 'Go and die.' "

CRITICAL COMMENTARY
Frederick J. Manning

In *The Boys in the Barracks*, Larry Ingraham has written of things certain to horrify American mothers, and probably a great many upper-middle-class fathers as well. He tells us that readers of the book in manuscript reacted with "shock, dismay, and even disgust" to this candid portrayal of barracks life. Such a reaction is perhaps the stuff of which today's best sellers are made, but I suspect it is one that the author, as a serious contributor to social science, could well do without, for it makes it all too easy for the reader to reject his theses and his suggestions for institutional change. Perhaps he recognizes the dissonance engendered by the notion that we have entrusted the defense of our nation to an army of such boys as he portrays, for he tells us that "the boys in the barracks are not deviants or delinquents . . . not made of defective protoplasm" in an attempt to cut off our escape at the "special case" pass. He asserts that it is the barracks rather than the boys that should be central to the issue of generality, for it is social structures rather than personalities and demographics that determine the behavior he describes. One of the goals of this "critical commentary" is to examine this assertion in the light of other studies of Army social structure, other works on drug and alcohol use, and other subcultures. A second goal is to examine the implications of this study for the Army and its leaders at all levels: what they have done since Ingraham began to show them his portrait of the barracks, what they still can do, and why they should do it. An additional issue, relevant to the generalization problem, and consequently to the need for change, is the question of method. Bluntly put, should a research report without numbers be considered science? It is with this issue that I should like to begin.

205

KNOWLEDGE AND MEASUREMENT

The Boys in the Barracks was conceived in a turbulent time. The late sixties and early seventies brought disillusionment in large doses—not only to the citizenry at large, but also to some cherished bastions of academic tranquility. One of these was social psychology's "Church of Latter-Day Empiricism." As in the rest of psychology, the "Experiment" had always been the one true path to knowledge. Yet Daniel Katz, one of the deans of social psychology, picked 1972 to observe that 20 years and thousands of experiments had produced only a few studies that supplied new information in a cumulative fashion (Katz, 1972). This sad lack of impact, he suggested, was due not to poor method, but to the paucity of good ideas. Brewster Smith came to a similar conclusion that same year (Smith, 1972), as did Leonard Berkowitz, who said "We seem to be somewhat at a loss for important problems to investigate and models to employ in our research and theory." Smith himself wrote that "the predominant experimental tradition of the field has contributed rather little of serious import in enlarging and refining our views of social man." It would seem that regardless of whether there can be research without numbers, there can hardly be a worthwhile science with numbers alone.

Prescriptions for remedying this state of affairs centered on a reduction in observing computer printouts and an increase in observing people. Lee Cronbach, for example, pointed out the advantage of incorporating field research into social psychology, even though he could not quite bring himself to call it science:

> The two scientific disciplines, experimental control and systematic correlation, answer formal questions stated in advance. Intensive local observation goes beyond disciplines to an open-eyed, open-minded appreciation of the surprises nature deposits in the investigative net. This kind of interpretation is historical more than scientific. I suspect that if the psychologist were to read more widely in history, ethnology, and the centuries of humanistic writings on man and society, he would be better prepared for this part of his work. (Cronbach, 1975, p. 125)

Daniel Katz went much further:

> The great contribution field research can make in supplying new ideas for the development of the field is in discovery. The strength of the laboratory experiment is in testing a hypothesis. But the hypothesis tested is often trivial or derived from some obvious commonsense observation, or it grows out of the technology of the experiment. The

discovery of new variables and new relationships is minimized in the laboratory. In field work, however, new issues and problems often confront the researcher. Discoveries are not assured by the conventional form of the hypothesis-testing experiment. To the extent that experimental social psychology cuts itself off from field research it will be deprived of a most important input for theoretical stimulation and growth. (Katz, 1972, p. 559)

Ingraham himself may have been guided by a similar view from the start, but one suspects, from his descriptions of the work's original design, that it was his work in the trenches that brought him to this view. He says quite honestly that, asked to find out something worth knowing about drug abuse in the Army, he turned to the literature first. Only when he discovered "there were no standardized measures of anything, few guiding theoretical ideas, and a tangled mass of confusing, conflicting, or incomparable results" did he conclude, "To honor our charge we had little choice but to go to an Army post and see for ourselves just what was going on" (Ingraham, 1975). This is eloquent testimony indeed to the tyranny of numbers under which our generation of psychologists had been trained.

Ironically, these remarks were uttered in Chicago, where sociology had a long tradition of down-to-earth qualitative research as a wellspring of theory. Grand Theory and grand measurement were not to be found, but students of the "Chicago school," starting in the twenties, were taught the inductive side of science, to venture out into the real world, complex as it might be, to bring in new information in quantity, and extract durable generalizations from it, preferably in standard layman's English (see Faris, 1967, for a first-hand account). *The Boys in the Barracks* shares a major theme with much of the work of this school—that human nature is a product of social living—"that a social problem is a malady of society, but that it is social rather than organismic processes that are deranged and in a pathological state" (Burgess and Bogue, 1964). Inspired principally by Robert Ezra Park and subsequently by Everett C. Hughes, William Foote Whyte, Howard Becker, Erving Goffman, and Elliot Liebow, these sociologists plunged into the apparent chaos of urban living looking for natural processes in the interactions of members of the crowds, directing attention, in the course of developing what Park called natural history, toward the typical rather than the unique. Such works as *The Hobo* (Anderson, 1923), Hughes' *French Canada in Transition* (1943), Frederick Thrasher's *The Gang* (1927), Becker's *Outsiders* (1963), William Whyte's *Street Corner Society* (1955), and Elliot

Liebow's *Talley's Corner* (1967) are from this urban anthropology mold, which today calls itself ethnography. Weppner's *Street Ethnography* (1977) provides a representative selection of this work, all of which bears a clear family resemblance to *The Boys in the Barracks*. This resemblance becomes even more striking when one considers the tongue-in-cheek definition of ethnography offered by Preble (quoted in Walters, 1980) on the basis of Greek etymology as "the study of heathens."

THE LIFE OF THE SOLDIER

As Ingraham quite rightly points out, the question of generality is a matter for future research. This does not mean, however, that we are not justified in looking to contemporary sources for verification. In fact, although *Boys* is a valuable contribution precisely because there have been so few serious descriptions, even autobiographical or fictional, of the life of the young enlisted soldier in the peacetime Army, there are numerous sources which bear on one or another small facet of this life. In this section I will draw on these in attempting to assess whether Ingraham has painted a generally valid picture of Army life in the early seventies, and to what extent this picture differs from ones drawn in previous years. I will defer to the next section the assessment of similarity to groups outside the military.

In one of the few other books dedicated solely to the life of the enlisted soldier, Moskos (1970) attempted to provide a much more sweeping view of the American enlisted man, providing relevant Army or Department of Defense statistics on occasion, but primarily relying on first hand observation and conversation with GIs in the U.S., Germany, Korea, and Vietnam. It is reassuring to discover so many points of similarity between this work, which might not unkindly be called broad and shallow, with the intense but narrow *Boys*. Indeed, after a review of the changing enlisted image as portrayed in fiction and film since World War II, Moskos begins his discussion of "the Enlisted Culture" by pointing out that "his [every soldier's] social horizon is largely circumscribed by activities occurring at the level of the company [around 200 men]." An order of magnitude larger than the 20 or so Ingraham proposes, but a difference which pales beside the approximately 1⅛ billion different four-person groups potentially available to a soldier in a division of 15,000. Another feature of Moskos's portrayal familiar to readers of *Boys* is "boomtown"—the "bar, laundries, tailor shops, car washes, souvenir stores, massage parlors, and houses of prostitution . . . a constituent part of the overseas military community." In Chapter 2, Ingraham suggests that it is only the souvenir shops that differentiate the overseas and domestic military "boomtowns." Indeed, much of Moskos's description of the overseas serviceman is remarkably consistent with Ingraham's picture of life at a U.S. post. Contrast, for example, the "short-timer's calendar" with servicemen counting days till their return to the states; the overseas soldier's lack of contact with foreign nationals and unfavorable comparison of all things foreign to the domestic soldier's similar behavior toward all things local; and the sexual exploits (both literal and figurative) of the *Boys* with Moskos's generalization that "it is the widespread opportunity for sexual promiscuity that most distinguishes overseas from stateside assignments." It would seem that "overseas" might best be seen as a slightly exaggerated version of "away from home" in terms of much of the soldier's interaction with the surrounding community. Indeed my own recent tour in Germany provided plenty of evidence that far and away the hardest aspect of a foreign tour for most young single soldiers was the inability to make weekend trips home.

Moskos provides other similarities, more important ones to Ingraham's theses. Though he describes military life as "characterized by an interracial equalitarianism of a quantity and kind that is seldom found in the other major institutions of American society," his description of off-duty behavior parallels Ingraham's exactly: both revolve around mutual racial exclusivism. Other, independent, evidence for both halves of this problem is readily available. Brown and Nordlie (1979) summarize Army surveys of 1972 and 1974, indicating a perception by blacks that "Race problems in the Army are not as bad as they are in the rest of society." Butler and Wilson (1978) also provide a two-process picture of racial attitudes in the Army. One process, found in both white and black samples, links frequent interracial contacts to positive racial attitudes, while the other, occurring only in their black sample, was a growing favorable attitude toward black separatism which led to a pattern of relatively infrequent off-duty contact in the Army. Whatever the cause, my own observations (Manning and Ingraham, 1980) in the late seventies, with blacks now constituting 25 to 30 percent of the Army, were that voluntary segregation was still the rule, and the de facto identifications of certain NCO and Enlisted Clubs as black or white (Moskos, p. 123) was still quite common.

One of the most important points made by Ingraham is the anti-Army norm of the barracks and the division—really a chasm—which has developed between the junior enlisted and the rest of the Army. Moskos also noted this cleavage, pointing out in fact that "the animosity between lower-ranking enlisted men and NCOs has come to override the traditional enlisted hostility toward officers." Indeed the statistics gathered during World War II by the Research Branch of the Information and Education Division of the U.S. Army, and later published in *The American Soldier* (Stouffer et al., 1974) consistently showed NCO attitudes toward leadership, the Army, the troops, and a wide range of other areas far more similar to those of the privates than to those of the officers.

Interestingly, nowhere in *The Boys in the Barracks* do we find mention of a similar rift which Moskos claimed was central to much of enlisted culture, namely that involving level of education. Bluntly stated, he asserts that it is only in the military that the middle-class college-educated youth finds himself subordinate to individuals from lower socioeconomic levels, and he finds this aspect of his service at least as difficult as the authoritarian nature of the service per se. His evidence is the basic juxtaposition of two sets of data from attitude surveys. In one, favorable attitudes toward nearly every aspect of Army life are negatively related to education. In the other we find a markedly higher proportion of enlisted men with at least some college responding affirmatively when asked if they would remain in the service if they were offered a commission as an officer. It is remarkable that such a pronounced phenomenon of the late sixties could disappear so rapidly with the switch to an all-volunteer force (In a 1978 work Moskos cites Army figures showing that less than 5 percent of its 1977 enlisted men had college degrees—less than one-third the 1964 level.)

Drugs and Drink: Extent and Frequency

Another pronounced phenomenon of the late sixties, which ironically appears to have gone unnoticed—or at least unnoted—by Moskos, was the frightening escalation in illegal drug use, both in and out of the Army. Civilian use will be treated in more detail below, not because it was or is in any real sense independent of drug use by soldiers, but only because my task at the moment is an examination of whether Ingraham's view of the soldier's life is consonant with that of others in a position to comment.

Although drug use in Vietnam did not gain national attention until 1971, when the House Subcommittee on Alcoholism and Narcotics held its official hearings, the fact of widespread marihuana use by American soldiers in Vietnam was well known by 1967. In June of that year Roffman (cited by Baker, 1971) found that 63 percent of the American servicemen imprisoned in Army stockades in Vietnam, excluding those convicted of a marihuana offense, reported having used marihuana. In 1970, Roffman and Sapol surveyed a population of Army enlisted men returning to the U.S. from Vietnam and found 29 percent willing to report having used marihuana while in Vietnam. Colbach and Wilson (1971) described the use of barbiturates by U.S. soldiers in Vietnam in the spring of 1969, and in November of that year, Stanton administered a survey to approximately 1200 arriving and 1200 departing soldiers. He found that 35 percent of enlisted men arriving in Vietnam, and 50 percent of those leaving said they had used marihuana before; 30 percent of those leaving reported using marihuana 200 or more times while in Vietnam. Cookson (cited by Holloway, 1974) conducted a "paper and pencil" survey in November 1970 with a sample of 1100 enlisted men from 19 randomly selected companies. He found 30 percent reporting marihuana use, with a third of these using daily. Institution of widespread urine screening, both in randomly selected units and as a prerequisite to returning to the U.S., revealed about 5 percent of U.S. troops positive for some opiate. By the fall of 1971, Ingraham was collecting data from U.S. soldiers caught by such screening.

Drug use was by no means confined to soldiers in Vietnam during this period, as an Army-wide study carried out by the Army Research Institute revealed: Hurst and coworkers (1973) found that only 40 percent of the 17,000 low-ranking enlisted men surveyed said they had *not* used cannabis in the previous month. A wide range of other drugs were reportedly in recent use by 9 to 15 percent of the respondents. More relevant to the question of whether *The Boys in the Barracks* is a representative study, Rohrbaugh and Press (1974) reported that their surveys of Fort Riley in 1972 and 1973 found over 50 percent of lower-ranking enlisted men reporting drug use in the previous month (30 percent reported use of a drug other than marihuana). Similar surveys reported at yearly intervals in Europe have shown monthly or more frequent marihuana use in about 20 percent of U.S. soldiers stationed in Europe from 1974 through 1978. Similar use of narcotics or other dangerous drugs was found to be about 7.5 percent. These figures, however, include responses from a representative sample of officers and senior NCOs, and restricting consideration to only the replies of personnel in the lower enlisted grades, age 21 and younger, roughly doubles the percentages. Taken as a whole, the studies cited here seem to provide adequate assurance that widespread use of drugs at Ingraham's "Fort Marshall" was not atypical for the time. I will defer for the moment the consideration of other observer's views on the cause and function of such drug use, and instead examine alcohol use by military personnel.

Drinking is a long and glorious tradition among military men. Farwell (1981) provides a look at some aspects of this tradition. The three principal amusements of the British soldier, he says, were "drink, women, and gambling." He cites the description of a private's life in the Edwardian army by Robert Legget of the Cameronians:

> There was ritual every evening. The men would make themselves absolutely spotless—uniform pressed, boots polished, hair plastered down, bonnet on just so—as if every one of them had a girl-friend waiting at the gate. They went straight down to the wet canteen and got drunk.

Apparently, not all companies went out drinking as neatly. According to Farwell, Robert Graves described Kipling's "Tommy" thus:

> He was known on the one hand for his foul mouth, his love of drink and prostitutes, his irreligion, his rowdiness and his ignorance; on the other for his courage, his endurance, his loyalty and skill with fusil and pike, or with rifle and bayonet.

Then as now, the businessmen in the neighborhood of military bases were a specialized lot. The area around the great training base at Aldershot in those mid nineteenth-century days was "a perfect network of public houses, dancing saloons, and vile houses." Although it would appear from the above that the Queen's men had no difficulty finding their own supplies of alcohol, it was thought quixotic, Farwell tells us, when in 1884, during his campaign to relieve Gordon at Khartoum, Wolseley decided to abolish the rum ration in favor of jam and marmalade. Queen Victoria upheld his action, over the bitter protests of the War Office (and the men, one must presume), but it must be noted that this was the only campaign in which Wolseley failed.

Victor Hicken's *The American Fighting Man* (1969) makes it clear that liquor has had no small part in the life of "Tommy's" U.S. counterpart. He claims that during Washington's time, drinking in the Continental Army was so common that the officers simply gave up all attempts to control it. A liquor store at Fort Riley was taken over by drunken soldiers in the early 1850s, and a newly recruited German immigrant of that time is quoted as saying, "The greater part of the Army consists of men who either do not care to work, or who, because of being addicted to drink, cannot find employment" (Hicken, 1969, p. 198). Periodic attempts at enforced temperance met with scant success. In 1895, the Surgeon General of the Army reported that 17 posts had more than 10 percent of their average strength under medical care for drunkenness. By 1899 the Secretary of War was advising the Army that facilities for drinking should be provided in order to stop the soldiers from imbibing in "vile resorts" (Hicken, 1969, p. 200).

Closer to the "Fort Marshall" situation perhaps are questionnaire data on alcohol use obtained by Cahalan and his colleagues (Cahalan, et al., 1971; Cahalan and Cisin, 1973). In their survey, 65 percent of Army enlisted men and 50 percent of the officers agreed that "It's all right to get drunk once in a while as long as it doesn't get to be a habit." Comparable figures for the Navy were 73 percent and 61 percent respectively. Even higher percentages in both services agreed that "Most of my friends don't mind a person getting drunk if he doesn't do things that disturb other people." Greden and his colleagues polled 1873 American soldiers in the U.S. and Vietnam during the early seventies (Greden, Frenkel, and Morgan, 1975). According to operational definitions based on both alcohol consumption and problem behaviors, 7 percent were classed as alcoholics, 5 percent as borderline alcoholics, and 24 percent as potential alcoholics. Younger and lower-ranking soldiers were disproportionately represented, and there was a positive relationship between drinking and use of illicit drugs. Very similar findings turned up on a yearly basis, from 1975 through 1978, in the U.S. Army in Europe (USAREUR). The USAREUR Personnel Opinion Survey annually questions a stratified random sample of Army personnel on a variety of subjects relevant to their health and well-being, including their use of drugs and alcohol and any personal difficulties that use may have caused. Dividing respondents into five categories on the basis of their answers to the alcohol questions consistently left 30 percent of the soldiers under 21 in the "problem drinker" or "alcohol addict" groups. Like that of Greden and coworkers, this study found a high degree of overlap between drug abusers and alcohol abusers, and noted that alcohol was clearly the drug of choice among USAREUR soldiers. The "heads" vs. "juicers" distinction reported to Ingraham (1974) by Vietnam veterans thus appears to be based primarily on abstention from illegal drugs rather than a propensity to use and abuse alcohol. In the face of all these reports, however, it is difficult to argue with the apparent ubiquity of drinking that he argues is part and parcel of barracks life.

Drugs and Drink: Functions

A far more important contribution, because of its originality, is Ingraham's theory of the functions which drug and alcohol serve for the barracks dwellers. Indeed, others have noted that the high levels of drinking characteristic of military groups seem to have something to do with group morale. Edwards and Dill (1974), for example, pointed out "a tendency to underestimate the socially derogatory and physically detrimental effects of excessive drinking, because it was viewed as a positive social amenity conducive to group cohesiveness and *esprit de corps.*" Jones and Johnson (1975), in discussing psychiatric problems encountered in their Vietnam experience, coined the term "disorders of loneliness" in referring to the high incidence of drug and alcohol abuse they witnessed in the early seventies (venereal disease was the third of the three disorders mentioned). Both of these characterizations, however, failed to provide much insight on how drugs and alcohol serve to facilitate group cohesiveness or ameliorate loneliness. Mirin and McKenna (1975) and Holloway (1974) come a bit closer to Ingraham, at least for drug use. The former, reporting on use of marihuana in Vietnam, assert that it "often became the sacrament that bound a group together," allowing "combat losses to be temporarily forgotten while new relationships were solidified." Holloway cites Tischler (1969) on anomie in new arrivals to Vietnam and incorporation of oneself into a "pseudo-community" as an escape from the stressful environment. Holloway mentions "heads," "juicers," and formal work groups as examples of such pseudo-communities, and while he concedes that membership in one of these groups did not preclude membership in another, he notes that a strong emotional allegiance was commonly expressed to one particular group. Bey and Zecchinelli (1971) made similar observations, based on their study of 20 soldier-patients in Vietnam, but the comments of Rohrbaugh and Press (1974) make it clear that it is not the stress of combat alone, which gives marihuana its appeal for soldiers or its effectiveness as a social facilitator:

> To us it is not surprising that the group membership offered by drug-taking behavior is alluring to the 17-21 year old enlisted man who, as often as not, is away from home for the first time, and is struggling with the normal adolescent issues of authority, dependence, and identity.

In regard to alcohol use, I could not find a single reference on military life that directly supported Ingraham's hypothesis on the mechanism by which drinking served to enhance group cohesiveness, i.e., by providing a history of distinctive events for a group, distinguishing them from other groups and providing grist for an impoverished conversational mill. However, I also could not find any observations which undermined it, and several studies of non-military youth groups have reported data extending the theory beyond the barracks walls. These studies will be taken up below.

One final assertion by Ingraham on drug and alcohol use by soldiers needs some supporting evidence, since it flies in the face of much middle-class, middle-age wisdom. This concerns what he has called elsewhere "the myth of illicit drug use and military incompetence" (Ingraham, 1979). Although a worldwide survey of nearly 16,000 soldiers in 1980 found 29 percent of junior enlisted personnel admitting to some kind of impairment of job performance at least once in the preceding 12 months due to alcohol, and 22 percent reporting impairment due to drug use (Burt, 1980), Ingraham alleges that most drug users are invisible to the leaders, and more importantly, have negligible consequences for garrison performance even if many or most inept and disaffected soldiers are also drug users. A very similar conclusion was reached nearly 50 years ago in a controlled study of Army marihuana users in the Panama Canal Zone (Siler, et al., 1933). Although marihuana smoking was reported as quite common among soldiers in Panama, no ill effects were observed in the six-day period during which subjects were hospitalized and allowed marihuana cigarettes as desired. They did note that reports from commanders in the field were quite negative about marihuana, claiming that it impaired unit morale. However, they concluded:

> The evidence obtained suggests that organization commanders in estimating the efficiency and soldierly qualities of delinquents in their commands have unduly emphasized the effects of marihuana, disregarding the fact that a large proportion of the delinquents are morons or psychopaths, which conditions of themselves would serve to account for delinquency.

Two reports from Vietnam observed that widespread use of marihuana had not seriously affected overall military effectiveness in the view both of mental health personnel (Colbach, 1971) and commanders (Staff Report, 1971). In the U.S., the Rohrbaugh and Press report from Fort Riley also reported that "unlike the inner city addict, the GI user is young, healthy, and in most cases able to carry out day-to-day work activities." In Europe, a 1978 survey of over 300 battalion and company commanders found that while two out of three considered drug and alcohol abuse detrimental to readiness, both ranked below two dozen other issues in their perceived impact. Further, a substantial portion of their impact stemmed from paperwork, counseling, and procedures for "processing" detected abusers (Farmer, 1978).

Appropriate conclusions from this short survey of the literature on drug and alcohol use and abuse in the military might be that considerable support exists for the picture of drinking and drug use portrayed by Ingraham. Surveys of the frequency and patterns of use of these substances, in Vietnam, Europe, and the U.S., as well as more subjective accounts of the functions apparently served by such use, make it difficult at least to view "Fort Marshall" as an aberration. The one completely unprecedented assertion is his theory that a major factor in the survival of heavy drinking as a dominant behavior pattern of barracks residents is the likelihood of a unique and memorable incident resulting, an episode which will then serve to bond the drinking group together. We will return to this theory below in discussion of research on the behaviors of some naturally occurring groups of young male civilians.

Affiliation

The central theme of *The Boys in the Barracks*, the author tells us, is affiliation; the central problems for the boys are finding companions, establishing status, and maintaining orderly interaction over time. He wonders aloud whether readers who experienced the U.S. Army of earlier years can possibly understand how these problems could arise, and he describes a few of the changes that have made today's Army so different from that depicted in *From Here to Eternity*. These changes in fact have been the central concern of military sociologists since the publication of Janowitz's *The Professional Soldier* in 1961. Moskos (1973, 1978) has crystallized much of this work in his presentation of the military as slowly shifting, or being pushed, from an institutional format to an occupational one. Military service, he says, is coming more and more to be defined as simply another job, performed during specified hours for wages determined by the mechanisms of the market place. Those who see military service as a "way of life" involving 24-hour dedication to "duty" and paternalistic systems of remuneration and administration are now in the minority (cf. Jacobs, 1978, on legal trends emphasizing the contractual and bureaucratic nature of military service). Despite impassioned arguments that the occupational model is not adequate to the task of defending the country in combat (e.g., Hauser, 1973; Bradford and Brown, 1973; Gabriel and Savage, 1978; Malone and Penner, 1980), the evidence continues to mount that "to the youth of the Western industrialized countries, serving in the military is not doing his duty but merely doing his job" (Van Doorn, 1975).

A major consequence of this shift has been a concomitant shift in emphasis from the military unit to the individual as the focus of mobility, training and performance. Cotton (1979) cites a group of students at the Canadian Land Forces Command and Staff College: "In general the Canadian Forces teach the individual soldier to carry out a particular task well enough . . . But well trained individuals do not in themselves mean a good Army." Molding those individuals into a "good Army" is made more difficult by the constant movement, again on an individual basis, characteristic of today's force. The Department of Defense, for example, reported to Congress that 1975 saw more than 1.8 million personnel changing stations of assignment. In addition to these signs that the institution is losing its fraternal nature (indeed perhaps it is one of the causes), there is also evidence that its newest members have extremely high levels of alienation from social institutions in general. Wesbrook (1980), for example, reported that:

1. 86 percent of the 425 junior enlisted combat arms soldiers surveyed believed that most people will take advantage of them if given the chance;
2. 51 percent felt most people cannot be trusted, and 19 percent were uncertain;
3. 69 percent believed most people are not concerned about others;
4. only half took issue with the statement that a person must do what is best for himself, even at the expense of others;
5. 33 percent believe there are no rules to live by, and 22 percent are uncertain;
6. 51 percent believe government is not concerned with people like themselves (21 percent unsure);
7. Only 18 percent believed they could count on their officers and senior NCOs to look out for soldiers' interests;
8. Only 25 percent believed their own platoons would make every effort to reach them if they were cut off in battle.

This transformation from a group-oriented, fraternalistic institution to an individualistic, contractual occupation has been paralleled by a decreasing emphasis on small-group solidarity in descriptions of enlisted relationships in combat, according to Moskos (1970). Historians like S.L.A. Marshall (1964), psychiatrists like Weinstein (1947), and sociologists like Samuel Stouffer (1949), as well as novelists (Manchester, 1981; Cowley, 1958), and journalists (Mauldin, 1945) are agreed on the overriding importance of interpersonal relationships in sustaining and motivating the World War II GI. Roger Little's firsthand observations of infantry men in Korea are generally considered the definitive word on interpersonal relationships in that war. His study (1964) emphasized the importance and ubiquity of two-man "buddy" relationships, in contrast to the squad or platoon bonds cited in World War II accounts. It is worth noting that it was during the Korean war that U.S. forces switched from a unit to an individual replacement system. In Vietnam, Moskos (1975) and Gabriel and Savage (1978) contend that the switch to individualism became complete. Although this view of enlisted cohesion in Vietnam is by no means uncontested (cf. Faris, 1977; Wermuth, 1977; Fowler, 1979; Caputo, 1977), a recent minority opinion contends that the whole notion of primary-group bonds in combat is best viewed as a secondary, strictly pragmatic outcome of the pursuit of personal survival (Moskos, 1975; Kviz, 1978; Renner, 1973). Kviz puts it in the language of social exchange theory: "Social status and social acceptance are private goods which groups may provide to individuals in exchange for collective good contributions" (i.e., helping the group survive). Although it downplays the need for social interaction as a basic human motive, an advantage of this representation of the mystical sounding "male bonding" is that it helps considerably in reconciling the striking similarities in the behaviors of Ingraham's "Boys" and small groups of soldiers observed by social scientists in and out of combat during World War II and Korea. Brotz and Wilson (1946), for example, note even more strongly than Ingraham that despite the seeming intimacy of Army life, an individual can be very isolated due to the impersonality of the "military method" and his sharply restricted mobility. As a result, they say, "It is rare to see a soldier or sailor alone . . . No amount of orientation courses can supplant the necessity for comradeship." They report that the complete severance of accustomed social relations leads to acquisition of "buddies," initially perhaps based solely on propinquity and the need to share the discomfits and perplexities of their new Army life. Berkman (1946) and Stone (1946) report similar pressures in somewhat different situations. Berkman described life aboard an armed guard ship, and Stone status and leadership among pilots in a fighter squadron. Both describe cliques with many of the same features as those described by Ingraham. The clique system of Stone's pilots was "organized around the ecological pattern of tents or rooms which housed the unit." It functioned to maintain the status system and . . . "at the same time, it functions as the agency for giving the new member firm ties within the group so that he learns the proper attitudes and actions." Only two men attempted to live outside the clique system, he tells us, and both were transferred out of the squadron. Although several "special-interest groups" crossed clique lines in such activities as "drinking, dating, card-playing, hobbies, and bull sessions" (marked by arcane flying terminology), members of a clique felt they belonged together because they had a history of shared experiences, combat experiences in this case.

Berkman (1946) also describes cliques, but those on board his ship centered on "liberty" experiences in various ports. Tales of adventures involving women and liquor are valuable social coin, and the new man quickly learns that acquiring "sea legs" and the "language of the sea" is not enough to be accepted as a real sailor. "To become identified with the group he is almost forced to take advantage of every leave opportunity."

Rose (1946) was another observer of the World War II Army who commented on the informal "underground" developed by enlisted men. Sometimes, he says, "the solidarity of enlisted men is so strong that an enlisted man can get something which his officer cannot get even for himself." This "underground," he claims, was a very natural result of the American tradition of "looking out for number one" in an institution bereft of rights for enlisted men.

The matter of barracks "norms" that are somewhat out of line with the larger organizations's conception of ideal behavior is also not without precedent. An anonymous contributor to a special issue of the *American Journal of Sociology* on Human Behavior in Military Society (1946), spelled out five "attitudes" which controlled life in the informal social groups of enlisted men he witnessed in several technical units at U.S. bases. Three of these were directly comparable to Ingraham's "regular guy" and anti-squealing norms. Another, concerning pass privileges, roughly parallels the norm on stealing apparently operative among the boys in the "Fort Marshall" barracks. The last, enjoining men who work together to cooperate in whatever is necessary to get the job done in the easiest manner for the whole group, has no obvious parallel in *Boys*, perhaps because previously common group punishment is no longer permissible. The observer reports that even mild social ostracism would bring an offender in line, for "the whole basis of his social life and status was in this one informal group . . . He belongs . . . or he is isolated."

Little's justly celebrated participant observation of an infantry platoon in Korea also emphasized the powerful control of informal group norms. He described a network of interpersonal linkages much like the network of ever-shifting dyads and triads portrayed by Ingraham as characteristic of the "Fort Marshall" barracks. "Buddy" for the infantryman was a term which had two distinct meanings: everyone in the unit who shared the risks and hardships of combat was a buddy, but conditions of actual or expected stress produced an unspoken choice of one man, on the same relative level in the organization, on whom special expectations of mutual loyalty were placed. Oddly, Little found very few true pairs, in which each member spontaneously named the other as his buddy. One of the norms of the buddy relationship in fact was that such choices were private and were to be kept private. As a result, Little says, buddy choices "never threatened the solidarity of the squad or platoon." Nevertheless, buddies had to be willing to listen when you wanted to talk, to understand you and be interested in your story. The third norm was that buddies never boasted of individual combat skills or compared combat proficiency. To talk about combat was to suggest a loyalty to the organization that must necessarily detract from loyalty to one another. The fourth and fifth norms explicitly described by Little follow up this implied choice: buddies never put one another on a spot by demanding such a choice, but if forced by circumstances it was understood that loyalty to buddies was primary. From the point of view of the larger organization, of course, this is highly undesirable. Indeed the longer a unit was "on the line" directly confronting the enemy, the more intensive their relationships became, and the more their behavior deviated from the norms of the larger organization. Paradoxically, when a unit reached this stage, Little says, it was described as having "low morale" and was withdrawn into reserve for "retraining."

With the benefit of hindsight it is possible to derive two additional "norms" that clearly exerted considerable influence within the platoon. Little's discussion of the "dud" and the "hero" makes it clear that, like the importance of "local interpretations" in following military standards which Ingraham describes and the World War enjoiner to cooperate in getting the job done in the easiest way for the whole group, there were definite performance limits—minimum and maximum—which had to be observed if one wanted buddies. Second and last, there were contrasting sets of attitudes toward personal property and Army property. Formal rules against theft of the former were reinforced, as at "Fort Marshall," by an elaborate system of attitudes concerning the care and use of such items (including a very powerful demand for sharing), while formal rules covering Army property were routinely abused.

In many respects, the barracks life of "Fort Marshall" in the early seventies bears a striking resemblance to that of the previous 30 years. Perhaps this is because many of the changes (such as more married enlisted men) have had as their major impact a simple reduction in the number or proportion of people living in the barracks. Perhaps it is because the loosening of ties to social institutions of all sorts in recent years has made some sort of informal group membership more important, even as the Army turned its focus away from communal living and working, and toward specialization and individual rights. Lastly, the recurrence of these common themes in descriptions of the social life of the enlisted soldier may be attributable to a couple of very basic constants: the youth of the average soldier and his sudden need to adjust to new living conditions far from home and his familiar social networks.

In any case, it is clear that many of the phenomena reported in detail in *The Boys in the Barracks* have been noted by other observers of military life over the years. As Ingraham concedes, the question of generality is indeed a matter for future research. It is, however, not a matter for future research alone; any model must not only predict, but also incorporate and perhaps help us to understand past observations as well. I would assert here that the past observations cited above are sufficient grounds for believing that the group of soldiers observed by Ingraham—support troops at that—stationed at a backwater post in the early 1970s, ought not to be dismissed too casually as unrepresentative of the Army as a whole. Another question concerns the extent to which "the Boys" are representative of modern American youth. In the next section, we will examine precisely this point, and in the words of Glaser and Strauss (1967) examine the possibility of Ingraham's substantive theory of enlisted life leading to a grounded formal theory of affiliation among young males.

THE BOYS OUTSIDE THE BARRACKS

It is uncivilized. It is anti-intellectual. It is a drug culture. It perpetuates racial stereotypes. It is sexist. The "it" referred to in these charges is not barracks living, but the fraternity house system of Dartmouth College, whose abolition Professor James Epperson was urging upon the board of trustees in 1978 (Merton, 1979). "I got sick on tequila my freshman year," one brother is quoted as saying. "I enjoyed breaking windows. I enjoyed burning couches. Destroying furniture was a spontaneous activity." A college pamphlet published about the same time quotes from a letter written by a female student:

> Friday night, everyone, and I mean everyone—goes out to the frats and gets totally shit-faced. It is literally impossible to have a good time at a fraternity if you're sober, because the things you observe totally bum you out. At least three-fourths of the guys are out to pick up a girl, any girl, and get into bed with her . . . they will tell their "frat brothers" about their real—or more often totally fictional—experiences in great detail . . . the other one-fourth of the guys, they have now "booted"— thrown up—supposedly a manifestation of "manhood." (Traynham, quoted in Merton, 1979)

These incidents are not meant to single out the Greek system, or Dartmouth, for abuse or contempt. Indeed, the St. Paddy's day trip to New York City described by Ingraham in Chapter 4 was primarily a college tradition in the sixties, nominally related to the National Invitational (basketball) Tournament. On the basis of extensive participant observation, the author can provide detailed testimony that the outrageous behavior of Gross, Barker, and Murphy, among others, was in fact the rule rather than the exception.

Likewise, Merton notes, "If you walked into any Holiday Inn at midnight and opened all the doors, what you saw would shock a lot of people." Consider also what one of the subjects of Howell's study of a white working-class neighborhood told him:

> You know, all this shit you're going to write in your book and all that you're going to put down, nobody's going to believe it . . . They're going to say people don't live like that. But . . . they don't know what the world is like. (Howell, 1973)

The fact that it is common in no way excuses sexist, racist, hedonistic, destructive behaviors. The point here is that the boys in the barracks are not so very different, even at their worst, from civilian youths in similar living conditions.

There are, however, several features of Merton's 1979 article on Dartmouth that bear particularly strongly on this similarity of living conditions: its relative isolation, its all-male tradition, and the "Dartmouth Plan." The similarity to "Fort Marshall" is perhaps too obvious to belabor in the case of the first two, though it may be useful to consider Dean Warner Traynham's words on isolation:

The community outside our gates is impotent. It exerts no pressure on us. Harvard and Columbia must respond to pressures from the cities which surround them; they have been forced to become more socially responsive. We have not. Dartmouth is a compound. (Merton, 1979)

The "Dartmouth Plan" completes the isolation of the student nearly as well as Army rotation practices for the soldier. The academic year is divided into four ten-week quarters, separated by two- or three-week holiday periods. During each quarter, about 25 percent of all students are either on vacation or studying off campus. From their sophomore through senior years, students must spend only eight quarters on campus, and they may spend them in any order. When a student returns to campus, he or she will be assigned a new dormitory room, and may find many former friends now off campus themselves or scattered to other dorms all over the campus. One result, according to Merton, is that fraternities provide "the strongest strand of social continuity in an atmosphere of flux and instability," a description which, if "fraternity" is taken to mean roughly a drinking, smoking, partying group that shares common quarters, paraphrases Ingraham quite closely.

Frat houses and college dorms are obviously not the only places one finds groups of young males. The street corner is an even more likely place to look, and it is a place whose population is far more likely to contribute to today's Army than is the campus. Here too we find adolescents struggling with the twin issues of becoming a man ("establishing status" in Ingraham's terms) and "maintaining orderly interaction over time." Several authors have described the subculture of the "gang" of the fifties and sixties in much the same way Ingraham has described the barracks subculture of the seventies. Gordon, for example, proposed that in groups in which interpersonal relations are insufficiently rewarding to be self-sustaining, group cohesiveness will depend upon activities other than the social skills valued by middle-class adults. In the case of street-corner gangs this is delinquent behavior:

a complex of techniques through which boys in a group strive to elicit nurturant, accepting and highly dependable responses from each other—perhaps to compensate for deprivation in family backgrounds or other institutional contexts—despite a generally reduced capacity on the part of those concerned to provide such responses. (Gordon, 1967)

One might argue that part of the definition of "lower-class," at least connotatively, is this reduced capacity to abide by the "interaction rituals" discussed by Goffman (1967). Both Howell (1973) and Miller (1958), for example, find "toughness" to be one of the focal concerns of lower-class culture. One of the consequences of this emphasis on masculinity is that expressions of affection and dependence by street-corner boys must be disguised, a job made much simpler by concocting tasks that justify dependence between even "manly" members and call for cooperation in common enterprises, such as fights and other adventures centered on alcohol, music, and sexual adventure (Gordon, 1967).

This sort of "action," according to Goffman, is a situation in which an individual has the opportunity to display to himself and others his style of conduct when the chips are down. "It is largely through such moments," he says, "that social life occurs." The spur is the possibility of affecting reputation, so it is perhaps not surprising that the quest for such "action" should be most intense among those with the least status in society and, because of age, education, economics, job or individual abilities, the fewest options for displaying character. "Extreme constraint," Goffman argues, forces the individual to "improper" ways of establishing and maintaining his self-image.

Couched in such general terms, it becomes possible to see Ingraham's observations as examples of behaviors characteristic of many subcultures, low-status ones in particular. Cohen (1955) attempted a general theory of subculture based precisely on the notion that they arise primarily as a solution to the inability of non-middle-class youth to achieve status in a middle-class society. The working-class youth, he argued, growing up in a working-class family and circle, is very likely to fare poorly when he tries to join the middle-class world. In a country where anyone can be president, and people are allegedly judged strictly by ability and not by ancestry, he then has a real problem explaining to himself and others why he is doing so poorly. A subculture provides a different set of criteria by which he can acquire status, albeit in a smaller group. These criteria, while they must necessarily contrast with middle-class standards (cf. Becker's description of the musician's subculture, 1963), do not necessarily have to be delinquent or illegal. Whyte's (1955) street corner society, for example, does not repudiate "college-boy" values so much as emphasize things which are incompatible with them, such as loyalty to neighborhood chums or spending money with friends. Eliot Liebow's classic study of "Negro street corner men" (1955) paints a similar portrait of adult black men who protect their self-esteem with a "shadow system of values . . . permitting them to be men" despite their failure as providers (and therefore as husbands and fathers). In their street-corner subculture, it is the number and depth of personal friendships that provide self-esteem, while the members bolster each other in their assertions of disdain for the goals of the larger society which have eluded them (a defensive mechanism akin to the Boys' norm of not saying anything about the Army unless you can say something bad?)

A prominent subculture in *The Boys in the Barracks* is that of the drug user/alcohol abuser. Although the author points out that neither drugs nor alcohol are central to the organization of barracks behavior itself, two of the six chapters are devoted to these topics, and any assessment of generality would be incomplete without addressing civilian drug subcultures.

I turn now to those studies which bear on how drinking and drug use affect what Ingraham identifies as "the central problems of the barracks-dwelling soldier: finding companions, establishing status, and maintaining orderly interactions over time." His own analysis emphasizes the contributions of drinking and smoking to the solution of the first of these, and it is by no means without support.

Preble and Casey (1969) came very close to Ingraham's explanation of heavy drinking in quoting a New York drug addict: "Drugs is a hell of a game; it gives you a million things to talk about." Numerous other authors have pointed out the essentially social nature of drug use without specifying a mechanism. Blum (1969), for example, writing about drug use by college students, alleges that "whatever private pleasure may be attributed to users' goals, these cannot be divorced from the pleasures of a social experience as such" (p. 178). Blum and Garfield (1969) even note that solitary smoking by college students may be predictive of discontinuation. Kandel (1974) points out that, among high school students at least, only age and gender serve as better predictors of friendship pairs than marihuana use, and conversely, that being married is one of the most important correlates of abstention among slightly older youth. She postulates that "most basically, the exchange of drugs among the young acts as a cementing of social solidarity, and may be the equivalent of the exchange of gifts in primitive societies." Marihuana use, she says, signifies acceptance of, and into the youth culture, vis-à-vis adulthood, an instant group identification much like Ingraham proposes from his observations of soldiers seeking companions without adopting the values and behaviors of the "lifers."

Students and soldiers are, of course, not the only subcultures to use drugs and ritualistic drinking (Keiser, 1969) as a means of companion identification. Becker (1963) described the use of marihuana among musicians in much the same manner. Fisher (1975) reported that Hindu devotees in Nepal use cannabis quite explicitly as a symbol of fellowship, while in Iran, opium smoking has long served this function, according to Mowlana (1974). Palgi (1975) provides an interesting view of this companion-identifying role of drugs in discussing the resistance to hashish by the traditional Jewish community in Morocco, where hashish use has been an accepted custom for centuries. In the eyes of these Jews, hashish smoking would have brought them into the Muslim social network, a situation they found threatening to their sense of identity. Immigration to Israel made this need for differentiation irrelevant, and those who did not find a place for themselves socially and economically in their new country turned to hashish, which Palgi considers to be a type of communication shared by the unskilled, the delinquents, and other "outsiders" in Israel.

Young soldiers are very much "outsiders" in the Army, despite the fact that they comprise a majority and, like immigrants, have cut their former social ties and left them far away. The allure of drug use as a quick and easy way of providing these missing ties is apparently not lost on either group, and there is ample evidence that it is not lost on the "tie-less" in other contexts. Battegay and his colleagues (1976) explicitly assert that drug abuse among modern European youth represents an attempt to overcome their loss of the clear sense of belonging to a certain culture which grew out of older patterns of education. In a similar vein, Murphy (1963) long ago described the heavy cannabis user in North Africa, India, and the U.S. as "the man in a marginal economic condition, cut off from satisfactory family ties and lacking stable residential roots."

More recently, Gorsuch and Butler (1976) concluded from an extensive review of the literature on social psychological factors predisposing individuals to drug use that lack of involvement in organized groups (family, school, religion, etc.) and a scarcity of close peer relationships were major influences on initial drug use. Conversely, Fitzpatrick (1975), in a study of drug use among Puerto Ricans in New York, marveled at the ability of so many slum residents to cope effectively with the all-pervasive presence of drugs. The power to resist, he felt, clearly lay in the Puerto Rican institutions of extended family and ritual kinship, and indeed claimed good results from a treatment program based primarily on strengthening these ties. Auerswald (1980) and Van Hasselt, Hersen, and Milliones (1978) came to similar conclusions from the treatment side and accordingly proposed radical changes in the direction of attack. Auerswald (1980) represents a substantial segment of a growing body of clinicians and scientists convinced that the family plays a major role in prevention, initiation and cessation of drug use (cf. Glynos, 1981). He argues that modern social conditions emphasizing individual freedom, mobility, specialization and competition fragment families and the support system they provide, leaving vacuums that become filled by chemicals and the superficial support provided by fellow users. He concluded that drug abuse should be attacked through measures that support close family life rather than by developing more treatment programs.

Van Hasselt and coworkers (1978) make more limited assertions of causality and suggest a more tightly focused intervention. They argue that there is convergent support for the hypothesis that both alcoholics (O'Leary, 1976; Sugerman, 1965) and drug addicts (Kraft, 1968; Lindblad, 1977) are "deficient in social skills," i.e., the ability to initiate and maintain conversations and to express both positive and negative feelings without suffering loss of social reinforcement. Although they do not explicitly present excessive drinking or drug use as attempts to compensate for lack of social skills, they review a number of studies in which specific training in this area was used successfully as part or all of a rehabilitation program.

There is yet another corpus of drug-taking literature, which bears on the second of Ingraham's "central problems": establishing status. To a large degree he has linked alcohol and drug use to the first of these problems—finding companions—and has concentrated on the role of physical and verbal "rough-housing" in the solution of the second. Verbal banter in particular has a longstanding and well-documented role in status achievement and maintenance. (See, for example, Berdie, 1947, on "playing the dozens"; Kochman, 1969, on "sounding and signifying"; and Goffman, 1967, on "aggressive facework" and "trial by taunting.") The status being established by such behaviors is, however, intragroup status, and there is considerable evidence, alluded to above, that the very existence of a drug use/alcohol abuser group is in part an effort to increase the self-esteem of members, none of whom can claim much status in the eyes of the "establishment."

Preble and Casey (1969), Feldman (1968), and Sutter (1966) were among the earliest to advocate this point of view, and Glaser (1971), Agar and Feldman (1980), Williams (1976), and Kaplan (1975) have added their voices in recent years. One of the first to challenge the "heroin use as pathological" doctrine of the mid-sixties, Feldman argued that slum youths used heroin not to escape problems or retreat from life, but to gain status in a street system that valued daring and resourcefulness highly. Preble and Casey's subjects told them that the problem with methadone is that "it takes all the fun out . . . you don't have to outslick the cops and other people." They point out further that even the type of criminal behavior an addict engaged in, and his success at it, determines to a large extent his status among fellow addicts and in the community at large. Glaser (1971) has pointed out that in lower-class neighborhoods drug-taking is often the basis for a third status system (after legitimate conventional economic success and organized crime).

While the status of the low-ranking enlisted soldier in society at large varies somewhat with the political and economic conditions of the country, there can be no doubt in the mind of anyone who has served that his status within the Army is low indeed. It is important in this context because Ingraham's observation on the pervasiveness of drinking and smoking cliques can therefore be seen not as oddities of military or even young male life, but as confirmation and extention of an oft-noted adaptation to the fact of low organizational status.

LEADERS, PROBLEMS, SOLUTIONS

Late in the book, Sergeant Wiley Fox, whose platoon Ingraham has made clear is noticeably closer than any of the others at "Fort Marshall," tells us:

> When I came in [30 years ago] the men felt close together. You could leave your billfold on your bunk for a week and it'd still be there when you came back.

This quote made a particularly strong impression on me because of a conversation I had not long ago with the commander of a National Guard unit which had been sent to Germany for two weeks to train with "the real Army" as he called it. When I met him, his company had been training at one of the major ranges for only three days, supported and supervised by a company of German-based "real Army" troops.

"Before we got here," he told me, "I was pretty scared. After all, we're just a bunch of hillbillies with no real Army experience, even though we've been spending weekends together for a long time. Here we are in Europe, where the rubber really meets the road and all! You know what?" he said as he looked around conspiratorially,

"We're every bit as good as these guys! And I'll tell you something else—we don't have to take our wallets to the shower with us!"

The main chore of the platoon sergeant, as Wiley Fox saw it, was creating this sense of community. "The important thing," he says, "is that the men talk to each other. Makes no difference who buys the beer, just so we have a reason to get together." His colonel knew better, knew that the future lay with the modern techniques of industrial management, standardization, and sophisticated bureaucracy. He knew the day had passed when leaders ate, slept, and breathed Army "25 hours a day," where everyone lived on the same post and were social friends as well as work associates.

The sergeants and officers closest to the troops, with few exceptions, knew these things too, but Ingraham tells us that it didn't keep them from grousing about the impersonal organizational climate, the changes in the legal system, the Army bureaucracy, and the morass of paper and regulations that sucked up so much of their time and energy. In fact their main concerns don't sound much different than those of the men they lead: "Where do I fit in this organization called the Army? Am I really important?"

Looking back now from the eighties, it seems that Wiley Fox, wherever he is, has won out after all. Management is now a dirty word in the Army, at least if mentioned without "leadership" in the same sentence (cf. Gabriel, 1978; Fallows, 1981; Webb, 1980). We recognize, or re-recognize, that leadership, as opposed to management, is an intensely personal process, something given to leaders not by their superiors, but by their subordinates (cf. Faris, 1981; Sarkesian, 1981).

Even more importantly, the Army has reaffirmed the legitimacy not only of Wiley Fox's techniques, but also of his goal: to create a sense of community within its units. It has heard and heeded, if not Wiley Fox, then men like General (Ret.) Andrew P. O'Meara (quoted in Meyer, 1981): "Until we destroy the myth that a collection of men with appropriate military occupational specialties constitutes a military unit, the Army is in deep trouble."

The present Chief of Staff of the Army has begun far-reaching initiatives to encourage the growth of just the sort of small-group bonding we have long known is both a product and a necessary ingredient of an effective fighting group (Meyer, 1982). Already underway is an extensive 19-company test of "cohesive operational readiness testing"—COHORT for short. The heart of the test is the effect of keeping entire companies intact throughout the entire enlistment of its members. Early data and testimony have been overwhelmingly favorable comparisons to the present "assembly line" system of plugging new trainees one at a time into holes in existing units (Gehlhausen and Timmerman, 1982). For a variety of reasons, nearly all highly defensible on grounds of efficiency, economy, and fairness, these holes now appear at rates which produce 60 to 100 percent turnover yearly in U.S.-based divisions (Meyer, 1982), turnover which not only makes unit bonding impossible but wreaks havoc with a progressive training system designed to move from individual to small unit to collective.

The Army is now in the process of implementing a new American Regimental System, which will institutionalize the COHORT aim of providing the stability of places and faces critical to any efforts of small-unit leaders to develop the sense of solidarity and community Wiley Fox so valued. In contrast to today's system, in which the average combat soldier's chances of serving even in the same division more than once in a 20-year career are vanishingly small, he'll join a regiment of three to four similar battalions (i.e., all infantry, all armor, all artillery), rather than "The Army," and except for occasional schooling or special assignments, serve out his career in his regiment, rotating overseas with his whole battalion, returning with his battalion to the same U.S. "home base," even maintaining his identity as a member of his regiment during schooling or special assignments by his distinctive uniform accoutrements. Many in the Army have protested that this movement will ultimately require extensive changes in nearly every aspect of personnel policy—recruitment, schooling, assignments, promotions, even awards. They are entirely correct in this, of course, for the present system is individual-oriented, not unit-oriented. An Air Force officer (Jacobowitz, 1980) has in fact provided a very creative road map of just how a real commitment to unit cohesion might affect recruiting, training, leadership and personnel policies. Should it be done anyway? Can it be done at all? Or is this the pipe dream of a frustrated idealist longing for "the good old days"?

In keeping with the theme of assessing the generalizibility of Ingraham's observations, in this case his view that many of the problems and unsavory aspects of barracks life stem from the Army's failure to provide its members with any real sense of belonging, let us turn briefly to some recent and some not-so-recent civilian writings to answer two questions on the desirability and feasibility of an American Regimental System. To start with the easier of these, let me quote the opening lines of a book by Vance Packard that was a bestseller when Ingraham and his surrogate investigators were haunting "Fort Marshall":

> Great numbers of [Americans] feel unconnected to either people [or] places and through much of the nation there is a breakdown in community living . . . a general shattering of small group life . . . We are becoming a nation of strangers. (Packard, 1972)

The less widely read but highly respected community psychologist Seymour Sarasen (1976) observed that he had never met anyone who did not understand what he meant by a psychological sense of community, because it was something nearly everyone wanted badly and could find for only fleeting moments. He points to the "flooding" of our language and literature with terms like alienation, anomie, and isolation, and to the proliferation of group therapy techniques, encounter movements, communes, and fundamentalist religious groups as evidence of "how earnestly people strive to be and feel part of a network of close relationships that gives one a sense of willing identification with some overarching values." (Sarasen, 1976).

A similar argument is made by Trippett (1980) on the basis of census figures showing small-town America (populations under 25,000) growing at twice the national rate, while big cites lost ground across the board. He points out that many of those pursuing the life they learned about from Norman Rockwell are disappointed, but he contends the sense of warm, intimate community can still be found, and that the need for it insures that the "small town will always haunt and invite the American mind."

Cast in small-town/big-city terms like this, it becomes apparent that Ingraham, far from merely offering a voyeur's view of an institution rapidly disappearing from the ken of the average middle-class American, has exposed yet another facet of one of sociology's central concerns. Toennies (1889), Durkheim (1893), and Spencer (1895) were arguing before the turn of the century over the role of industrialization in the transformation of the dominant social order from one of *Gemeinschaft* (based on intimacy, personal attraction, and shared values) to one of *Gesellschaft* (based on formal organization, rules and procedures). Park and Burgess (1921), Louis Wirth (1938), and others of the "Chicago School" cited earlier keyed on urbanization and specialization. Nisbet (1953), Stein (1960), Warren (1963), and others added further valuable points to the debate, but voices arguing that the decline of community was either imaginary or not undesirable have been few and far between (see, however, Fischer et al., 1977).

On the more difficult question of feasibility it might be assumed that a hundred-year history of decrying the loss of "Gemeinschaft" is itself eloquent testimony to its inevitability. On the other hand, several of the major features of the "Great Change in American Communities" (Warren, 1963) are currently faltering or under attack. Increased specialization and division of labor, for example, have been indicted as major contributors to shoddy workmanship by some major industries, and steps have been taken to help the worker regain his image as a craftsman. Voters elected a President whose major appeal was his belief that "less government is better government." School boards and tax collectors have seen more and more demands for return of local and neighborhood control. Bureaucracy has become a derisive term. We have witnessed the previously mentioned population shift from big cities to suburbs and small towns, the proliferation of group movements from communes to "Moonies," and perhaps most important to ever-practical Americans, the successful adoption by several major U.S. corporations of a Japanese management style based on "trust, subtlety, and intimacy" (Ouchi, 1981).

In the final analysis, however, the Army simply has no choice but to try its reforms, for as Ingraham implies in his opening chapter, come the fighting, both the soldier and the Army will depend on them. The Army's premier historian, S. L. A. Marshall, has this to add:

> I hold it to be one of the simplest truths of war that the thing which enables an infantry soldier to keep going with his weapon is the near presence or the presumed presence of a comrade . . . It is far more than a question of the soldier's need of physical support from other men. He must have at least some feeling of spiritual unity with them if he is to do an efficient job of moving and fighting. Should he lack this feeling for any reason . . . he will become a castaway in the middle of a battle and as incapable of effective offensive action as if he were stranded somewhere without weapons.

REFERENCES

Agar, M., and Feldman, H. A Four-City Study of PCP Users: Methodology and Findings, in Akins, C., and Beschner, G. (eds.), *Ethnography: A Research Tool for Policymakers in the Drug and Alcohol Fields* (DHHS Publication No. ADM 80-946). Washington, D.C.: U.S. Government Printing Office, 1980

Anderson, N., *The Hobo.* Chicago: University of Chicago Press, 1923.

Auerswald. E.H. Drug use and families in the context of twentieth century science, in Ellis, B.G. (ed.), *Drug Abuse from the Family Perspective* (DHHS Publication No. 80-910). Washington, D.C.: U.S. Government Printing Office, 1981.

Baker, S.L. Drug abuse in the United States Army. *Bulletin of the New York Academy of Medicine* 47:541–549, 1971.

Battegay, R., Ladewig, D., Muhlemann, R., and Weidmann, M. The culture of youth and drug abuse in some European countries. *International Journal of Addictions* 11:245–261, 1976.

Becker, H.S. *Outsiders.* New York: The Free Press, 1963.

Berdie, R.F. Playing the dozens. *Journal of Abnormal and Social Psychology* 42:120–121, 1947.

Blum, R.H., *Students and Drugs.* San Francisco: Jossey-Bass, 1969.

———, and Garfield, E. A Follow-up Study, in Blum, R. (ed.), *Students and Drugs,* San Francisco: Jossey-Bass, 1969, p. 185–194.

Bradford, Z., and Brown, F. *The United States Army in Transition.* Beverly Hills, Cal.: Sage Publications, 1973.

Brotz, H., and Wilson, E. Characteristics of military society. *American Journal of Sociology* 51:371–375, 1946.

Brown, D.K., and Nordlie, P.G. *Changes in Black and White Perceptions of the Army's Race Relations/Equal Opportunity Program, 1972.* McLean, Va.: Human Sciences Research, 1975.

Burgess, E.W., and Bogue, D.J. *Contributions to Urban Sociology.* Chicago: University of Chicago Press, 1964, p. 488.

235

Burt, M.R., and Biegel, M.M., *Worldwide Survey of Nonmedical Drug Use and Alcohol Use Among Military Personnel, 1980.* Bethesda, Md.: Burt Associates, 1980.

Butler, J.S., and Wilson, K.L. *The American Soldier* revisited: Race relations and the military. *Social Science Quarterly* 59(3):451–467, 1978.

Caputo, P. *A Rumor of War.* New York: Holt, Rinehart, & Winston, 1977.

Cohen, A.K., *Delinquent Boys.* New York: Free Press, 1955.

Colbach, E. Marijuana use by GIs in Viet Nam. *American Journal of Psychiatry* 128:204–207, 1971.

Cotton, C.A. *Military Attitudes and Values of the Army in Canada.* Report 79-5, Canadian Forces Personnel Applied Research Unit, Willowdale, Ontario, 1979.

Cowley, M. *The Literary Situation.* New York: Viking Press, 1958.

Cronbach, L.J. Beyond the two disciplines of scientific psychology. *American Psychologist* 30:116–127, 1975.

Durkheim, E. *The Division of Labor in Society.* New York: Free Press, 1933.

Edwards, J.D., and Dill, J.E. Alcoholism clinic in a military setting: A combined disulfiram and group therapy outpatient program. *Military Medicine* 139:206–209, 1974.

Fallows, J. A military without mind or soul. *The Washington Monthly,* April 12–27, 1981.

Faris, J.H. Leadership and Enlisted Attitudes, in Buck, J.H. and Korb, L.J. (eds.), *Military Leadership.* Beverly Hills, Cal.: Sage Publications, 1981.

———. An alternative perspective to Savage and Gabriel. *Armed Forces and Society* 3:457–462, 1977.

Faris, R.E.L. *Chicago Sociology, 1920–1932.* Chicago: University of Chicago Press, 1967.

Farmer, M.B. Special Survey of Commanders, May 1978. Office of the Deputy Chief of Staff, Personnel. Headquarters, U.S. Army Europe, Heidelberg, 1978.

Feldman, H.W. Ideological support to becoming and remaining a heroin addict. *Journal of Health and Social Behavior* 9:131–139, 1968.

Fischer, C.S., Jackson, R.M., Stueve, C.A., Gerson, K., Jones, L.M., and Baldassare, M. *Networks and Places.* New York: Macmillan, 1977.

Fisher, J. Cannabis in Nepal: An Overview, in Rubin, V. (ed.). *Cannabis and Culture.* The Hague: Mouton, 1975.

Fitzpatrick, J. P. *Puerto Rican Addicts and Non-Addicts: A Comparison.*

New York: Institute for Social Research, Fordham University, 1975.

Fowler, J.G. Combat cohesion in Viet Nam. *Military Review* 59:22–32, 1979.

Gabriel, R.A. Combat cohesion in Soviet and American military units. *Parameters—Journal of the U.S. Army War College* 8(4):16–27, 1978.

———, and Savage, P. *Crisis in Command.* New York: Hill & Wang, 1978.

Gehlhausen, L.M., and Timmerman, F.W., Jr. Cohesion is watchword in trailblazing B Co. *Army,* May 1982, 52–60.

Glaser, B.G., and Strauss, A.L. *The Discovery of Grounded Theory.* Chicago: Aldine, 1967.

Glynn, T.J. (ed.). *Drugs and the Family* (NIDA Research Issues Publication No. 29) Washington, D.C.: U.S. Government Printing Office, 1981.

Goffman, E. Characteristics of total institutions, in Rioch, D. (ed.), *Symposium on Prevention and Social Psychiatry.* Washington, D.C.: Walter Reed Army Institute of Research, 1957.

———. *Interaction Ritual.* Garden City, N.Y.: Doubleday, 1967.

Gordon, R.A. Social level, social desirability, and gang interaction. *American Journal of Sociology* 73:42–62, 1967.

Gorsuch, R.L., and Butler, M.C. Initial drug abuse: A review of predisposing social psychological factors. *Psychological Bulletin* 83:120–137, 1976.

Greden, J.F., Frenkel, S.I., and Morgan, D.W. Alcohol use in the army: Patterns and associated behaviors. *American Journal of Psychiatry* 132:11–16, 1975.

Hauser, W. *America's Army in Crisis.* Baltimore: Johns Hopkins University Press, 1973.

Holloway, H. Epidemiology of heroin dependency among soldiers in Vietnam. *Military Medicine* 139:108–113, 1974.

House of Representatives, Ninety-Fourth Congress. *Department of Defense Appropriations for 1976; Hearing before Subcommittee of the Committee on Appropriations,* First Session (part 3, p. 364), 1975.

Howell, J.T. *Hard Living on Clay Street.* Garden City, N.Y.: Anchor Books, 1973.

Hurst, P.M., Walizer, D.G., Ridono, W., and McKendry, J. *Assessment of Drug Abuse Prevalence.* HRB-Singer Report No. 4664-1. Springfield, Va.: National Technical Information Service, 1973.

Ingraham, L.H. Sense and nonsense in the Army's drug abuse prevention effort. *Parameters* 11:60–70, 1981.

———. Introduction to symposium on problems with laboratory

training in approaching real world research situation. Presented at the annual meeting of the American Psychological Association, Chicago, 1975.

———. "The Nam" and "the World": heroin use by U.S. enlisted men serving in Vietnam. *Psychiatry* 37:114–128, 1974.

———. The myth of illicit drug use and military incompetence. *Medical Bulletin of the U.S. Army, Europe,* 36(4):18–21, 1979.

Jacobowitz, D.W. Alienation, anomie, and combat effectiveness. *Air University Review* 31:23–34, 1980.

Jacobs, J.B. Legal change within the United States armed forces since World War II. *Armed Forces and Society* 4:391–421, 1978.

Janowitz, M. *The Professional Soldier.* New York: Free Press, 1961.

Johnston, L.D., Bachman, J.G., and O'Malley, P.M. *Highlights from Drug Use among American High School Students, 1975–77* (DHEW Publication No. ADM 79-621) Washington, D.C.: U.S. Government Printing Office, 1978.

Kandel, D. Interpersonal Influences of Adolescent Drug Use, in Josephson, E., and Carroll, E. (eds.), *The Epidemiology of Drug Abuse.* Washington, D.C.: Winston, 1974.

———. Illicit drug use as adolescent behavior. Paper presented to the National Academy of Sciences, Committee on Substance Abuse and Habitual Behavior. Washington, D.C., February 1981.

Kaplan, H.B. Self-Esteem and Self-Derogation Theory of Drug Abuse, in Lettieri, D.J., Sayers, M., and Pearson, H.W. (eds.), *Theories on Drug Abuse* (NIDA Research Monograph 30). Washington, D.C.: U.S. Government Printing Office, 1980.

Katz, D. Some Final Considerations about Experimentation in Social Psychology, in C.G. McClintock (ed.), *Experimental Social Psychology.* New York: Holt, Rinehart & Winston, 1972.

Keiser, R.L. *The Vice Lords: Warriors of the Streets.* New York: Holt, Rinehart & Winston, 1969.

Kochman, T. "Rapping" in the black ghetto, *Trans-action* 6:26–34, 1969.

Kraft, T. Social anxiety and drug addiction. *British Journal of Social Psychiatry* 2:192–195, 1968.

Kvis, F.J. Survival in combat as a collective exchange process. *Journal of Political and Military Sociology* 6:219–232, 1978.

Liebow, E. *Talley's Corner.* Boston: Little, Brown, 1967.

Lindblad, R.A. *Self-Concept and Drug Addiction: A Controlled Study of White Middle Socioeconomic Status Addicts.* Washington, D.C.: U.S. Government Printing Office, 1977.

Little, R.W. Buddy Relations and Combat Performance, in Janowitz,

M. (ed.), *The New Military: Changing Patterns of Organization*. New York: Russell Sage Foundation, 1964.

Malone, D.M., and Penner, D.D. You can't run an army like a corporation. *Army*, February 1980, pp. 39–41.

Manchester, W. *Goodbye Darkness*. New York: Little, Brown, 1979.

Manning, F.J., and Ingraham, L.H. Personnel attrition in the U.S. Army in Europe. *Armed Forces and Society* 7:256–270, 1981.

———. Assessment of unit cohesion and its relation to unit performance, in Belenky, G.L. (ed.) *Contemporary Studies in Combat Psychiatry*. Boston: Kluwer Nijhoff, 1983.

Marshall, S.L.A. *Men Against Fire*. New York: Morrow, 1964.

Mauldin, W. *Up Front*. New York: Holt, Rinehart & Winston, 1945.

Merton, A. Hanging on (by a jockstrap) to tradition at Dartmouth. *Esquire*, June 19, 1979, pp. 57–67.

Meyer, E.C. The unit, Defense 82. Arlingon, Va.: Armed Forces Information Services, February 1982.

Miller, W.B. Lower class culture as a generating milieu of gang delinquency. *Journal of Social Issues* 14(3):5–19, 1958.

Mirin, S.M., and McKenna, G.J. Combat zone adjustment: the role of marihuana use. *Military Medicine* 140:482–485, 1975.

Moskos, C.C. *The American Enlisted Man*. New York: Russell Sage Foundation, 1970.

———. The emergent military: Civil, traditional, or plural? *Pacific Sociological Review* 6:255–280, 1973.

———. The American combat soldier in Vietnam. *Journal of Social Issues* 31:25–27, 1975.

———. The Enlisted Ranks in the All-Volunteer Army, in Keely, J.B. (ed.), *The All-Volunteer Force and American Sociology*. Charlottesville: University of Virginia Press, 1978.

Mowlana, H. The Politics of Opium in Iran: A Social-Psychological Interface, in Simmons, L., and Said, A. (eds.), *Drugs, Politics and Diplomacy: The International Connections*. Beverly Hills, Cal.: Sage Publications, 1974.

Murphy, H.B.M. The cannabis habit: a review of recent psychiatric literature. *Bulletin on Narcotics* 15:15–23, 1963.

Nisbet, R.A. *The Quest for Community*. New York: Oxford University Press, 1969.

O'Donnell, J.A., Voss, H.L., Clayton, R.R., Slatin, G.T., and Room, R.G.W. *Young Men and Drugs—A Nationwide Survey* (NIDA Research Monograph 5). Springfield, Va.: National Technical Information Service, 1976.

O'Leary, D.E., O'Leary, M.R., and Donovan, D.M. Social skill acquisition and psychosocial development of alcoholics: a review. *Addictive Behaviors* 1:111–120, 1976.

Ouchi, W.G. *Theory Z: How American Business Can Meet the Japanese Challenge.* Reading, Mass.: Addison-Wesley, 1981.

Packard, V. *A Nation of Strangers.* New York: McKay, 1972.

Palgi, P. The Traditional Role and Symbolism of Hashish Among Moroccan Jews in Israel and the Effects of Acculturation, in Rubin, V. (ed.), *Cannabis and Culture.* The Hague: Mouton, 1975.

Park, R.E., and Burgess, E.W. *Introduction to the Science of Sociology.* Chicago: University of Chicago Press, 1921.

Preble, E., and Casey, J.J., Jr. Taking care of business: The heroin user's life on the street. *International Journal of Addictions,* 4:1–24, 1969.

Renner, J.A. The changing patterns of psychiatric problems in Viet Nam. *Comprehensive Psychiatry* 14:169–177, 1973.

Roffman, R.A., and Sapol, E. Marihuana in Vietnam: A survey of use among Army enlisted men in two southern corps. *International Journal of Addictions* 5:1–43, 1970.

Rohrbaugh, M., and Press, S. The Army's war on stateside drug use: A view from the front. *Journal of Drug Issues,* Winter 1974, 32–43.

Rouse, B. Johns Hopkins University national survey of college drug use. *Drinking and Drug Practices Surveyor* 4:6–7, June 1971.

Rouse, B.A., and Ewing, J.A. Marijuana and other drug use by women college students: Associated risk taking and coping activities. *American Journal of Psychiatry* 130:486–491, 1973.

Rouse, B.A., and Ewing, J.A. Marijuana and other drug use by graduate and professional students. *American Journal of Psychiatry* 129, 75–80, 1972.

Sarasen, S. *The Psychological Sense of Community.* San Francisco: Jossey-Bass, 1976.

Sarkesian, S. A Personal Perspective, in Buck, J.H., and Korb, L.J. (eds.), *Military Leadership.* Beverly Hills, Cal.: Sage Publications, 1981.

Siler, J.F., Sheep, W.L., Bates, L.B., Clark, G.F., Cook, G.W., and Smith, W.A. Marihuana smoking in Panama. *The Military Surgeon* 73:269–280, 1933.

Smith, M.B. Is experimental social psychology advancing? *Journal of Experimental Social Psychology* 8:86–96, 1972.

Spencer, H. *The Principles of Sociology.* New York: Appleton, 1895.

Staff Report on Drug Abuse in the Military: Subcommittee on Alcoholism and Narcotics of the Committee on Labor and Public

Welfare, 92nd Congress, First Session: Military Drug Abuse. U.S. Government Printing Office, Washington, D.C., June 1971.

Stein, M.R. *The Eclipse of Community.* Princeton, N.J.: Princeton University Press, 1960.

Stouffer, S.A., Lumsdaine, A.A., Lumsdaine, M.H., Williams, R.M., Jr., Smith, M.B., Janis, I.L. Star, S.A., and Cottrell, L.S. Jr. *The American Soldier,* Vol. II: *Combat and Its Aftermath.* Princeton, N.J.: Princeton University Press, 1949.

Sugerman, A.A., Reilly, D., and Albahary, R.S. Social competence and essential—reactive distinction in alcoholism. *Archives of General Psychiatry* 12:552–556.

Surgeon General of the Army. *Report to the Secretary of War for the Fiscal Year Ended June 30, 1895.* Washington, D.C.: U.S. Government Printing Office, 1895.

Sutter, A.G. The world of the righteous dope fiend. *Issues in Criminology* 2:177–222, 1966.

Thrasher, F.M. *The Gang.* Chicago: University of Chicago Press, 1927.

Tischler, G.L. Patterns of Psychiatric Attrition and Behavior in a Combat Zone, in Bourne, P. (ed.), *The Psychology and Physiology of Stress.* New York: Academic Press, 1969.

Toennies, F. *Fundamental Concepts of Sociology.* New York: American Book Company, 1940.

Trippett, F. Small town, U.S.A.: Growing and groaning. *Time,* September 1, 1980, pp. 38–39.

Van Doorn, J. The decline of the mass army in the West: General reflections. *Armed Forces and Society* 1:147–157, 1975.

Van Hasselt, V.B., Hersen, M., and Milliones, J. Social skills training for alcoholics and drug addicts: A review. *Addictive Behaviors* 3:221–233, 1978.

Warren, R.L. *The Community in America.* Chicago: Rand McNally, 1963.

Webb, E.L. (ed.). Leadership Issue. *Military Review* 60(7), 1980.

Weinstein, E.A. The function of interpersonal relations in the neurosis of combat. *Psychiatry* 10:307–314, 1947.

Wermuth, A.L. A critique of Savage and Gabriel. *Armed Forces and Society* 3:481–490, 1977.

Wesbrook, S.D. Sociopolitical alienation and military efficiency. *Armed Forces and Society* 6:170–189, 1980.

Williams, J.R. *Effects of Labeling the "Drug-Abuser": An Inquiry* (NIDA Research Monograph 6). Rockville, Md.: National Institute on Drug Abuse, 1976.

Wirth, L. Urbanism as a way of life. *American Journal of Sociology* 44:3–
    24, 1938.
Whyte, W.F. *Street Corner Society*, ed. 2. Chicago: University of
    Chicago Press, 1955.